SCHOOLCRAFT COLLEGE LIBRARY
W9-BSU-706

Modern Studies in Philosophy

HEGEL

Modern Studies in Philosophy is a series of anthologies presenting contemporary interpretations and evaluations of the works of major philosophers. The editors have selected articles designed to show the systematic structure of the thought of these philosophers and to reveal the relevance of their views to problems of current interest. These volumes are intended to be contributions to contemporary debates as well as to the history of philosophy; they not only trace the origins of many problems important to modern philosophy, but also introduce major philosophers as interlocutors in current discussions.

Modern Studies in Philosophy is prepared under the general editorship of Amelie Oksenberg Rorty, Livingston College, Rutgers University.

Alasdair MacIntyre has taught at Oxford, the University of Essex, and Princeton, and is currently teaching philosophy at Brandeis University.

Modern Studies in Philosophy

AMELIE OKSENBERG RORTY, GENERAL EDITOR

HEGEL

A Collection of Critical Essays

EDITED BY

ALASDAIR MACINTYRE

1972

ANCHOR BOOKS

Doubleday & Company, Inc.

Garden City, New York

This anthology has been especially prepared for Anchor Books and has never before appeared in book form.

Anchor Books edition: 1972

Library of Congress Catalog Card Number 71-171335

Printed in the United States of America
First Edition

CONTENTS

I. *The Contemporary Relevance of Hegel,*
J. N. Findlay 1

II. *The Hegel Myth and Its Method,*
Walter Kaufmann 21

III. *The Young Hegel and Religion,*
Walter Kaufmann 61

IV. *Hegel: A Non-Metaphysical View,*
Klaus Hartmann 101

V. *Hegel's Concept of* "Geist,"
R. C. Solomon 125

VI. *The Opening Arguments of the* Phenomenology,
Charles Taylor 151

VII. *Notes on Hegel's "Lordship and Bondage,"*
George Armstrong Kelly 189

VIII. *Hegel on Faces and Skulls,*
Alasdair MacIntyre 219

IX. *The Formalization of Hegel's Dialectical Logic,*
Michael Kosok 237

X. Hegel on Freedom,
RICHARD L. SCHACHT 289

XI. Hegel Revisited,
SHLOMO AVINERI 329

Select Bibliography 349

INTRODUCTION

No philosopher has suffered more from enthusiastic misrepresentation than Hegel, sometimes by professed followers, but more often by would-be critics; and no philosopher—not even Plato or Marx—has aroused more-violent passions, occasionally idolatrous, usually denigratory. The result is the existence of a very odd literature about Hegel. He has been blamed for so much—for liberalism, the bombing of London, modern atheism, the concentration camps, communism, to give a few examples—and so many strange and different views have been ascribed to him that an uninformed reader who guessed that there was more than one philosopher called Hegel could be forgiven.

One of these Hegels would be the rationalist metaphysician, invented by Russell, who believed that "only minds and mental events can exist" (*History of Western Philosophy,* chapter XVI) and that "if enough was known about a thing to distinguish it from all other things, then all its properties could be inferred by logic" (op. cit., chapter XXII). Russell's Hegel is in fact vaguely recognizable as J. M. E. McTaggart seen through a glass darkly. Russell had, however, never heard of the Hegel who criticized logical atomism (in Section I of the *Phenomenology*) a hundred years before Russell formulated it. Another of these Hegels would be the rather different rationalist metaphysician invented by Kierkegaard, who seems never to have read the *Phenomenology* either and so to have missed the criticisms of Kierkegaard's existentialism in more than one section of that work, which

Hegel assembled thirty years before Kierkegaard formulated his views.

Not all the Hegels of philosophical fiction are rationalist metaphysicians. There is Hegel the ancestor of phenomenology, even Hegel the existentialist and Hegel the Marxist. It is therefore important that we recover the Hegel of fact from the Hegels of fiction and that we recover him as a living philosopher concerned with genuine issues. These are the two criteria that have dominated the selection of the present essays. I am grateful to my contributors not only for their contributions, but also for their advice and their patience.

Alasdair MacIntyre

HEGEL

I. THE CONTEMPORARY RELEVANCE OF HEGEL

J. N. Findlay

I WISH this evening[1] to defend the proposition that Hegel is an extremely important philosopher, well deserving the closest of contemporary study, and not at all belonging to what some have called the 'palaeontology' of philosophical thought. To defend this proposition in the present climate of opinion still requires a certain expenditure of energy and personal authority, though much less than it did a little while ago. There has been, as you know, ever since the beginning of the century, a Hegel-renaissance in Germany, which has increased rather than declined in strength: it is now culminating in a really authoritative edition of Hegel's work, with a correct, unjumbled use made of the invaluable notes of his various students. There has also been a Hegel-renaissance in France ever since M. Hyppolite produced his excellent translation of the *Phenomenology of Spirit*, and Sartre's philosophical production is as much influenced by what I regard as the healthy philosophizing of Hegel as by the somewhat morbid, if interesting, philosophizing of the German existentialists. In Anglo-Saxon countries a Hegel-renaissance has been made more difficult by the comparative recency of a period in which Hegel's prestige was immense, though his doctrine and

Reprinted from Findlay, J. N., *Language, Mind and Value* (Allen & Unwin Ltd., London, 1963), by permission of the author and the publisher.

[1] Lecture first given at a Colloquium on Contemporary British Philosophy in London, September 1959.

method were very imperfectly understood. Hegel is a philosopher whose misfortune it has been to fascinate philosophers of a wholly different and much less subtle cast of mind, who have then created a one-sided image of his thought to fit their rather limited horizons, and who have involved Hegel in the discrediting reaction which their own views ultimately provoked. No one probably now wants to revive the Spinozistic absolutism of Bradley, the time-denying monadism of McTaggart, the febrile subjectivism of Croce and Gentile, even the optimistic rationalism of Royce: what is not realized is how very remote all these philosophers are from the toughness, the empirical richness, the logical brilliance and the astonishing self-subversive movement of Hegel's dialectical thought. Whatever these thinkers may have learnt from him, most of them never learnt to think dialectically at all. What they hold has always a final definiteness of assertion, a systematic stability and clarity, an elimination rather than living suspension of conflict, which stamps it as a 'still', a product of 'understanding', rather than of what Hegel understood by 'dialectic' or 'reason'. Had Hegel known of these thinkers, he would have disposed of each of them in a few paragraphs of his system.

A Hegel-renaissance has also been made difficult in the Anglo-Saxon world by the immense prestige of mathematical logic: since 1911 one may say that we have all lived in the noble shadow of *Principia Mathematica.* Hegel is, however, believed, chiefly by those who have not read him, to have been grievously contumacious as against that sort of logic, and in particular against the logical law of non-contradiction, and by such contumacity to have corrupted all clear thinking at its source. It was in this connection, probably, that Ryle said, on some occasion in the past, that Hegel did not deserve study, even as error. Ryle was, however, completely misguided, since few philosophers have so well understood, and so eloquently admired, the peculiar genius of the mathematicizing understanding, when at work on its own tasks and at its own level, and the indispensability of its clarifying, fixing, separating, equational activities, its moves that really serve to maintain immobility, from the point of view of exposing the limitations of each thought-position and of making it possible to progress to the next. The fact, further, that Hegel uses superficially self-contradictory language in an illuminating manner, simply shows that Hegelian contradiction, like Hegelian identity, is not the nugatory, self-stultifying notion of the mathematical logician, but has an entirely different, valuable role. Hegelian dialectic has, in fact, a function complementary to the thought of *Principia Mathematica* and similar systems: it is the thought of the *interstices* between clear-cut notions, fixed axioms and rigorous deductive chains, the interstices where we are as yet unclear as to what our notions cover and what they do not, where we constantly stretch or retract them as we try them out on new material, where we are concerned to look at them from the outside, and see how well or how ill they do certain conceptual work, where we are concerned with innumerable loose, inexact, sliding, shading relations of notions to one another which are not less important for being loose. Hegel's dialectic corresponds to the sort of informal, non-formalizable passages of comment and discussion in a book like *Principia Mathematica*, rather than its systematic text, and it has the immense importance of that interstitial comment. The decisions and moves of thought that precede formal statement, and that lead us to discard one formal statement for another, are in fact the only part of a mathematicized system that has genuine philosophical interest, and all these are certainly dialectical in the Hegelian sense.

Having said so much in mitigation of initial prejudice, I wish to range my remarks on Hegel under three distinct heads: I wish to discuss dialectic as a feasible philosophical method which we might to some extent use on our modern problems, I wish to say something about the Hegelian use of the notions of internality and totality which differs so utterly from the not very useful employment of these notions by Bradley and the British Idealists, and I wish lastly to say something about the remarkable general perspective in which Hegel sees experience and the world, a perspective much more closely adjusted to the tough and tender aspects of experience, much less inclined to soar over them to some non-empirical beyond, than almost any other philosophical system, and a perspective which is, moreover, utterly misrepresented by what is generally thought to be the connotation of its name, i.e. 'absolute idealism'. In the sense in which other philosophers are idealists and absolutists, Hegel is not one at all: a perspectival rationalist or spiritualist, with a strong realist, empiricist and even materialist infusion might describe him better.

I shall now attempt to say what I think are the basic characteristics of Hegel's dialectical method, as actually evinced in his philosophical practice. The textbook accounts of thesis, antithesis and synthesis are descriptive nullities idly repeated by people who have for the most part no real acquaintance with the actual writings of Hegel or the real workings of his thought. I should say that the basic characteristic of the dialectical method is that it always involves *higher-order comment* on a thought position previously achieved. What one does in dialectic is first to operate at a given level of thought, to accept its basic assumptions, and to go to the limit in its terms, and then to proceed to stand outside of it, to become conscious of it, to become clear as to what it really has achieved, and how far these achievements do or do not square with its actual professions. In dialectic one sees what can be said *about* a certain thought-position that one cannot actually say *in* it. And the sort of comment made in dialectic is not a comment on the correctness or truth of what is said in a certain manner or in terms of certain concepts, but a comment on the adequacy or logical satisfactoriness of the conceptual approaches or instruments one has been employing. In dialectic one criticizes one's mode of conceiving things, rather than the actual matter of fact that one has conceived. One is, if one likes to use Moorean terms, giving a series of deepening analyses of ordinary matters of fact, whose 'truth' in the common-or-garden sense is never questioned, or one is, if one likes, putting forward a series of 'linguistic recommendations' each of which illuminates matters of fact more intensively and more widely. Hegel would of course never have expressed himself in either of these ways, but with his uncanny prescience for later philosophical developments, he very often comes close to it. His official description of what he is doing is that he is giving a series of improving definitions of the Absolute.

What Hegel does is in fact extraordinarily like what is done in modern syntactics or semantics or similar formal studies, when we pass from discourse *in* a language to discourse *about* that language, when we make a language an object-language *for* a metalanguage. It includes of course the further willingness to make what is brought out in this manner itself part of a widened object-language, but this is likewise something regularly done in many metalinguistic exercises. What is further important to realize is that such metalinguistic dialectical comment always involves the possible emergence of definite novelties of principle, things not formally entailed by what one has done at the lower level. Sometimes these novelties are slight, mere reaffirmations or endorsements or particularly stressed versions of what one had previously thought: sometimes, however, they involve an ironical swing-over to what is totally contrary, the assertion *about* X of something which is just the opposite of what X itself intends or asserts, as when we assert from a higher level the complete nullity of a distinction which a lower level vehemently makes: sometimes again they involve the making clear of a conceptual inadequacy, and the concealed need for some sense-making, saving complement. Sometimes, still more remarkably, they involve a reversal of perspective which turns a problem into an explanation: we come to see in certain very difficult contrasts and oppositions the 'very nature' of something which requires just these contrasts and oppositions and so renders them acceptable. This last step resembles the falling in love with a woman for the very features which at first made her unattractive. The central nerve of Hegel's dialectic is in fact of this sort: it consists in finding absoluteness, finality and infinity *precisely* in what at first promised *never* to be so.

The building set up by thought's perpetual self-transcendence is in fact not an erect but a tapering structure: it is a widening, top-heavy building in which the higher storeys extend farther and farther beyond their base. *More* entities, *more* concepts and principles are in fact always needed to cope with the entities, concepts at a given level than are to be found at that level, a fact well known to those who construct formal systems, but strangely ignored by all those nominalists, reductionists, phenomenalists, etc., who think it incumbent on them to keep the higher storeys of the conceptual building well *within* its supporting base. Fortunately the principles of logical stability are not those of architecture, since there is not in their case any overwhelming urge towards the ground.

Two of the greatest logico-mathematical discoveries of fairly recent times may in fact be cited as excellent and beautiful examples of Hegelian dialectic: I refer to Cantor's generation of transfinite numbers, and to

Goedel's theorem concerning undecidable sentences. In the case of Cantor we first work out the logic of the indefinitely extending series of inductive, natural numbers, none of which transcends finitude or is the last in the series. We now pass to contemplate this series from without, as it were, and raise the new question as to how many of these finite, natural numbers we have. To answer this we must form the concept of the first transfinite number, the number which is the number *of* all these finite numbers, but is nowhere found *in* them or among them, which exists, to use Hegelian language, *an sich* in the inductive finite numbers, but becomes *für sich* only for higher-order comment. And Cantor's generation of the other transfinite numbers, into whose validity I shall not here enter, are all of exactly the same dialectical type. Goedel's theorem is also through and through dialectical, though not normally recognized as being so. It establishes in a mathematicized mirror of a certain syntax-language that a sentence declaring itself, through a devious mathematicized circuit, to be unproveable in a certain language system, is itself unproveable in that system, thereby setting strange bounds to the power of logical analysis and transformation. But the unproveable sentence at the same time soars out of this logico-mathematical tangle since the proof of its unproveability in *one* language is itself a proof of the same sentence in *another* language of higher level, a situation than which it is not possible to imagine anything more Hegelian.

There are countless other good examples of such a dialectical swing-over in the history of philosophy: Descartes's Cogito which turns universal first-order doubt into absolute higher-level certainty, Anselm's similar transformation of the God doubted by the fool into a being that even the philosopher cannot doubt, Hume's ironic claim that the hideous pantheism of Spinoza was in fact indistinguishable from the belief in an underlying substantial soul, Wittgenstein's solipsism which by eliminating the possibility of talking about another person's experiences ends by making it impossible to speak of one's own, etc. etc. We perform similar dialectical moves when we recognize concreteness to be an extraordinarily abstract notion, the idea of beauty to be profoundly unbeautiful in its non-sensuous remoteness, the militancy of the 'free world' to be in danger of becoming tyrannical, the null-class or class devoid of members to be itself a perfectly good member of a class of higher order, the absence of the *doux printemps d'autrefois* to be itself lamentably present, the wonderful abstractness and gratuitous purity of a behaviourist theory to testify unwittingly and unwillingly to the existence of what can never be fully evinced in behaviour, etc. etc. I am not, however, concerned to make dialectic reputable, but to make plain what it is. It is a method in which step 2 is a true and inevitable and sometimes ironic comment on what has been present at step 1, step 3 a true and inevitable comment on what has been present at step 2, and so on. If at any stage in this proceeding, a step is not a true and inevitable comment on what went before, wrung from it by reflection, then the step in question is not valid. Hegel's dialectic is not an amusing or boring parlour game of setting up arbitrary oppositions among notions, and then arbitrarily 'overcoming' them. The emergence of the oppositions and their overcoming must be the inevitable fruit of reflection on what the notions are, if it is to be valid at all: it must, as Hegel says, be the *Erfahrung*, the experience of a previous phase, or, more radically, it must be simply what is involved in the conscious view that the previous phase *has* gone before, much as, on a plausible analysis of time, the content of the present simply *is* the pastness of whatever has gone before it.

You will no doubt now feel that I should to some extent illustrate all these sweeping assertions regarding Hegel's dialectic, the fruit, I may say, not of pondering over commentaries, nor of armchair reconstruction, but of reading and repeated reading of Hegel's actual text, over a large number of years, and of repeated dissections of his arguments with several seminars of intelligent students. I do not shrink, as some commentators shrink, from this sort of test, but the extent to which I can submit myself to it this evening is unfortunately (or perhaps fortunately) very limited. I shall therefore refer to, rather than actually expound, a few of Hegel's dialectical sequences, so that you can see how the pattern works in practice. Let us begin with the famous beginning of the Logic, where we start with the mere notion of 'being', the sort of notion we have when we collide with an object in the dark without making out what it is, when we face the world after a swoon without as yet construing it, or when we have a vague 'objectless' affect directed merely to 'something'. This notion gives itself out to be positive and rich in content, and the most opposed to the mere absence of anything. Seen from a higher point of view it reveals itself, however, as utterly empty and abstract, and as not really differing in content from the total absence it excludes. To think merely of *some* object, one knows not what, does not differ significantly from thinking of *no* object at all. The 'truth' of the indeterminate first something is therefore nothing, in Hegel's intriguing language, and the 'truth' of this *last* affirmation is simply the impossibility of keeping emptily abstract notions apart, their tendency to lose their would-be distinctness and to flow over into one another. Logical instability, marginal fluidity, notional becoming is in short the 'truth' of hard-and-fast abstractness carried to extremes. The whole phantasmagoric flux points, however, inexorably to definite being, the being of an object united with a determining feature, which is a being-this or a being-such or a being-there rather than a *mere* being. The dialectic here grasps at the differentiatedness from which it is possible to abstract, and apart from which references to an *a* and a *b*, to something and something else, such as we make in pure mathematics, make no sense at all.

I have now shown you the working of the dialectic in Hegel's famous first triad, that through being, nothing and becoming to determinate being, which has been so much misunderstood and abused. Let me now take a flying leap to the beginning of the Doctrine of Essence where Hegel dwells on the notion of identity and shows it to be senseless unless connected with essential difference: it only makes sense to say that *A*, e.g. the Buddhist religion, is one and the same, if *A* is also differentiated into co-ordinate forms A_1, A_2, A_3, A_4, Theravada Buddhism, Mahayana Buddhism, Zen Buddhism, etc., *in* which it can be identical. Hegel is here recalling the strayed sheep of formal logic, which try to be so independent and self-sufficient, to the fold of ordinary usage and understanding. This essential difference is at first mere difference, the diversity of things in the world which have nothing to do with one another: it is plain, however, on unblinkered reflection, that each different form only is what it is by virtue of what it excludes, and this makes the hidden 'truth' of mere difference lie in polar opposition. Polar opposition brings to a focus what all difference less obviously illustrates. Opposition, however, reveals itself, on deeper examination, as not so 'head-on', so crass, as it superficially gives itself out to be. Opposites depend wholly for their being on their contrast, as is brought out saliently in opposites like east and west, and this means, if we reflect on it, that each opposite really has *its* opposite built into itself, has its whole being in opposing that opposite. This leads, on a profounder examination, to the insight that all opposition is in a sense veiled equivalence, the *A* of a *B* facing the *B* of an *A*, a proposition whose import modern psychoanalysis has used to the full in its studies of sexual permutations.

A last flying leap will now take us to the very different final triad of the Logic where the idea of life, as the passing on of an organic type or pattern through a variety of individuals is shown to involve the possible separation of that type in and for a mind. The natural world is essentially a petrified, externalized version of an order which science internalizes and abstracts and makes its notional own. One cannot understand the natural world, and certainly not its highest organic phases, except as a series of universals sunk in matter which must be lifted into full consciousness in the medium of science. Science, however, shows us mind in the ever unfinished endeavour of subordinating the natural world to rational explanatory patterns of various sorts, but always finding the fathomless individuality of things eluding the net of its patterns. What intelligent activity aims at, however, practical activity achieves, i.e. the complete mastery of *individual* natural reality by rational pattern. The 'truth' of theory, as Marx was afterwards plagiaristically to repeat, lies in practice. Practice, however, also is unable to complete the rationalization of an alien order—to do so would lead to its own destruction—and needs the help of a final injection of theory, the view of the world in all its theoretical and practical imperfection as the eternal foil or battleground required by rationality in order to deploy itself fully and become fully conscious of itself. In all these dialectical transitions there is no entailment in the formal logical sense, and yet no stringing together of random observations. At each stage we see the sense or the truth of the previous stage, what it did not try to be yet was, or what it was not but tried to be, and by so seeing things we see them in an ever changing and enriched perspective. Some of Hegel's transitions are no doubt much more far-fetched and questionable than others: sometimes they are so far-fetched as to seem arbitrary and irrational. Dialectical movement, however, is not inference, but notional deepening of what has gone before, and deepening may have many varying grades of relevance and illumination. On the whole, however, the experienced Hegelian finds profound illumination even in the most far-fetched of Hegel's transitions: it is illuminating, e.g., to see the profound analogy between a syllogism, which attaches a universal to an individual by way of some suitable middle term, with a scientific object, which is merely a syllogism turned on its head, an individual illustrating various specific and generic concepts. Likewise to find in historical and other changes a gross carrying out of the self-criticism present in dialectical thought is by no means unhelpful and absurd. The fact, further, that we can question or criticize Hegel's transitions shows that there is something in his method. A purely arbitrary, illogical stringing together of ideas would not be open to criticism.

I wish now to lay some stress on the use throughout Hegel's system of an appeal to implications, internal relations among concepts, which are not the entailment-relations dominant in formal logic. Hegel assumes throughout that, while we can and must blinker our gaze in using each limited concept—we must think in terms of abstract identity when we are doing formal logic, in terms of mere quantity when we are doing mathematics, in terms of pushes and pulls and weights when we are doing mechanics, in terms of mere realism when we are studying nature, in terms of abstract rights when we are studying jurisprudence, etc. etc.—that our notions are none the less not without a profound and necessary relevance to other notions not included in their purview, that they require these other notions to make sense, and that this requirement reveals itself in dialectic as soon as we examine each notion from above or from without. We can see, for instance, that the abstractions of logic and mathematics are nothing without a qualitatively variegated world, that mechanics is an imperfect illustration of connections more clearly exhibited at the organic and teleological levels, that the natural order ultimately needs the scientific intelligence to interpret it, that abstract rights can only obtain in a much more closely knit, not merely juridical unity, etc. etc.

The internal relations I am citing must be carefully distinguished from the internal relations appealed to by writers of the school of Bradley, and I shall try to indicate the main ways in which they are different. In the first place, the internality appealed to by a writer like Bradley is universal, and of equal intimacy throughout: it is more a reflection of Spinozism and of nineteenth-century determinism than of Hegelianism. For Bradley, etc., there are no external relations, no irrelevances, nothing could have been different without disrupting the whole: the most trivial fact of experience is as closely linked with other similar facts as are the most fundamental features of experience. In Bradley, we may say, the universal sway of internal relations reduces them all to non-significance, it does not differ from the sway of the most absolute externality. It is like the situation aptly put in Gilbert and Sullivan, where when everybody's somebody then no one's anybody. In Hegel there is nothing of this sort. It is held that there are vast reaches of experience where contingency ranges unchecked, where the philosopher must strenuously avoid the temptation of trying to prove that things *must* be so and not otherwise. And even at the level where rational implication obtains, the connections studied are still open to empirical exception, even on a large scale. They represent norms, paradigms, completely rounded out cases needed to make full sense of everything, but not necessarily realized everywhere and always. Thus Hegel's idealism, which holds that the natural world has an inner affinity for mind, and that it necessarily produces minds to which it will, after a struggle (like the sea-god Proteus) deliver its secrets and reveal itself in its true notional form—this idealism is compatible with the view that mind was the last thing in time to appear on the world-stage, and that there were long ages of past existence when there were *no minds at all.* Hegel as an idealist is infinitely far from both Berkeley and Kant, and he is more nearly a dialectical materialist than most Hegelians have realized.

The inner connections which link one notion to another are therefore rather carried out in limiting or fully perfected cases than in any and every instance: they are goals towards which cases move, rather than concomitances they always satisfy. And Hegel believes like Aristotle that one cannot understand the richer, more developed case from the more meagre and less developed: the developed, fully rounded case has the priority in explanation. If Hegel's view of internality differs from Bradley's in being liable to much empirical exception, and being much more limited in scope, it differs from it also in laying no stress on an all-embracing *whole.* The word 'universe' is hardly ever mentioned in Hegel, and then only at some definite phase of thought such as that of the 'object'. What is infinite and absolute in Hegel is always the individual concrete reality, pinned down in time and space, especially when it is conscious of itself. It is infinite and absolute not by losing itself in the 'whole', but by concentrating the whole in itself, by demoting the 'universe' with its trivial, dispersed being to a condition of its own self-conscious, rational life. For Bradley philosophy is a dumb grasping at the Absolute, for Hegel philosophy is the Absolute. It is in and for the rational activities of conscious human individuals that everything 'cosmic' may be held ultimately to exist.

If you now ask me whether I actually believe in all this mild internality, the answer is that I do believe it, and that I believe that a philosopher should look for it everywhere. Philosophy should not be an experimental playing about with logical possibilities and a seeking to make them more numerous than they at first seem to be: it should aim at a judicious reduction of them, at finding them much less numerous than they at first seem to be. I am encouraged in this attitude by the extent to which even modern logical empiricism or analytic philosophy has deferred to it in practice, if not always in theory. For modern logical empiricism and analysis, as for Hegelianism, it is not merely an accident that our sense-experience exemplifies regularly recurrent patterns: without it there would be no identifiable objects, and objectively oriented discourse would not be possible. The occasional loose sense-experience exists, and radical looseness is not logically self-contradictory, but it is implied by all our discourse that it will not obtain. In the same manner logical empiricism like Hegelianism admits the non-accidental character of the existence of persons other than the speaker: all our standards of truth and significance are implicitly public. Wittgenstein, throughout his life a prey to dialectical *Umschwünge,* after dallying long with solipsism passed over to what may be called radical publicism, the doctrine that it is impossible to talk purely to oneself in a language framed only for one's private use. I do not myself accept this extreme swing of dialectic—I believe that in a world where publicity exists privacy also has its possibility and its legitimacy—but I mention it to indicate the degree to which modern philosophy covertly admits non-analytic connections. Personally, as I have said, I believe them to exist everywhere, and to penetrate far down into the detail of experience: practically everywhere one finds, if one seeks for them, extraordinary analogies, affinities and relations of mutual complementarity among the most seemingly disparate, disconnected things.

I now wish, in the limited time at my disposal, to say something about Hegel's central affirmation, his so-called absolute idealism. This is not the belief that all things exist only in and for a consciousness, but that all things must be seen either as necessary conditions of, or as stages towards, self-conscious rationality, towards the conscious rational use of universals, or, as Hegel calls it, *Geist* or Spirit. What does Hegel mean by saying that Geist is the truth of everything, and is such an affirmation in any way valid or acceptable? The whole of our study of Hegel's dialectic shows that this assertion is not to be metaphysically understood: it does not go beyond the facts of human experience, its sense lies in the daylight of our conscious rational life. Geist is in fact exemplified in the three forms of Art, Religion and Philosophy: it is there and nowhere else that Hegel's Absolute is to be found. And that Geist is the truth of everything does not mean that Geist engineered the world, or was causally responsible for it: Geist makes its appearance at a comparatively late stage in the world's history, its supreme stage, philosophy, is even said to arrive in the world when the shades of night are falling. Clearly the sense in which Geist is the truth of everything in the world is a perspectival sense: it is an *Ansicht,* a peculiar view of the facts of experience—Hegel sometimes characterizes it as the removal of an illusion—not something which underlies the universe or is causally responsible for it.

The precise way in which this *Ansicht,* this crowning perspective, arises, is not left obscure by Hegel. When we fully realize that the various unspiritual things in the world are *necessary conditions* for the emergence of Geist, of rational conscious activity, their apparent unspirituality vanishes: they become mere adjuncts and aspects of rational subjectivity, things built into it and inseparable from it. This insight is again and again achieved in relation to different kinds of material. We start, for instance, by treating the material of sense-experience as something alien and external to our minds: we painfully struggle to impose on it the rational pattern of perception or scientific law. This venture succeeds continously, but is never finally successful: each triumph of scientific explanation creates new problems for the scientist. But on the endless approximations of science a mystical insight supervenes: we realize that the struggle with recalcitrant sensory materials is *necessary* to the being of science, that if all nature could be reduced to a tautology, without irreducible elements of sense-given individuality, rational science would wither away and die. In this insight lies also the way to the absolute: we realize that the recalcitrance of sense is only (as it were) a sham recalcitrance, a recalcitrance presupposed by and necessary to science, the shadow cast by its own abundant life. It will be always there, because science will always be there—perhaps with some cosmic intermissions—but to realize its merely shadow-character is to overcome its alienness, to see it as a mere adjunct of rational science.

In the same way, our practical life starts in a welter of instincts and personal interests of which no rational deduction is possible. Practical life consists in subjecting these instincts and interests to individual and social discipline, in weaving them into great, ordered projects, a task which again can never be finally completed. On this welter of passion, and on this everlasting approximation of practice, a mystical vision supervenes: we see the passions as the mere raw stuff for rational control and planning, as being there to be organized and subjected, as themselves rational *because* they are the necessary conditions, the raw material of reason. In much the same manner, our social life starts in a brutal struggle with other individuals, which at first tends to the enslavement of individuals or classes of individuals by other individuals or classes of individuals, at a later stage to the co-ordination of persons in various social unities. This co-ordination, too, can never be carried to completion: there will always perhaps be excluded individuals and repressed classes. But on the broken arcs of the social unity and the class-struggle a higher vision supervenes: we see that the deep gulf between persons and classes of persons is a necessary condition of their emergent rationality. Only because people are rent apart in atomic privacy can the rational life of science bridge their differences of insight and experience, only because they live immured in selfish interests, can morality and social obligation arise among them. The distinctness of persons is therefore a *necessary condition* of the rational life common to them all, and is therefore a *part* of that life. If it did not exist, it would have to be imagined or invented. In the same way, lastly, we begin to see the whole material world, with its ladder of forms rising from the inert and mechanical to the purposively organized and organic, as a mere hieroglyph of the order found in conscious rationality, as a mere preparation for that rationality itself. In this crowning vision all discrepancies, frustrations, resistances, conflicts are seen as necessary conditions of the final rational outcome, as in fact already part of it. Can we accept this Hegelian *Ansicht,* and is it in some sense the ultimately *right* perspective in which to view life and the world?

I shall here merely say that I think there are several strong grounds for being an Hegelian, and that I doubt whether there are equally strong grounds for being anything else. One *should* be an Hegelian because, as a rational being, one *must* be one anyway, because one must at least *act* as if all theoretical discrepancies could be removed, all irrational impulses controlled, all differences of personal insight and interest adjusted, the natural world deprived of its alienation and remoulded to serve the rational purposes of man. There is, I think, a good practical ground for being an Hegelian, and for those who believe in the unity of thought and practice, this should be sufficient. There is, however, also a good theoretical ground for preferring Hegel's perspective to any other, and this lies in the fact that rational subjectivity alone demands, requires, presupposes all the other toward and untoward factors in life and experience, whereas they do not seem to demand, require, presuppose rational activity. It explains them as they do not explain it. Rational activity is in a sense the most dependent of all things in the world: not only the stresses of Hitler's concentration camps, but a mere breakdown in the central heating may suffice temporarily to disrupt it. But its dependence on everything can be seen, by a rational change of perspective, to be a dependence of everything on it: the world either has no explanation at all, or is explained only by it. Either the world is merely a bad tragedy, a series of episodes, everything which is the case, or it has its 'sense' in Spirit.

What shall I recommend you to believe? And what do I myself believe? In my not infrequent moods of exaltation I am certainly an Hegelian. When I do hard theoretical work and succeed in communicating its results to others, I feel that the whole sense of the world lies in endeavours such as mine, that this is the whole justification of its countless atrocious irritants. I feel clear too that the world *has* a sense, and that no other philosophy expresses this sense satisfactorily. But in my more frequent mood of mild depression I am not an Hegelian, I regress to a materialism which is not, I fear, at all dialectical. I see the world as bereft of sense, and I submit masochistically to its senselessness, even taking more comfort in its cold credibility than in the rational desirability of Hegelianism. I am not even convinced that there is one best or right perspective in which the world should be viewed: it seems a provocative staircase figure always idly altering its perspective. Being myself uncertain, I shall not try to turn you into Hegelians. But what I shall insist on is the need of keeping Hegel, despite all his difficulty and the difficulty of getting anyone to teach him properly, in our philosophical curriculum, for to miss his illumination is to miss one of the greatest pleasures and treasures of civilized life.

II. THE HEGEL MYTH AND ITS METHOD

Walter Kaufmann

Hegel's importance. Hegel was not a pagan like Shakespeare and Goethe but a philosopher who considered himself Christian and tried to do from a Protestant point of view what Aquinas had attempted six hundred years earlier: he sought to fashion a synthesis of Greek philosophy and Christianity, making full use of the labors of his predecessors. Among these he counted not only the great philosophers from Heraclitus and Plato down to Kant, Fichte, and Schelling but also such world-historic individuals as Paul and the men who had made the French Revolution. As he saw it, philosophy did not stand between religion and poetry but above both. Philosophy was, according to him, its age comprehended in thought, and—to exaggerate a little—the philosopher's task was to *comprehend* what the religious person and the poet *feel.*

Hegel's enormous importance becomes clear as soon as we reflect on his historic role. There is, *first,* his direct influence, which appears not only in philosophic idealism, which, at the turn of the last century, dominated British and American philosophy—Bradley, Bosanquet, McTaggart, T. H. Green, and Royce, to give but five examples—but also in almost all subsequent histories of philosophy, beginning with the epoch-making works of Erdmann, Zeller, and Kuno Fischer. It was Hegel who established the history of philosophy as a central academic discipline and as

Reprinted by permission of Faber and Faber Ltd. from *The Owl and the Nightingale* and by permission of the author.

part of the core of any philosophic education. It was also Hegel who established the view that the different philosophic systems that we find in history are to be comprehended in terms of development and that they are generally one-sided because they owe their origins to a reaction against what has gone before.

Secondly, most of the more important philosophic movements since his death have been so many reactions against Hegel's own idealism and cannot be fully understood without some grasp of his philosophy. The first two great revolts were those of Kierkegaard and Marx, who swallowed easily as much of his philosophy as they rejected: notably, his dialectic. Today Marx's dialectic dominates a large part of the total population of the globe, while Kierkegaard's has been adapted by some of the most outstanding thinkers of the free world, notably Heidegger and Tillich, Barth and Niebuhr.

Two later revolts against Hegelianism dominate English and American philosophy in the twentieth century: pragmatism and analytic philosophy. William James, though occasionally he attacked Hegel himself, reconstructed Hegel somewhat in the image of his Harvard colleague, Royce, who was then the outstanding American idealist; while Moore, at Cambridge, who was joined by Russell, led the fight against the influence of Bradley and McTaggart.

One of the few things on which the analysts, pragmatists, and existentialists agree with the dialectical theologians is that Hegel is to be repudiated: their attitude toward Kant, Aristotle, Plato, and the other great philosophers is not at all unanimous even within each movement; but opposition to Hegel is part of the platform of all four, and of the Marxists, too. Oddly, the man whom all these movements take to be so crucially important is but little known to most of their adherents; very few indeed have read as many as two of the four books that Hegel published.

Hegel is known largely through secondary sources and a few incriminating slogans and generalizations. The resulting myth, however, lacked a comprehensive, documented statement till Karl Popper found a place for it in his widely discussed book, *The Open Society and Its Enemies.* After it had gone through three impressions in England, a revised one-volume edition was brought out in the United States in 1950, five years after its original appearance.

2

Critique of a critic. To explode the popular Hegel legend one can hardly do better than to deal in some detail with Popper's Hegel chapter. This involves a temporary departure from religion and poetry, but the development "from Shakespeare to existentialism" cannot be understood without some grasp of Hegel and some discussion of the widely accepted image of Hegel. Moreover, Hegel is so frequently mentioned in contemporary discussions that it is intrinsically worth while to show how wrong many widespread assumptions about him are. Thirdly, our study should include some explicit consideration of questions of method, and especially of common pitfalls. Finally, we shall have occasion, as we develop Hegel's actual views, to call attention to the religious roots of some of his most characteristic notions.

Those who nevertheless prefer to skip this chapter to pick up the thread in the next should at least take note of the author's awareness that gross falsifications of history are not the monopoly of Miniver Cheevy. Forward-looking liberals and even believers in "piecemeal social engineering," like Popper, often distort history, too. And so, alas, did Hegel.

A detailed critique of Popper's sixty-nine pages on Hegel may be prefaced with a motto from Nietzsche's *Ecce Homo:* "I only avail myself of the person as of a strong magnifying glass with which one can render visible a general but creeping calamity which it is otherwise hard to get hold of."

The calamity in our case is twofold. First, Popper's treatment contains more misconceptions about Hegel than any other single essay. Secondly, if one agrees with Popper that "intellectual honesty is fundamental for everything we cherish" (p. 253), one should protest against his methods; for although his hatred of totalitarianism is the inspiration and central motif of his book, his methods are unfortunately similar to those of totalitarian "scholars"—and they are spreading in the free world, too.

3

Scholarship. Although the mere presence of nineteen pages of notes suggests that his attack on Hegel is based on careful scholarship, Popper ignores the most important works on his subject. This is doubly serious because he is intent on psychologizing the men he attacks: he deals not only with their arguments but also—if not altogether more—with their alleged motives. This practice is as dangerous as it is fashionable, but in some cases there is no outright evidence to the contrary: one can only say that Popper credits all the men he criticizes, except Marx, with the worst possible intentions. (Marx he credits with the best intentions.)

In the case of Hegel, there is voluminous evidence that Popper ignores: beginning with Dilthey's pioneering study of 1906 and the subsequent publication of Hegel's early writings, ample material has been made available concerning the development of his ideas. There is even a two-volume study by Franz Rosenzweig, the friend of Martin Buber, that specifically treats the development of those ideas with which Popper is concerned above all: *Hegel und der Staat.*

Furthermore, Popper has relied largely on *Scrib-*

ner's Hegel Selections, a little anthology for students that contains not a single complete work. Like Gilson in *The Unity of Philosophical Experience* (p. 246), Popper takes over such a gross mistranslation as "the State is the march of God through the world," although the original says merely that it is the way of God with the world that there should be the State, and even this sentence is lacking in the text published by Hegel and comes from one of the editor's additions to the posthumous edition of *The Philosophy of Right*—and the editor admitted in his Preface that, though these additions were based on lecture notes, "the choice of words" was sometimes his rather than Hegel's.

Popper also appears to be unaware of crucial passages, if not entire works, that are not included in these *Selections;* for example, the passage on war in Hegel's first book, which shows that his later conception of war, which is far more moderate, was not adopted to accommodate the king of Prussia, as Popper maintains. The passage on war in Hegel's *Phenomenology of the Spirit,* in the section on "The Ethical World," was written when Hegel—a Swabian, not a Prussian—admired Napoleon and was published in 1807, a year after Prussia's devastating defeat at Jena. Hegel's views on war will be considered soon (in section 11); but questions of method require our attention first.

4

Quilt quotations. This device, used by other writers, too, has not received the criticism it deserves. Sentences are picked from various contexts, often even out of different books, enclosed by a single set of quotation marks, and separated only by three dots, which are generally taken to indicate no more than the omission of a few words. Plainly, this device can be used to impute to an author views he never held.

Here, for example, is a quilt quotation about war and arson: "Do not think that I have come to bring peace on earth; I have not come to bring peace, but a sword. . . . I came to cast fire upon the earth. . . . Do you think that I have come to give peace on earth? No, I tell you. . . . Let him who has no sword sell his mantle and buy one." This is scarcely the best way to establish Jesus' views of war and arson. In the works of some philosophers, too—notably, Nietzsche—only the context can show whether a word is meant literally.

The writings of Hegel and Plato abound in admittedly one-sided statements that are clearly meant to formulate points of view that are then shown to be inadequate and are countered by another perspective. Thus an impressive quilt quotation could be patched together to convince gullible readers that Hegel was—depending on the "scholar's" plans—either emphatically for or utterly opposed to, say, "equality." But the understanding of Hegel would be advanced ever so much more by citing one of his remarks about equality *in context*, showing how it is a step in an argument that is designed to lead the reader to a better comprehension of equality and not to enlist his emotions either for it or against it.

Even those who would not reduce all philosophy to such analyses should surely grant the ambiguity of words like equality and freedom, good and God—and also that philosophers can be of service by distinguishing some of the different meanings of such terms instead of aping politicians by assuring us that they are heartily in favor of all four. Popper writes like a district attorney who wants to persuade his audience that Hegel was against God, freedom, and equality—and uses quilt quotations to convince us.

The first of these (p. 227) consists of eight fragments of which every single one is due to one of Hegel's students and was not published by him.

Although Popper scrupulously marks references to Gans's additions to the *Philosophy of Right* with an "L" and invariably gives all the references for his quilt quotations—e.g., "For the eight quotations in this paragraph, cf. *Selections* . . ."—few readers indeed will recall when they come to the Notes at the end of the book that "the eight quotations" are the quilt quotations that they took for a single passage. And Popper advises his readers "first to read without interruption through the text of a chapter, and then to turn to the Notes."

Quilt quotations invite comparison with composite photographs. In a campaign for a seat in the U. S. Senate, one such photograph was used that showed one candidate shaking hands with the head of the Communist party. It matters little whether it was labeled in fine print "composite photograph."

To be sure, quotations and photographs that are not patched together may be grossly unfair, too; and in rare cases, composite ones might not be unfair. But a self-respecting candidate will not use patched-up photographs of his opponent; and a scholar should not use a quilt quotation to indict the men he criticizes.

5

"*Influence.*" No conception is bandied about more unscrupulously in the history of ideas than "influence." Popper's notion of it is so utterly unscientific that one should never guess that he has done important work on logic and on scientific method. At best, it is reducible to *post hoc, ergo propter hoc.* Thus he speaks of "the Hegelian Bergson" (p. 256 and n. 66) and assumes, without giving any evidence whatever, that Bergson, Smuts, Alexander, and Whitehead were all interested in Hegel, simply because they were "evolutionists" (p. 225 and n. 6).

What especially concerns Popper—and many another critic of German thinkers—is the "influence" that the accused had on the Nazis. His Hegel chapter is studded with quotations from recent German writers, almost all of which are taken from *The War Against the West* by Kolnai. In this remarkable book Friedrich Gundolf, Werner Jaeger (Harvard), and Max Scheler are pictured as "representative of Nazism or at least its general trend and atmosphere." Kolnai is also under the impression that the men who contributed most "to the rise of National Socialism as a creed" were Nietzsche "and Stefan George, less great but, perhaps because of his homosexuality, more directly instrumental in creating the Third Reich" (p. 14); that Nietzsche was a "half-Pole" (p. 453); that the great racist H. S. Chamberlain "was a mellow Englishman tainted by noxious German influences" (p. 455); and that Jaspers is a "follower" of Heidegger (p. 207). It would seem advisable to check the context of any quotations from Kolnai's book before one uses them, but Kolnai generally gives no references. Popper writes:

> I am greatly indebted to Kolnai's book, which has made it possible for me to quote in the remaining part of this chapter a considerable number of authors who would otherwise have been inaccessible to me. (I have not, however, always followed the wording of Kolnai's translations.)

He evidently changed the wording without checking the originals or even the context.

Popper uses quotation after quotation from Kolnai to point out supposed similarities with Hegel, but never stops to ask whether the men he cites had read Hegel, what they thought of him, or where, in fact, they did get their ideas. Thus we are told that the idea of "fame is revived by Hegel" (p. 266), for Hegel spoke of fame as a "reward" of the men whose deeds are recorded in our history books—which would seem a trite enough idea that could also be ascribed to scores of sincere democrats—but Popper goes on: "and Stapel, a propagator of the new paganized Christianity, promptly [i.e., one hundred years later] repeats [*sic*]: 'All great deeds were done for the sake of fame or glory.'" This is surely quite a different idea and not trite but false. Popper himself admits that Stapel "is even more radical than Hegel." Surely, one must question the relevance of the whole section dealing with Stapel and other recent writers; this is not history of ideas but an attempt to establish guilt by association on the same page—in the hope, it seems, that *semper aliquid haeret.*

It is also the height of naïveté. A quick dip into a good dictionary of quotations would have shown Popper a great many closer parallels to Stapel than he found in Hegel. Perhaps the most extreme, and also the most memorable, formulations are found in some poets whose influence would be hard to gauge. Shakespeare writes:

Let fame, that all hunt after in their lives,
Live register'd upon our brazen tombs.

And though these lines occur in one of his comedies, *Love's Labour's Lost,* he certainly did not think meanly of fame. Ben Jonson even went a step further in *Sejanus* (I, ii): "Contempt of fame begets contempt of virtue." And Friedrich Schiller voiced a still more radical view—in a poem that many German school children learn by heart, *Das Siegesfest,* which deals with the Greeks' celebration of their triumph over Troy:

Of the goods that man has cherished
Not one is as high as fame;
When the body has long perished
What survives is the great name.

For every Nazi who knew Hegel's remarks about fame there must have been dozens who knew these lines. Does that prove Schiller a bad man? Or does it show that he was responsible for Nazism?

Besides, Popper often lacks the knowledge of who influenced whom. Thus he speaks of Heidegger and "his master Hegel" (p. 271) and asserts falsely that Jaspers began as a follower "of the essentialist philosophers Husserl and Scheler" (p. 270). More important, he contrasts the vicious Hegel with superior men "such as Schopenhauer or J. F. Fries" (p. 223), and he constantly makes common cause with Schopenhauer against the allegedly protofascist Hegel, whom he blames even for the Nazis' racism—evidently unaware that Fries and Schopenhauer, unlike the mature Hegel, *were* anti-Semites.

Hegel's earliest essays, which he himself did not publish, show that he started out with violent prejudices against the Jews. These essays will be considered in the next chapter; but they are not represented in *Scribner's Hegel Selections* and hence were not exploited by Popper. Nor have they exerted any perceivable influence. When Hegel later became a man of influence, he insisted that the Jews should be granted equal rights because civic rights belong to man because he is a man and not on account of his ethnic origins or his religion.

Fries, who was Hegel's predecessor at the University of Heidelberg, has often been considered a great liberal, and Hegel has often been condemned for taking a strong stand against him; it is rarely, if ever, mentioned in this context that Fries published a pamphlet in the summer of 1816 in which he called for the "extermination" of Jewry. It appeared simultaneously as a review article in *Heidelbergische Jahrbücher der Litteratur* and as a pamphlet with the title "How the Jews endanger the prosperity and the character of the Germans." According to Fries, the Jews "were and are the bloodsuckers of the people" (p. 243) and "do not at all live and teach according to Mosaic doctrine but according to the Talmud" (p. 251) of which Fries conjures up a frightening picture. "Thus the Jewish caste . . . *should be exterminated completely* [*mit Stumpf und Stiel ausgerottet*] *because it is obviously of all secret and political societies and states within the state the most dangerous*" (p. 256). "Any immigration of Jews should be forbidden, their emigration should be promoted. Their freedom to marry should . . . be limited. . . . It should be forbidden that any Christian be hired by a Jew" (p. 260); and one should again force on them "a special mark on their clothing" (p. 261). In between, Fries protests: "Not against *the Jews,* our brothers, but against *Jewry* [*der Judenschaft*] we declare war" (p. 248).

This may help us to understand why Hegel, in the Preface to his *Philosophy of Right,* scorned Fries's substitution of "the pap of 'heart, friendship, and enthusiasm'" for moral laws. It would certainly have been unwise of the Jews to rely on Fries's brotherly enthusiasm.

Hegel's often obscure style may have evened the way for later obscurantism, but Fries's and Schopenhauer's flamboyant irrationalism was, stylistically, too, much closer to most Nazi literature. It does not follow that Fries influenced the Nazis. He was soon forgotten, till, in the twentieth century, Leonard Nelson, a Jewish philosopher, founded a neo-Friesian school that had nothing to do with Fries's racial prejudices. The one influential thinker whom Nelson succeeded in leading back to Fries was Rudolf Otto, the Protestant theologian, who is best known for his book on *The Idea of the Holy.* What makes that book so notable is its fine description of the "numinous" experience; but the confused discussion of "The Holy as an A Priori Category" and the romantic notions about "divining" are indebted to Fries.

Popper, though he has written an important book on *Die Logik der Forschung,* "The Logic of Research," does not find it necessary to check his hunches by research when he is concerned with influences in his Hegel chapter. He simply decrees that Hegel "represents the 'missing link,' as it were, between Plato and the modern form of totalitarianism. Most of the modern totalitarians are quite unaware that their ideas can be traced back to Plato. But many know of their indebtedness to Hegel" (p. 226). Seeing that the context indicates a reference to the Nazis and that all the totalitarians cited in this chapter are Fascists, not Communists, Popper only shows his ignorance of this brand of totalitarianism.

Hegel was rarely cited in the Nazi literature, and, when he was referred to, it was usually by way of disapproval. The Nazis' official "philosopher," Alfred Rosenberg, mentioned, and denounced, Hegel twice in his best-selling *Der Mythus des Zwanzigsten Jahrhunderts.* Originally published in 1930, this book had reached an edition of 878,000 copies by 1940. In the same book, a whole chapter is devoted to Popper's beloved Schopenhauer, whom Rosenberg admired greatly. Rosenberg also celebrates Plato as "one who wanted in the end to save his people [*Volk*] on a racial basis, through a forcible constitution, dictatorial in every detail." Rosenberg also stressed, and excoriated, the "Socratic" elements in Plato.

Plato, unlike Hegel, was widely read in German schools, and special editions were prepared for Greek classes in the *Gymnasium,* gathering together allegedly fascist passages. In his introduction to one such selection from the *Republic,* published by Teubner in the series of *Eclogae Graecolatinae,* Dr. Holtorf helpfully listed some of his relevant articles on Plato, including one in the *Völkischer Beobachter,* which was Hitler's own paper. Instead of compiling a list of the many similar contributions to the Plato literature, it may suffice to mention that Dr. Hans F. K. Günther, from whom the Nazis admittedly received their racial theories, also devoted a whole book to Plato—not to Hegel—as early as 1928. In 1935, a second edition was published.

Whether Hegel did, or did not, influence the Nazis may not be particularly relevant to Popper's central theses in his book—but then most of his book is not. His often stimulating ideas are amalgamated with a great deal of thoroughly unsound intellectual history; and Section V of his Hegel chapter (eighteen pages) is representative of the latter. It is also representative of scores of similar attempts by authors who have less to offer than Karl Popper.

6

Vituperation and allegation of motives. Although Popper, in his introduction, speaks of "the application of the critical and rational methods of science to the problems of the open society" (p. 3), he writes about Hegel in the accents of a prosecutor who addresses a jury. He says of Fichte and Hegel, "such clowns are taken seriously" (p. 249); he demands, "I ask whether it is possible to outdo this despicable perversion of everything that is decent" (p. 244); and he denounces "Hegel's hysterical historicism" (p. 253; cf. p. 269).

Hegel certainly has grievous faults. Among these is his obscure style, but it is dry and unemotional in the extreme. A detailed account of his almost incredibly unemotional style as a lecturer has been given by one of his students, H. G. Hotho, and is quoted in Hermann Glockner's *Hegel* (I, 440 ff.), and in Kuno Fischer's *Hegel*, too. If "hysterical" means, as Webster says, "wildly emotional," Popper deserves this epithet much more than Hegel. For all of Hegel's shortcomings, it seems wildly emotional indeed to say that "he is supreme only in his outstanding lack of originality" and was not even "talented" (p. 227). And "the critical and rational methods of science" could hardly establish Popper's contention that the philosophy of Jaspers is a "gangster" philosophy (p. 272). Nor is this proved by a note on "the gangster philosophy" in the back of the volume, which turns out to furnish us with a quilt quotation (see above) from Ernst von Salomon's book, *The Outlaws*, which bears no perceivable relation to Karl Jaspers—not to speak of Hegel.

Popper's allegation of motives is scarcely distinguishable from vituperation. Hegel is accused of "a perversion . . . of a sincere belief in God" (p. 244), but no evidence whatever is given to substantiate this charge. "Hegel's radical collectivism . . . depends on Frederick William III, king of Prussia" and his "one aim" was "to serve his employer, Frederick William of Prussia" (pp. 227 f.); and it is hinted that Hegel misused philosophy as a means of financial gain (p. 241); but Popper ignores the literature on this question, which includes, in addition to the volumes cited above, T. M. Knox's article on "Hegel and Prussianism" in *Philosophy*, January 1940, and his discussion with Carritt in the April and July issues.

Hegel, we are told, "wants to stop rational argument, and with it, scientific and intellectual progress" (p. 235), and his dialectics "are very largely designed to pervert the ideas of 1789" (p. 237). When Hegel explicitly comes out in favor of the things that, according to his accuser, he opposed, this is called "lip service" (ns. 11 and 43). Thus Popper claims—like Bäumler in his Nazi version of Nietzsche—that the man whom he professes to interpret did not mean what he clearly said. Quilt quotations are used to establish a man's views, and his explicit statements are discounted when they are inconvenient.

In the name of "the critical and rational methods

of science," one must also protest against such emotional *ad hominem* arguments as that Heidegger's philosophy must be wrong because he became a Nazi later on (p. 271), or that "Haeckel can hardly be taken seriously as a philosopher or scientist. He called himself a free thinker, but his thinking was not sufficiently independent to prevent him from demanding in 1914 'the following fruits of victory . . .'" (n. 65). By the same token, one might seek to discredit Popper's philosophy of science by pointing to his treatment of Hegel, or Newton's physics by calling attention to his absorbing concern with magic, which Lord Keynes has described in his *Essays and Sketches in Biography*.

Popper's occasional references to "the doctrine of the chosen people," which he associates with totalitarianism, show little knowledge of the prophets though a great deal of emotion, and his references to Christianity are also based on sentiment rather than the logic of research. He is "for" Christianity, but means by it something that is utterly at variance with the explicit teachings of Paul, the Catholic Church, Luther, and Calvin.

Hegel's rejection of the adequacy of conscience as a guide in moral questions is countered by Popper's parenthesis, "that is to say, the moralists who refer, for example, to the New Testament" (p. 262)—as if no crimes had ever been committed in the name of the New Testament. Julius Streicher, in his violently anti-Semitic paper, *Der Stürmer*, constantly quoted the Gospel according to St. John.

One of the most important criticisms of Popper's approach, and of the large literature that resembles his attack on Hegel, might be summed up by citing Maritain's epigram from *Scholasticism and Politics* (p. 147): "If books were judged by the bad uses man can put them to, what book has been more misused than the Bible?"

7

Hegel's metaphysics. Two simple points may illustrate how thoroughly Popper misunderstands the whole framework of Hegel's thought. First, he claims that Hegel taught that "self-evidence is the same as truth" (p. 237), although Hegel's first book begins with the denial of this view and Hegel never changed his mind about this.

The second point is more important because Hegel has so often been misunderstood in this way. "Hegel believes, with Aristotle, that the Ideas or essences are *in* the things in flux; or more precisely (as far as we can treat a Hegel with precision), Hegel teaches that they are identical with the things in flux: 'Everything actual is an Idea,' he says" (p. 231). Yet one need not look farther than Royce's helpful article on Hegel's terminology in Baldwin's *Dictionary of Philosophy and Psychology* to find that "actual" is, in Hegel's work, a technical term (as its equivalent was in Plato's and Aristotle's), and that he very emphatically did not claim that Ideas—another technical term—"are identical with the things in flux."

The dictum around which these misinterpretations have been woven most persistently, beginning when Hegel was still alive, occurs in the Preface to his *Philosophy of Right* and reads: "What is rational, is actual; and what is actual, is rational."

This dictum is very similar to Leibniz's idea that this world is the best of all possible worlds. Without sympathizing in the least with either of these two ideas, one should realize that both are rooted in religion. In the third edition of his *Encyclopaedia* (1830; §6) Hegel himself said of his epigram:

> These simple sentences have seemed striking to some and have excited hostility—even from people who

> would not wish to deny some understanding of philosophy, not to speak of religion. . . . When I have spoken of actuality, one might have inquired, without being told to do so, in what sense I use this expression; after all, I have treated actuality in an elaborate *Logic* and there distinguished it precisely not only from the accidental, which, of course, has existence, too, but also, in great detail, from being there, existence, and other concepts.

Alas, this passage was not included in *Scribner's Selections;* hence these distinctions are overlooked by Popper, who reiterates the popular myth that, according to Hegel, "everything that is now real or actual . . . must be reasonable as well as good. And particularly good is, as we shall see, the actually existing Prussian state."

It would prevent some confusion if Hegel's term *wirklich* were translated *actual,* seeing that he opposed it to *potential* rather than to *unreal* or *nonexistent.* An acorn, though certainly real enough in the usual sense of that word, is not, as Hegel uses that term, *wirklich.* Only that is actual in Hegel's sense which fully realizes its own nature or, as Hegel might say, the "idea" of which most existent things fall short. And the Prussian state, though, according to Hegel, more rational than a state that is based on slavery, yet fell short in some respects, as his *Philosophy of Right* makes clear, of the "idea" of the state.

8

The State. When Hegel speaks of "the State" he does not mean every state encountered in experience. Immediately after first offering his epigram about the rational and actual, he himself continued:

> What matters is this: to recognize in the semblance of the temporal and transient the substance which is

> immanent and the eternal which is present in it. For the rational (which is synonymous with the Idea), in its actuality, also embeds itself in external existence and thus manifests itself in an infinite wealth of forms, appearances, and figures, shrouding its core in a multicolored rind. Our consciousness first dwells on this rind, and only after that does philosophic thinking penetrate it to detect the inward pulse and to perceive its beat even in the external forms. The infinitely varied relations, however, which take shape in this externality . . . this infinite material and its organization are not the subject matter of philosophy.

Thus Hegel would distinguish between the Idea of the State, which he means when he speaks of "the State," and the many states around us. But the Idea, he claims, does not reside in a Platonic heaven, but is present, more or less distorted, in these states. The philosopher should neither immerse himself in the description and detailed analysis of various historical states, nor turn his back on history to behold some inner vision: he should disentangle the rational core from the web of history.

Hegel is not driven to "juridical positivism" and the approbation of every state with which he is confronted, as Popper supposes (p. 252): he can pass judgment. Hegel makes a sharp distinction between such philosophic judgment and the arbitrary criticisms that reflect personal idiosyncrasies and prejudices. This would not involve any difficulty if he were willing to restrict himself to internal criticism, pointing out the multifarious inconsistencies that are so striking in the utterances of most statesmen, in the platforms of most parties, and in the basic convictions of most people. Hegel, however, goes further.

He believes in a rational world order and in his ability to understand it. For him, life is not "a tale told by an idiot"; and history, not merely, although also, a succession of tragedies. There is an ultimate purpose —freedom—and this furnishes a standard of judgment.

A few quotations from the *Philosophy of Right* may illustrate this. "One may be able to show how a law is completely founded in, and consistent with, both circumstances and existing legal institutions, and yet is truly illegitimate and irrational" (§3). Hegel also speaks of "*unalienable*" rights and condemns, without qualification,

> slavery, serfdom, the disqualification from holding property or the prevention of its use or the like, and the deprivation of intelligent rationality, of morality, ethics, and religion, which is encountered in superstition and the concession to others of the authority and full power to determine and prescribe for me what actions I am to perform . . . or what duties my conscience is to demand from me, or what is to be religious truth for me [§66].

According to the addition of Gans, the editor, Hegel remarked in his lectures in this connection that "the slave has an absolute right to liberate himself" (cf. also §77).

Hegel is not inconsistent when he writes: "the State cannot recognize conscience [*Gewissen*] in its peculiar form, i.e., as subjective knowledge [*Wissen*], just as in science, too, subjective opinion, assurance, and the appeal to subjective opinion have no validity" (§137). Conscience is fallible; and, while no government or church has the right to dictate to our conscience, no government can afford to recognize conscience as a legal standard. As several of his interpreters have pointed out, Hegel, when he wrote the *Philosophy of Right*, was concerned about the recent assassination of the poet Kotzebue by a student who was convinced that the poet was a Russian spy and deserved death.

We are bound to misunderstand Hegel when we apply his remarks about conscience within the framework of the Nazi state. It would be more pertinent if we thought of the German Republic before 1933 and of the conscience of Hitler. For by "the State" Hegel means one in which freedom is realized and "a human being counts because he is a human being, not because he is a Jew, Catholic, Protestant, German, Italian, or the like"—and this "is of infinite importance" (§209; cf. §270 n.). Hegel would consider rational the conscience of an opponent of Hitler who recognized his own absolute right to make himself free and to realize his unalienable rights—but not the conscience of a fanatic impelled by personal motives or perhaps by an equally objectionable ideology.

It is no wonder that the Nazis found small comfort in a book that is based on the conviction that "the hatred of law, of right made determinate by law, is the shibboleth which reveals, and permits us to recognize infallibly, fanaticism, feeble-mindedness, and the hypocrisy of good intentions, however they may disguise themselves" (§258 n.). In his Preface, too, Hegel called the law "the best shibboleth to distinguish the false brothers and friends of the so-called people." One may agree with Herbert Marcuse when he says in *Reason and Revolution: Hegel and the Rise of Social Theory:* "There is no concept less compatible with Fascist ideology than that which founds the state on a universal and rational law that safeguards the interests of every individual, whatever the contingencies of his natural and social status" (pp. 180 f.).

In sum: Popper is mistaken when he says, like many another critic, that, according to Hegel, "the only possible standard of judgment upon the state is the world historical *success* of its actions" (p. 260). Success is not the standard invoked in the *Philosophy of Right* when Hegel speaks of "bad states." "The State" does not refer to one of "the things in flux," but to an Idea and a standard of judgment, to what states would be like if they lived up fully to their *raison d'être*. This reason is to be found partly "in a higher sphere" (§270) for which Hegel himself refers the reader to his system as outlined in his *Encyclopaedia*. The whole realm of Objective Spirit and human institutions that culminates in the State is but the foundation of a higher realm of Absolute Spirit that comprises art, religion, and philosophy.

The discussion of "the State" in the *Philosophy of Right* opens with the pronouncement: "The State is the actuality of the ethical idea." If he were a Platonist, he would mean justice; but Hegel means freedom: not that freedom from all restraints which, at its worst, culminates in anarchy, license, and bestiality, but, rather, man's freedom to develop his humanity and to cultivate art, religion, and philosophy. He considers the State supreme among human institutions because he would subordinate all such institutions to the highest spiritual pursuits and because he believes that these are possible only in "the State." He himself says: "To be sure, all great human beings have formed themselves in solitude—but only by assimilating what had already been created in the State."[1] One might nevertheless insist, as Hegel does not, that conformity should be discouraged beyond the necessary minimum, and one might dwell, as Nietzsche did half a century later, on the dangers of the State.

It would be absurd to represent Hegel as a radical individualist; but it is equally absurd to claim, as Popper does (p. 258), that Hegel's State is "totalitarian, that is to say, its might must permeate and control the whole life of the people in all its functions: 'The State is therefore the basis and center of all the concrete elements in the life of a people: of Art, Law,

[1] *Die Vernunft in der Geschichte*, ed. Lasson, p. 92; *Reason in History*, transl. Hartman, p. 51.

Morals, Religion, and Science.'" Popper's claim simply ignores Hegel's emphatic insistence on the sphere of "subjective freedom," which he himself considered a decisive advance over Plato. The quotation from Hegel, of course, does not at all prove the preceding contention: it means—and the context in the lectures on the *Philosophy of History* (Preface) makes this quite clear—that the State alone makes possible the development of art, law, morals, religion, and science. And Hegel's formulation here shows less the influence of Plato, whom Popper represents as a terrible totalitarian, than the impact of Pericles, whom Popper admires. The sentence Popper quotes could almost come from Thucydides' version of Pericles' most famous speech.

Hegel's philosophy is open to many objections, but to confound it with totalitarianism means to misunderstand it. Ernst Cassirer puts the matter very clearly in *The Myth of the State* (1946), a book dealing with much the same material as Popper's, but in a much more scholarly manner. His Hegel chapter ends: "Hegel could extol and glorify the state, he could even apotheosize it. There is, however, a clear and unmistakable difference between his idealization of the power of the state and that sort of idolization that is the characteristic of our modern totalitarian systems."

9

History. Hegel, like Augustine, Lessing, and Kant before him and Comte, Marx, Spengler, and Toynbee after him, believed that history has a pattern and made bold to reveal it. All these attempts are controversial in detail and questionable in principle; but a sound critique of Hegel should also take into account his remarkable restraint: he did not attempt to play the prophet and was content to comprehend the past.

Popper says that his own book could be "described

as a collection of marginal notes on the development of certain historicist philosophies" (p. 4); and, as we have seen, he accuses Hegel of "hysterical historicism." But according to Popper's definition, Hegel was no historicist at all: he was not one of those who "believe that they have discovered laws of history which enable them to prophesy the course of historical events." This addiction to predictions is what Popper means by historicism (p. 5).

We are told that Hegel was guilty of

> historical and evolutionary relativism—in the form of the dangerous doctrine that what is believed today is, in fact, true today, and in the equally dangerous corollary that what was true yesterday (*true* and not merely "believed") may be false tomorrow—a doctrine which, surely, is not likely to encourage an appreciation of the significance of tradition [p. 254].

Hegel, of course, excelled in his appreciation of the significance of tradition; in his books and lectures he took for granted its essential rationality, and he condemned as arbitrary any criticism of the past or present that was not accompanied by an appreciation of the significance of tradition.

He did not maintain "that what is believed today is, in fact, true today" but insisted that many of his contemporaries, both philosophers and "men in the street," held many mistaken beliefs. And "what was true yesterday . . . may be false tomorrow" is, in a sense, a commonplace—as when we take such statements as "it is raining" or "the Americans, while saying that all men are endowed by their Creator with certain unalienable rights, including liberty, hold slaves" or "another war might well spread the ideals of the French Revolution, without endangering the future of civilization." The same consideration applies to many a generalization about a nation and about war.

Hegel did not believe that such propositions as "two plus two equals four" were true at one time but not at another; he thought that the truth comes to light gradually and tried to show this in his pioneering lectures on the history of philosophy. He emphasized not how utterly wrong his predecessors had been but how much truth they had seen; yet Plato's and Spinoza's truths were not "all of the truth" but were in need of subsequent qualification and amendment.

Hegel's approach is not amoral. Although he finds the aim of history in its "result" (p. 260) and considers the history of the world the world's court of justice (p. 233 and n. 11), he does not idolize success. His attitude depends on his religious faith that in the long run, somewhere, somehow freedom will and must triumph: *that* is Hegel's "historicism." Those of us who lack his confidence should still note that he does not believe that things are good because they succeed, but that they succeed because they are good. He finds God's revelation in history.

This point is best illustrated by Hegel's polemic against Von Haller in the *Philosophy of Right* (§258). Throughout, he tries to avoid the Scylla of that revolutionary lawlessness that he associates with Fries and the Wartburg festival and the Charybdis of conservative lawlessness that he finds in Von Haller's *Restauration der Staatswissenschaft.* He cites Von Haller (I, 342 ff.): "As in the inorganic world the greater represses the smaller, and the mighty, the weak, etc., thus among the animals, too, and then among human beings, the same law recurs in nobler forms." And Hegel interposes: "Perhaps frequently also in ignoble forms?" He then quotes Von Haller again: "This is thus the eternal, immutable order of God, that the mightier rules, must rule, and always will rule." And Hegel comments: "One sees from this alone, and also from what follows, in what sense might is spoken of here: not the might of the moral and ethical, but the accidental force of nature."

Popper quotes Hegel: "A people can only die a violent death when it has become naturally dead in itself" (p. 263); and Hegel continues, "as e.g. the German Imperial Cities, the German Imperial Constitution" (n. 77). Applied to the collapse of the Holy Roman Empire in 1806, Hegel's remark makes sense, while his bold generalization invites criticism. But one should take into account that Hegel is in agreement with a religious tradition that extends from Isaiah to Toynbee.

Intent on dissociating Hegel from this religious tradition and on associating him with the Nazis instead, Popper fastens on Hegel's conception of world-historical peoples. He quotes (p. 258) Hegel's *Encyclopaedia* (§550) as saying that "the Spirit of the Time invests its Will" in "the self-consciousness of a particular Nation" that "dominates the World." This would seem to be another instance where Popper improved a translation without checking the original (cf. section 5 above). The passage in the *Encyclopaedia* reads: "The self-consciousness of a particular people is the carrier of the current stage of development of the universal spirit as it is present, and the objective actuality into which this spirit lays its will." In *Scribner's Hegel Selections,* this becomes ". . . in which that spirit for a time invests its will." And in Popper, finally, we suddenly encounter "the Spirit of the Time." His profuse capitalization of nouns in his quotations from Hegel is apparently intended to make Hegel look silly.

Hegel goes on to say, though Popper does not quote this, that the spirit "steps onward" and "delivers it over to its chance and doom." His position depends on his assumption that ultimate reality is spiritual and that the spirit reveals itself progressively in history. The stages of this revelation are represented by different peoples, but by only one people at any one time.

This strange notion was adapted by Stefan George and, with the individual prophet in the place of a whole people, became part of the creed of his Circle:

> *In jeder ewe*
> *Ist nur ein gott und einer nur sein künder.*

This idea that "in every epoch, there is but one god, and but one his prophet" is even more obviously false than Hegel's view; and it is doubly ironical because, even in the relatively small field of German poetry, George was no solitary giant but was eclipsed by his contemporary, Rilke.

Hegel's notion was surely suggested to him by the way in which the Romans succeeded the Greeks—and perhaps also the Greeks, the Persians; and the Persians, the Babylonians.

> This people is the *dominant* one in world history for this epoch—*and it can be epoch-making in this sense only once.* Against this absolute right which it has to be the embodiment of the current stage of development of the world spirit, the spirits of the other peoples have no right, and they, even as those whose epoch has passed, do not any longer count in world history.[2]

Above all, Hegel was probably also influenced by the Christian conception of the relation of Christianity to Jew and Greek.

Hegel's conception is dated today: we know more than he did about the history of a great number of civilizations. We can no longer reduce world history to a straight line that leads from the Greeks via the

[2] *Philosophy of Right,* §347.

Romans to ourselves; nor can we dispose of ancient Asia as "The Oriental Realm" and understand it simply as the background of the Greeks. We are also aware of ambiguities in the conception of a *Volk* or nation and should not apply such terms to the carriers of Greek or Roman civilization. We understand the flowering of medieval philosophy in terms of the interaction of Jews, Muslims, and Christians against a Greek background, and should not care to say who in that epoch represented the world spirit. Some of us have even lost all belief in a world spirit.

All this does not imply that Hegel's views are wicked or that his basic error is due to his alleged nationalism or tribalism. Toynbee's conception of separate civilizations is open to almost the same objections.

With the exception of entirely isolated communities, no unit can be understood completely without reference to others. But any unit whatever, whether it be Western civilization, France, Athens, or the Burlington Railroad, can be made the object of a historical study. In each instance, one will introduce other units as sparingly as possible and only to throw light on the history of the unit under consideration.

Hegel's whole conception of "world history" is arbitrary and amounts to an attempt to study the development of his own civilization. But here he was at one with almost all of his contemporaries and predecessors who were also under the influence of the Bible. For it is from the Bible that the Western idea that history has a single beginning and moves along a single track toward a single goal received its impetus and sanction. Today we are apt to be more agnostic about the beginning; we are bound to deny the single track; but we may once again think in another sense of the unity of world history—a unity that is established by the present confluence of hitherto independent streams.

Hegel was not impeded by the recognition that

some of the ancestors of his own civilization had made their epoch-making contributions simultaneously. Homer may have been a contemporary of the earliest prophets; Thales and Jeremiah wrote at the same time; and Stoicism flourished while Christianity developed out of Judaism. Elsewhere, Confucius and the Buddha were contemporaries. A pluralistic perspective is needed, as is more respect for individual units. There is no single plan into which all data can be fitted, and Hegel was certainly something of a Procrustes.

Any attempt, however, to read into Hegel's conception of "world domination" an exclusively political or even military sense in order to link him with Hitler is quite illegitimate. It is doubly misleading when one does not emphasize that Hegel was not making predictions or offering suggestions for the future but was scrupulously limiting himself to an attempt to understand the past. Pedagogically, the single-track conception has the virtue of simplicity; and it is still adopted almost universally in the field of Hegel's primary competence—the history of philosophy.

10

Great men and equality. Hegel's conception of world-historical peoples is closely related to his notion of world-historical personalities. Both notions are justifiable up to a point. Some peoples have had little effect on anybody outside themselves, while the Greeks and the Jews, for example, have affected the history of the world out of all proportion to their numbers. Similarly, Socrates and Caesar might well be called world-historical personalities.

It is the rankest emotionalism when Popper writes:

> Glory cannot be acquired by everybody; the religion of glory implies antiequalitarianism—it implies a re-

> ligion of "Great Men." Modern racialism accordingly "knows no equality between souls, no equality between men" (Rosenberg). Thus there are no obstacles to adopting the Leader Principles from the arsenal of the perennial revolt against freedom, or as Hegel calls it, the idea of the World Historical Personality [pp. 266 f.].

Popper implies that we ought to be "for" equalitarianism; but if it involves the belief that no man can achieve anything that cannot be achieved by everybody else, too, it is simply silly. In any sense in which it is at all worth while, equalitarianism is entirely compatible with belief in great men.

According to Popper,

> Hegel twists equality into inequality: "That the citizens are equal before the law," Hegel admits, "contains a great truth. But expressed in this way, it is only a tautology; it only states in general that a legal status exists, that the laws rule. But to be more concrete, the citizens . . . are equal before the law only in the points in which they are equal *outside the law* also. *Only that equality which they possess in property, age, . . . etc., can deserve equal treatment before the law. . . .* The laws themselves presuppose unequal conditions. . . . It should be said that it is just the great development and maturity of form in modern states which produces the supreme concrete inequality of individuals in actuality" [p. 239].

The omissions in the Hegel quotation are Popper's, and Popper explains them in the very next sentence:

> In this outline of Hegel's twist of the "great truth" of equalitarianism into its opposite, I have radically abbreviated his argument; and I must warn the reader that I shall have to do the same throughout the chap-

ter; for only in this way is it at all possible to present, in a readable manner, his verbosity and the flight of his thoughts (which, I do not doubt, is pathological).

A look at the *Encyclopaedia* (§539) shows that Hegel is not "for" or "against" equality but tries to determine in what sense it can be embodied in the modern state.

> With the appearance of the State, inequality enters; namely, the difference between the governing forces and the governed, authorities, magistrates, directories, etc. The principle of equality, carried out consistently, would repudiate all differences and thus be at odds with any kind of state.

It is in the following discussion that we find the sentence italicized by Popper, and it seems best to quote it without omissions and with Hegel's, rather than Popper's, italics:

> Only that equality which, in whatever way, *happens to exist independently,* regarding wealth, age, physical strength, talents, aptitude, etc., or also crimes, etc., can and should justify an equal treatment of these before the law—in regard to taxes, liability to military service, admission to public office, etc., or punishment, etc.

Hegel's sentence, though hardly elegant, is carefully constructed and exhibits a crucial parallelism. Only those with equal wealth should be taxed equally; age and physical strength should be taken into account by draft boards; talents and aptitudes are relevant qualifications for public service; and so forth. Or should we have equal punishment for all, regardless of whether they have committed equal crimes? Should we induct children into the armed forces and exact equal taxes from the poor and the rich? Is it Hegel that is guilty of a "twist"?

To return to "great men": Hegel said, according to Gans's addition to section 318: "Public opinion contains everything false and everything true, and to find what is true in it is the gift of the great man. Whoever tells his age, and accomplishes, what his age wants and expresses, is the great man of his age." (Popper's "translation" of this passage [p. 267] makes nonsense of it: "In public opinion all is false and true. . . .") Hegel's passage ends, in Popper's translation: "He who does not understand *how to despise public opinion*, as it makes itself heard here and there, will never accomplish anything great." Popper's italics as well as his comments appeal to the reader's prejudice in favor of the supremacy of public opinion, though he previously appealed to the prejudice in favor of the supremacy of conscience. These two standards, however, are very different; and Hegel recognized the fallibility of both because he did not believe, as Popper alleges (p. 237), that "self-evidence is the same as truth." Hegel argued, in the body of section 318, that "to be independent of [public opinion] is the first formal condition of anything great and rational"; and he had the faith that public opinion "will eventually accept it, recognize it, and make it one of its own prejudices."

In the above quotation from Gans's addition, Popper finds an "excellent description of the Leader as a publicist"; and since he has introduced it with a reference to "the Leader principle," one is led to think of the *Führer* and to consider Hegel a proto-Nazi. The quotation, however, is not at odds with a sincere belief in democracy and fits beautifully not only Franklin D. Roosevelt's "interventionism" but also Lincoln's great speeches; for example, "A house divided against itself cannot stand" or "With malice toward none; with charity for all." And it is true of Lincoln, too, when

Hegel says of the world-historical personalities, "They were practical, political men. But at the same time they were thinking men, who had an insight into the requirements of the time–into what was ripe for development."

Hegel found that world-historical individuals are always propelled by some passion ("Nothing Great in the World has been accomplished without *passion*") and that their motivation is rarely entirely disinterested. The latter point he expressed in terms of "the cunning of reason." The individual may be motivated not only by profound insights but also by "private interests" and even "self-seeking designs." Alexander was passionately ambitious; but in the long run his private interests furthered Western civilization. The same consideration applies to Caesar and to Franklin D. Roosevelt; in *The American Political Tradition*, Richard Hofstadter has shown how Lincoln, too, was fired by political ambitions until he was elected president.

Popper links Hegel with "the fascist appeal to 'human nature' [which] is to our passions" and proposes that we call this appeal the *"cunning of the revolt against reason"* (p. 268). Yet he himself evidently believes that Napoleon, whose motivation was hardly entirely disinterested and whose methods could scarcely be approved by a devotee of "the open society," was furthering Western civilization to such an extent that the German uprising against him must be labeled "one of these typical tribal reactions against the expansion of a supernational empire" (p. 250).

11

War. Without accepting Hegel's view of war, one should distinguish it clearly from the Fascists'. Three points may suffice here.

First, Hegel looks back, not forward. He is not less

interested than Popper in "the furthering of civilization" (p. 268) but finds that our civilization has been furthered by any number of wars in the past; for example, the Greeks' war against the Persians, Alexander's wars of conquest, some of the Romans' wars, and Charlemagne's conquest of the Saxons. Believing that it is the philosopher's task to comprehend "that which is"—to cite the Preface to the *Philosophy of Right*—and not to construct utopias, Hegel speaks of war as one of the factors that have actually furthered civilization.

Second, we should not confuse Hegel's estimate of the wars that had occurred up to his own time with a celebration of war as we know it today or imagine it in the future.

Third, Hegel's attitude is not fully comprehensible when considered apart from its religious roots. He considered all that is finite ephemeral. According to Gans's addition to section 324, he said: "From the pulpits much is preached concerning the insecurity, vanity, and instability of temporal things, and yet everyone . . . thinks that he, at least, will manage to hold on to his possessions." What the preachers fail to get across, "Hussars with drawn sabres" really bring home to us. (Popper writes "glistening sabres" [p. 269]; and the change, though slight, affects the tone of the passage.)

These three points are sufficient to show how Popper misrepresents Hegel's view. "Hegel's theory," we are told, "implies that war is good in itself. 'There is an ethical element in war,' we read" (p. 262). This is a curious notion of implication: from Hegel's contention that "there is an ethical element in war, which should not be considered an absolute evil" (§324), Popper deduces that Hegel considered war "good in itself." Hegel attempted to solve the problem of evil by demonstrating that even evil serves a positive function. He accepted Goethe's conception of "that force which would/Do evil evermore and yet creates the good." It is of the very essence of Hegel's dialectical approach to penetrate beyond such assertions as that war is good or evil to a specification of the respects in which it is good and those in which it is evil. Today the evil so far outweighs any conceivable good that we are apt to be impatient with anyone who as much as mentions any good aspects; but in a concrete predicament, the majority still feels that the good outweighs the evil, even if this point is made by speaking of "the lesser evil."

The one passage in which Hegel does consider the question of future wars is not well known and is worth quoting. It is found in his Berlin lectures on aesthetics:

> Suppose that, after having considered the great epics of the past [the *Iliad, Cid,* and Tasso's, Ariosto's, and Camoëns' poems], which describe the triumph of the Occident over the Orient, of European measure, of individual beauty, and of self-critical reason over Asiatic splendor, . . . one now wished to think of great epics which might be written in the future: they would only have to represent the victory of the living rationality which may develop in America, over the incarceration into an infinitely progressing measuring and particularizing. For in Europe every people is now limited by another and may not, on its part, begin a war against another European people. If one now wants to go beyond Europe, it can only be to America.[3]

In his lectures on the philosophy of history, Hegel also hailed the United States as "the land of the future."[4] Plainly, he did not believe that world history

[3] *Werke,* ed. Glockner, XIV, 354 f.

[4] *Ibid.,* XI, 128 f.

would culminate in Prussia. His lectures on history do not lead up to a prediction but to the pronouncement: "To this point consciousness has come."

This may also be the clue to the famous expression of resignation at the end of the Preface to the *Philosophy of Right*—a passage that, at first glance, seems at odds with the subsequent demand for trial by jury and for a real parliament with public proceedings, institutions then still lacking in Prussia. But apparently Hegel did not believe that Prussia, or Europe, had any real future: "When philosophy paints its grey on grey, a form of life has grown old, and with grey on grey it cannot be rejuvenated, but only comprehended. The owl of Minerva begins its flight only at dusk."

12

Nationalism. On this point Popper's account is particularly confused. "When nationalism was revived a hundred years ago [about 1850?], it was in one of the most mixed regions of Europe, in Germany, and especially in Prussia" (p. 245). A page later, we hear of "the invasion of German lands by the first national army, the French army under Napoleon." Three pages later we are told that Fichte's "windbaggery" gave "rise to modern nationalism." Fichte died in 1814. Contemptuous of the concept of nationality, Popper maintains that it is a common belief in democracy, "which forms, one might say, the uniting factor of multilingual Switzerland" (p. 246). Why, then, have the Swiss no wish to unite with any democratic neighbor? Popper's opposition to many features of modern nationalism is well taken; but those who are interested in its development, or who wish to understand it, will do better to turn to Hans Kohn's *The Idea of Nationalism* (1944) and to his chapter on "Nationalism and the Open Society" in *The Twentieth Century* (1949).

One of the major themes of Popper's Hegel chapter is that "Hegelianism is the renaissance of tribalism" (p. 226). Popper's use of "tribalism" and "nationalism" is emotional rather than precise, and he accuses Hegel of both. Even so he must admit that Hegel "sometimes attacked the nationalists" (p. 251). Popper cites Hegel's *Encyclopaedia* where the so-called nation is condemned as rabble:

> And with regard to it, it is the one aim of a state that a nation should *not* come into existence, to power and action, as such an aggregate. Such a condition of a nation is a condition of lawlessness, demoralization, brutishness. In it, the nation would only be a shapeless wild blind force, like that of a stormy elemental sea, which however is not self-destructive, as the nation—a spiritual element—would be.

The Nazis concluded quite correctly that Hegel was unalterably opposed to their conception of the *Volk* and that his idea of the State was its very antithesis.[5]

Popper, on the other hand, is so intent on opposing Hegel that he immediately seeks to enlist the reader's sympathies on the nationalist side when he finds Hegel criticizing it. Thus Popper is not content to point out, quite correctly, that Hegel is referring "to the liberal nationalists" but must add, "whom the king hated like the plague." Hegel's attitude, of course, cannot be understood or reasonably evaluated in terms of the emotional impact of such words as "liberal" and "king." What is wanted is a profile of the movement condemned by Hegel; and that may be found in Herbert Marcuse's *Reason and Revolution* (pp. 179 f.):

> There was much talk of freedom and equality, but it was a freedom that would be the vested privilege of

[5] Cf., e.g., Rosenberg's *Mythus*, p. 527.

> the Teutonic race alone. . . . Hatred of the French went along with hatred of the Jews, Catholics, and "nobles." The movement cried for a truly "German war," so that Germany might unfold "the abundant wealth of her nationality." It demanded a "savior" to achieve German unity, one to whom "the people will forgive all sins." It burned books and yelled woe to the Jews. It believed itself above the law and the constitution because "there is no law to the just cause." The state was to be built from "below," through the sheer enthusiasm of the masses, and the "natural" unity of the *Volk* was to supersede the stratified order of state and society. It is not difficult to recognize in these "democratic" slogans the ideology of the Fascist *Volksgemeinschaft.* There is, in point of fact, a much closer relation between the historical role of the *Burschenschaften,* with their racism and antirationalism, and National Socialism, than there is between Hegel's position and the latter. Hegel wrote his *Philosophy of Right* as a defense of the state against this pseudo-democratic ideology.

The "liberal" Fries called for the extermination of Jewry (section 5 above), while Hegel denounced the nationalistic clamor against the extension of civil rights to the Jews, pointing out that this "clamor has overlooked that they are, above all, human beings" (§270 n.). Are we to condemn Hegel because he agreed with the king, or praise Fries because he called himself liberal?

13

Racism. Popper's most ridiculous claim—and the last one to be considered here—is that the Nazis got their racism from Hegel. In fact, the Nazis did not get their racism from Hegel, and Hegel was no racist (see section 5 above).

The Nazis did find some support for their racism in Schopenhauer, with whom Popper constantly makes common cause against Hegel, and in Richard Wagner, who Popper eccentrically insinuates was something of a Hegelian (p. 228) though he was, of course, a devoted disciple of Schopenhauer. Popper declares that one W. Schallmeyer, when he wrote a prize essay in 1900, "thus became the grandfather of racial biology" (p. 256). What, then, is the status of the rather better known and more influential Gobineau and Chamberlain and any number of other writers who publicized their views before 1900 and were widely read and constantly quoted by the Nazis?

Popper offers us the epigram: "Not 'Hegel + Plato,' but 'Hegel + Haeckel' is the formula of modern racialism" (p. 256). Why Haeckel rather than Bernhard Förster, Julius Langbehn, Hofprediger Stöcker, Chamberlain, Gobineau, or Wagner? Why not Plato, about whose reflections on breeding the Nazis' leading race authority, Dr. Hans F. K. Günther, wrote a whole book—and Günther's tracts on race sold hundreds of thousands of copies in Germany and went through several editions even before 1933? (See section 5 above.) And why Hegel?

Decidedly, Hegel was no racialist; nor does Popper adduce any evidence to prove that he was one. Instead, Popper says: "The transubstantiation of Hegelianism into racialism or of Spirit into Blood does not greatly alter the main tendency of Hegelianism" (p. 256). Perhaps the transubstantiation of God into the *Führer* does not greatly alter Christianity?

One can sympathize with G. R. G. Mure when he says that the increasingly violent and ill-informed attacks on Hegel have reached a point in Popper's Hegel chapter where they become "almost meaninglessly silly."[6] But familiarity with Hegel has waned to

[6] *A Study of Hegel's Logic*, p. 360.

the point where reviewers of the original edition of *The Open Society and Its Enemies*, while expressing reservations about the treatment of Plato and Aristotle, have not generally seen fit to protest against the treatment of Hegel; and on the jacket of the English edition Bertrand Russell actually hails the attack on Hegel as "deadly"—for Hegel. Since the publication of the American edition in 1950, John Wild and R. B. Levinson have each published a book to defend Plato against the attacks of Popper and other like-minded critics, and Levinson's *In Defense of Plato* goes a long way toward showing up Popper's methods. But Popper's ten chapters on Plato, although unsound, contain many excellent observations, and his book is so full of interesting discussions that no exposé will relegate it to the limbo of forgotten books. *The Open Society* will be around for a good long while, and that is one reason why its treatment of Hegel deserves a chapter.

What is ultimately important is not the failing of one author but the increasing popularity of the Hegel myth and of the methods on which it depends. To cite Nietzsche's *Ecce Homo* once more: "I only avail myself of the person as a magnifying glass with which one can render visible a general but creeping calamity which it is otherwise hard to get hold of."

Popper should be allowed the last word. And any critic of his work could do worse than to cite in his own behalf what Popper says to justify his own critique of Toynbee:

> I consider this a most remarkable and interesting book. . . . He has much to say that is most stimulating and challenging. . . . I also agree with many of the political tendencies expressed in his work, and most emphatically with his attack upon modern nationalism and the tribalist and "archaist," i.e., culturally reactionary tendencies, which are connected

with it. The reason why, in spite of this, I single out . . . [this] work in order to charge it with irrationality, is that only when we see the effects of this poison in a work of such merit do we fully appreciate its danger [pp. 435 f.].

III. THE YOUNG HEGEL AND RELIGION

Walter Kaufmann

How to approach Hegel. To find an approach to Hegel's later philosophy is extremely difficult. Taking their cue from him, some of the best Hegel scholars have attempted a historical approach. Richard Kroner, for example, wrote two volumes on the development *Von Kant bis Hegel,* while G. R. G. Mure devoted the first half of his *Introduction to Hegel* to Aristotle. Both procedures are illuminating, but we could also begin with Plato, Proclus, or Spinoza. The crucial question remains: How did Hegel come to relate his own philosophy so closely to that of his predecessors? How did he arrive at his unique conception of the close relation of systematic philosophy to the history of philosophy? What led him—the hyperbolic expression is almost justified—to the discovery of the history of philosophy, a discipline that he established with his lectures on that subject that were published by his students in three volumes after he had died?

Many studies, of course, have bypassed any historical approach and have plunged immediately into the *Logic*—the center of attention in the English literature—or, more judiciously, into the *Phenomenology,* which has more and more become the favorite of Continental scholars, not only in Germany. When we are thus confronted with Hegel's full-fledged philosophy, however, we find Hegel constantly reminding us that it is very difficult to make a beginning: wher-

Reprinted by permission of Faber and Faber Ltd. from *The Owl and the Nightingale* and by permission of the author.

ever he begins, all the rest is presupposed. He keeps comparing his philosophy to a circle and says in effect with T. S. Eliot: "In my beginning is my end" and "Every phrase and every sentence is an end and a beginning."

He insists on having a system but denies that it is based on assumptions he could fairly state at the outset—or anywhere. Hegel is unintentionally obscurantist at this point. His central assumption is indeed different from a mathematician's axioms, or even from Spinoza's: he takes for granted the essential truth of all the great philosophies of the past. Heraclitus and Parmenides, Plato and Aristotle, Descartes, Spinoza, and Kant had all seen the truth, but not all of the truth: their insights were partial. What is needed is the crowning integration of their visions, a synthesis of all that has gone before. Thus, Hegel's beginning, by presupposing his vision of the whole history of philosophy from the pre-Socratics to Schelling, presupposes his subsequent exposition.

It is only in Hegel's early essays that we encounter him without any such premise. In fact, at first his attitude was just the opposite of this. He himself did not publish these essays. It was only in 1906 that Dilthey called attention to them in his *Jugendgeschichte Hegels;* and, in the following year, this material was made available in a separate volume, admirably edited by one of Dilthey's students, Hermann Nohl. Unfortunately, Nohl gave the book a very misleading title: *Hegels theologische Jugendschriften.*

Just as interest in Hegel was thus being revived in Germany after a long lapse, Hegel went into eclipse in England and in the United States; it took forty-two years before two of these essays appeared in an English translation by T. M. Knox as Hegel's *Early Theological Writings.* What distinguishes these writings from Hegel's later works is, in part, that they are antitheological. A new reading of these antitheological essays furnishes the best introduction to Hegel's later works; it leads to a new conception of his intellectual development; and it helps to correct a far-reaching and fateful fasification of German cultural history.

2

The antitheological essays. It will be best to consider the four titles in the German volume one by one. The first two are omitted from the English edition, which features a sixty-six-page introduction by Richard Kroner. This is as scholarly as one would expect it to be in view of his earlier two-volume work—but equally subjective. Even as the title of the larger work suggested simultaneously Kroner's own development "from Kant to Hegel," the Introduction to the *Early Theological Writings* intimates Kroner's subsequent development into a mystic and a theologian. Hegel is now envisaged as "a Christian mystic" (p. 8) and a "Romanticist" (p. 14).

Are these early papers really theological? Only insofar as Webster defines one meaning of theology as "the critical, historical, and psychological study of religion and religious ideas." By the same token, Gibbon's *Decline and Fall,* Nietzsche's *Antichrist,* and Freud's *Future of an Illusion* could also be called "theological writings"—which would certainly be most misleading.

Hegel's essays are not antireligious but consistently depreciate theology in any customary sense of that word. We shall begin by considering five fragments that the German editor printed under the title *Folk Religion and Christianity.* Like the other so-called theological writings, they were not intended for publication by Hegel himself but are more interesting than many things he did publish. The next four sections deal with these earliest fragments, which are not available in English, under systematic headings.

3

Subjective and objective religion. Hegel begins with this contrast.

> Objective religion is *fides quae creditur,* . . . can be systematized, presented in a book or a lecture; subjective religion expresses itself only in feelings and acts [p. 6]. Subjective religion is all that matters. . . . Let the theologians quarrel about dogmas, about that which belongs to objective religion [p. 8]. Subjective religion is pretty much the same in all good human beings, while their objective religion can have almost any color whatever [p. 10].

In support, Hegel cites Lessing's *Nathan,* the greatest drama of the German Enlightenment. It has three heroes, a Christian, a Muslim, and a Jew, Nathan, who is modeled after Lessing's friend, Moses Mendelssohn. The moral of the play is stated in Nathan's version of the fable of the three rings: we cannot know which religion is true, we should respect other religions, and, above all, we should be moral. This is the work cited most often in these so-called theological writings—invariably with approval. And Hegel says expressly: "the most venerable human beings are assuredly not always those who have speculated most about religion and who very often transform their religion into theology" (p. 10).

Hegel goes on to denounce "the self-important conceit that characterizes the sectarian spirit which deems itself wiser than all human beings of other parties," finds an example in Tertullian, and expresses his admiration for Socrates. Of his more sarcastic remarks, one example may suffice:

> What a bald and forced remark it is when the good

> Gellert says somewhere that today any small child knows more about God than the wisest pagan—just like Tertullian. . . . As if the compendium of morals in my closet there, which I can use at will to wrap a stinking cheese, had more value than the, perhaps at times unjust, heart of Frederick II. For the difference between Tertullian's *opifex* [artisan] or Gellert's child, into whom the theological leaven has been beaten with the catechism, and the paper on which morals have been printed, is after all none too great in this respect: any consciousness gained through experience is lacking almost equally in all three cases [pp. 11 f.].

4

Hegel's difference with Kant. In his antitheological attitude, Hegel is at one with Lessing and other protagonists of the Enlightenment, and his insistence on the sole importance of subjective religion may remind us of Kant's dictum about the sole intrinsic value of the good will. Yet Hegel differed with Kant in some important respects, even in these earliest fragments.

> The understanding serves only objective religion. By purifying principles and by representing them in their purity, the understanding has produced splendid fruit, such as Lessing's *Nathan*, and it deserves the eulogies heaped on it. But the understanding can never transform principles into practice. The understanding is a courtier who obeys his master's moods and knows how to provide justifications for any passion and for any enterprise.

Here we are reminded of David Hume's famous formulation in his *Treatise* (Book II, Part III, §3): "Reason is . . . the slave of the passions." The understanding can rationalize any kind of conduct. "Enlightenment of the understanding makes more clever but not better" (p. 12).

What is needed to bring about moral conduct is, at least for the mass of the people, something in man's passional nature; and "love, though it is a pathological principle of action, is unselfish" (p. 18). The word "pathological" refers to Kant's usage: according to Kant, conduct motivated by love rather than by sheer respect for reason is not moral because its motivation is not rational but pathological, by which he means that it is grounded in the passions.

Moral teachings, says Hegel, must indeed be "authorized by the universal reason of man"; but they must also be "so human that they correspond to that stage of morality which a people has attained" (p. 21). Kant's ethics thus seems unrealistic. Mere respect for the moral law will not do; nor, Hegel thinks, will Christianity.

5

Hegel's vitriolic treatment of Christianity. In these fragments Hegel's hostility was not confined to Christian *theology;* and his sarcastic jibes about Christianity invite comparison with Voltaire, with Kierkegaard's *Attack on Christendom,* and with Nietzsche. Stylistically, too, he is much closer to these powerful polemicists than to the intricate and frequently obscure prose of his later years.

What distinguishes him from Voltaire and Kierkegaard, though not from Nietzsche, is the recurrence of sardonic contrasts of Christianity with ancient Greece.

> Not only does one train the Christian mob from childhood on to pray constantly; one also tries continually to persuade them of the supreme necessity of prayer by promising its sure fulfillment. And one has piled

up such a heap of reasons for comfort in misfortune . . . that we might be sorry in the end that we cannot lose a father or a mother once a week. . . . It might be very interesting to compare all this with the faith of the Greeks. . . . For them, misfortune was misfortune, pain was pain . . . [pp. 22 f.].

The popular feasts of the Greeks were all religious feasts. . . . Everything, even the excesses of the bacchanals, was sacred to some god. . . . At our greatest public feast, one approaches the enjoyment of the holy host in the color of mourning, with downcast eyes. At the very feast which ought to be the feast of universal brotherhood, many are afraid that through the brotherly goblet they might be infected with a venereal disease by someone who drank from it before. And lest one's mind remain attentive, God forbid, wrapt in a holy feeling, one must reach into one's pocket in the midst of things and put one's offering on a plate—whereas the Greeks, with the friendly gifts of nature, wreathed with flowers, clothed in the colors of joy . . . [pp. 26 f.].

This is the friend of Hölderlin, the hymnic poet who loved Greece and found the modern world a desert—a Hegel unknown to the mass of those who write about him. Nor did the young Hegel spare Christ, whom he contrasts cuttingly with Socrates, of whom he says:

Of course, one did not hear him deliver sermons on a platform or a mount: How could it even have occurred to Socrates, in Greece, to deliver sermons? He aimed to enlighten [!] men. . . . The number of his closer friends was indeterminate: the thirteenth, fourteenth, and the rest were as welcome as the preceding ones. . . . Socrates did not live in them and was not the head from which they, as the members,

> received the juice of life. He had no mold into which he wished to pour his characters and no rule according to which he might have desired to even out their differences: for that only small spirits would have been at his disposal; and he cared for these, too, but they certainly did not become his closest friends. He had no mind to polish for himself a small corps that might be his bodyguard, with the same uniform, drill, passwords—a corps that would have one spirit and bear his name forever. . . . Each one of his students was himself a master: many founded schools of their own; several were great generals, statesmen, heroes of all kinds . . . not heroes in martyrdom and suffering, but in action and in life. Besides, whoever was a fisherman, remained a fisherman; nobody was to leave his home; with each he started with his handicraft and thus led him from the hand to the spirit. . . . He developed concepts out of the soul of man, where they had been all along and needed nothing but a midwife. He gave nobody cause to say: How now? Is not this the son of Sophroniscus? Where did he attain such wisdom that he dares to teach us? He did not offend anyone by swaggering self-importance or by using high-flown and mysterious phrases of the sort that impress only the ignorant and credulous [pp. 33 f.].

Later, Hegel cites Montesquieu's *Esprit des loix* to the effect that one should not enumerate the evils that religion has produced without admitting that it has had good effects, too; and he tries to look at Jesus' teachings in a more positive way. Even so, he considers them impossible as social norms, and irony wins the upper hand again:

> One has never yet heard that a man whose coat was stolen, but who was able to save his vest and pants, was reproached by a Christian teacher for not giving

these up, too. And in the case of oaths, where the clergy must surely know of Christ's explicit prohibition, this very clergy has to play the most solemn part. What was it that excited more than anything else the hatred of the scribes and the counsels of the Jews against Christ? Was it not his individualistic way both of acting himself and of judging the actions of others when they conflicted not only with sacred customs but also with civil laws? When it was a matter of judging a case in accordance with the law of the courts, Christ attacked the administrators of these laws. But even if they had been the most irreproachable of men and quite of his own mind, they still would have had to judge irrespective of that, in accordance with the laws. The judge must often speak differently from the human being and condemn what as a human being he might pardon. From all this it should be clear that the teachings and the principles of Jesus were really suitable only for the education of single human beings, and intended only for this [p. 41].

Jesus' command to the young man to distribute his wealth to the poor would lead

to consequences far too absurd than that one could ever think of extending it to a large people. And if a group constitutes itself among another people, like the early Christians, under a law of this sort, holding all possessions in common, then the spirit of such a command disappears precisely at the moment when such institutions are established: not only does it awaken, by introducing compulsion, the desire for concealing something, as it did in Ananias, but it also restricts the benefit of this renunciation to the members of the group . . . and thus it stands opposed to the spirit of love that pours out its blessings on the circumcised and the uncircumcised [this sounds like

> Paul, but Hegel goes on], on the baptized and the unbaptized [pp. 41 f.].

Although Hegel finds something in Jesus' teachings that he can admire and respect, he is opposed not only to theology but also to all Christian institutions—not only to the Catholic Church, for which he never developed any sympathy, but also to the Reformers. He excoriates "the presumption to try the reins and heart and to judge and punish consciences" and finds its seeds "in the first origins of Christianity, since that which is possible only in a small family was falsely extended to civil society"; and he denounces "confession, church ban, penance, and the whole series of such debasing monuments of human degradation."

"The Reformers," too, are reproached for their establishment of "Christian police institutions. . . . The establishment of church power as the champion of the freedom of conscience against the power of the princes never occurred to them: they subjected Christianity to worldly power." They never rose above

> the concept of the church as a kind of state within the state, as a visible homogeneous community and a union in a common rite. How far Luther, for example, was from any idea of the worship of God in spirit and truth, is apparent in his sorry quarrels with Zwingli, Oecolampadius, and the rest. He took from the clergy the power to rule by force, over men's purses, too, but he himself still wanted to rule over their opinions [p. 42].

Hegel condemns Protestantism for substituting "theological prejudices concerning an innate corruption of human nature" for "a real knowledge of the human heart"; and he says of "theological compendia" that "one must be ashamed that all this art and scholarship has been devoted to a matter which mere common sense grasps in a quarter of an hour." The seeds of all later ills he finds "already in the first undeveloped draft" for a "Christian society." These seeds were nursed and utilized "by the lust for domination and hypocrisy" (pp. 43 f.).

Hegel concludes that Christianity cannot raise the masses to a higher level of morality any more than Kantian respect for reason.

> Institutions and laws of a small society, where each citizen retains the freedom to be, or not to be, a member, are in no way admissible when extended to a large civil society and cannot coexist with civil liberty. . . . Nothing is more intolerable than publicly employed guardians of morals. Whoever acts with a pure heart is always the first to be misunderstood by the people with the moral and religious yardstick [pp. 44 f.].

6

Folk religion. What is needed, according to the young Hegel, is not Christianity or mere reason but a folk religion. This conception, influenced by Hegel's idealized picture of classical Greece and perhaps also by Herder, differs from contemporary romanticism by insisting on the primacy of morals and the sovereignty of reason. "The highest end of man is morality, and among his dispositions for promoting this end, his disposition for religion is one of the most outstanding" (p. 48). "We consider it a necessary requirement for a folk religion that it does not force its teachings upon anyone, nor does violence to any human conscience." Its doctrines "must not contain anything that universal human reason does not recognize—no certain or dogmatic claims which transcend the limits of reason, even if their sanction had its origin in heaven itself" (p. 50). Incomprehensible doctrines and mysteries, though backed by the most venerable traditions, "reason must repudiate; in its demands for moral goodness it cannot compromise" (p. 52).

Hegel also expressly rejects any doctrines that are said to "transcend reason without contradicting reason." Perhaps "the doctrines as such do not contradict reason, but it contradicts reason to believe them" (pp. 53 f.).

Some of this is even more rigoristic than Kant. What is less rigoristic, however, is Hegel's concern with "the education of mankind"—to cite the title of one of Lessing's essays—and the concern with the whole human being, including the imagination. While the appeal to art and what Schiller called "aesthetic education" was the most characteristic solution of the seventeen-nineties, Hegel looked to religion. But it is hardly surprising that he could not give us any concrete picture of such a purely rational folk religion and was hence unable to complete any of the drafts considered here.

7

Hegel's "romanticism." It is important to recognize the full extent of Hegel's early affinity with, and debt to, the Enlightenment, both to gain a better understanding of his intellectual development and to bridge the great cultural gap between Germany on the one hand and the English-speaking peoples on the other. Most modern German writers depreciate the Enlightenment as shallow and un-German and mistakenly read their own antipathy into their heroes. Yet most of the greatest Germans were sympathetic toward the Enlightenment. This is true not only of Leibniz and Frederick the Great, of Lessing and Kant, but also of Goethe and Schiller, Fichte and Hegel, and, as I have tried to show in my book on him, of Nietzsche.

Seen in this perspective, it is doubly regrettable that Kroner should claim in his long Introduction to these essays that the fragments just reported on, but omitted in his edition, show how Hegel opposed Christianity "as the religion of the Enlightenment dominated by reason" (p. 3). As we have seen, Hegel subjects Christianity to vitriolic strictures, in large part because he took it to be utterly at odds with the ideals of the Enlightenment.

The romanticized picture of the young Hegel can be traced back to Dilthey. It was his interest in the early German romantics—he wrote celebrated essays on Novalis and Schleiermacher—that led him to the early Hegel. We can still be grateful to him for calling attention to Hegel's first essays, but we must give up the misconception that these writings are theological and that, to cite Kroner once more, "during Hegel's young manhood he was an enthusiastic Romanticist" (p. 14).

It is with this claim that Kroner's section on "Romanticism" begins, and this sentence sums up the whole section. Even so, Kroner admits rightly that Hegel "was realistic enough to see the weaknesses of past civilizations, and he was anti-Romantic in glorifying the present as the fruitful moment or the *kairos* given to his generation" (p. 16). One may also safely agree that "Hegel was called upon to transcend the horizon of the Romanticists, to reconcile their revolutionary message with the more sober views of Enlightenment. . . . He was called upon to intellectualize Romanticism and to spiritualize Enlightenment" (pp. 20 ff.). But perhaps this is truer of Hegel's later intentions than it is of his actual achievement.

Whether the young Hegel was a romantic or not depends, of course, on the meaning one attaches to "romanticism." Kroner maintains, like a great many other scholars, that the "philhellenic affection is in itself a

Romantic trait" (p. 16). This popular view overlooks the crucial difference between the peculiar "classicism" of Goethe and Schiller, of which Goethe's *Iphigenia* (1790) is the outstanding example, and the romanticism of the Schlegels, Tieck, and Novalis, who coined the word "romanticism" in its modern sense and who, before the end of the century, abandoned "philhellenism" for Germanic models, especially of the medieval period.

Hegel never aligned himself with the romantics against Goethe and Schiller. The formative influences on the young Hegel were Goethe and Schiller and, besides Kant, above all Lessing. The philhellenism of his panegyric on Socrates with its many blasphemies against Christ is surely anything but romantic. And least of all is it theological.

8

The Life of Jesus. This is the title of Hegel's second effort, written in 1795 and never translated into English. It begins with the singularly untheological and unromantic declaration, reminiscent of Robespierre: "Pure reason, incapable of any limitation, is the deity itself." Jesus' "parents were Joseph and Mary" (p. 75); and the account closes, pointedly, with Jesus' burial (p. 136). In between we find—as Knox says in accounting for his omission of the essay—"little more than a forced attempt to depict Jesus as a teacher of . . . Kant's ethics" (p. v).

Thus the young Hegel lets Jesus say:

> What you can will to be a universal law among men, valid also against yourselves, according to that maxim act—this is the basic law of ethics, the content of all legislation and of the sacred books of all peoples [p. 87].

> What I teach I do not offer as my ideas or property. I do not demand that anyone should accept it on my authority. . . . I subject it to the judgment of universal reason [p. 89].

> This inner law is a law of freedom to which, as given by himself, man subjects himself voluntarily: it is eternal, and in it we find the feeling of immortality [p. 98].

> Oh, that men had stopped there and never added to the duties imposed by reason a lot of other burdens to bedevil poor humanity [p. 102].

> Thus many . . . who worshipped Zeus, or Brahma, or Wotan, will find grace before the judge of the world [p. 107].

Hegel's Jesus knows no authority but that of reason, rejects faith, and demands only "the service of reason and virtue" (p. 122). While there are no references to Kant in the footnotes, it is significant, as will be seen later (in section 13), that the authorities cited include, besides the Gospels, not only Lessing's *Nathan* (p. 100) but also Goethe's *Iphigenia* (p. 98).

What is the motivation of this tour de force? Surely, this is Hegel's attempt to write the scripture of his folk religion. Moral demands are strengthened psychologically by the thoroughly humanized figure and story of Jesus. The strange result should be compared not only with the Gospels but also with Kant, who is here made readable and palatable for the people. Theology is still rejected, and Jesus is employed to propagate Kant's ethics.

9

The Positivity of the Christian Religion. This essay was also written in 1795. Hegel says at the outset that it is his basic assumption "that the end and essence of all true religion, and of our religion, too, is the morality of man" (p. 153). Again he makes common cause with Kant and the Enlightenment against romanticism and theology. "Positive" he defines as meaning "founded on authority and placing the worth of man not at all, or at least not only, in morality" (p. 155). He has in mind a contrast that is very similar to that which Erich Fromm has developed between "humanistic" and "authoritarian" religion in his Terry Lectures on *Psychoanalysis and Religion.*[1]

Kroner claims that "obviously, Hegel was fighting especially against the Roman Catholic church"; and in support of this false contention he quotes Hegel: "Great men have claimed that the fundamental meaning of 'Protestant' is a man or a church which has not bound itself to certain unalterable standards of faith but which protests against all authority in matters of belief" (p. 8). But Kroner does not mention that Hegel immediately goes on to disagree with these great men by insisting that the Protestant churches have, as a matter of fact, not lived up to any such "negative determination" (p. 199).

Not only does Hegel include Protestantism in his indictment, but he aims to show that the seeds of positivity, or authoritarianism, must be found in the teachings and the conduct of Jesus himself. Here Hegel goes far beyond Fromm, who pictures not only Jesus but also "early Christianity" as a prime example of humanistic, nonauthoritarian religion. The charges against Jesus are pressed in considerable detail and amount to a formidable indictment; yet Hegel does not blame Jesus, but his contemporary audience, the Jews, who, according to Hegel, were impervious to any other approach.

[1] 1950. For a detailed criticism of Fromm's contrast, see my *Critique,* §77.

After Jesus, Hegel considers the church. Before long, he includes Protestantism in his indictment and says, for example, that "the Protestant church is a state as much as the Catholic one, regardless of the fact that it dislikes that name" (p. 181).

> In some Protestant states a so-called Act Concerning Confirmation has been introduced, and the child renews the baptismal bond; i.e., in its fourteenth or fifteenth year it enters voluntarily into a contract with the church and does solemnly what the witnesses at the baptism could only promise—only, the church has carefully arranged things to ensure that the child will not have become acquainted with anything but the faith of its church, and the church . . . accepts the child's babbling of the formulas of faith, which is generally not informed by any real understanding, as if it were an expression of the free choice of the understanding [p. 182].

Hegel goes into considerably more detail, but this example may suffice to show that his strictures are neither directed at Catholicism alone nor only against the Lutheranism of his own time. He is concerned with "the positivity of the Christian religion" and not merely with occasional lapses from grace.

Some German scholars have tried to square the facts with their antipathy against the Enlightenment by seeking to connect Hegel's essays with all sorts of spiritualistic, and even theosophic, elements that, they say, were still alive at Tübingen when Hegel attended the theological seminary. However that may be, it deserves emphasis how very close to the spirit of the Enlightenment the young Hegel was. Hegel expressly regrets that "In almost all Catholic as well as Protestant countries the church state with its right has prevailed over the civil state" (p. 184), and he draws this contrast: "the state demands it as a duty that the rights of men of other faiths must be respected," while "the officials of the tolerating church (including the Protestants) always speak of kindness, of pity, and of love which should be extended to those who err—of inclinations which cannot be commanded as duties but which ought to be shown voluntarily" (p. 185). Surely, his stand here is not that of the sectarians but that of a protagonist of the Enlightenment.

The same is possibly still more obvious three and four pages later. "Every man brings into the world not only the right to a mere animal existence but also the right to develop his capacities, to become a human being." The state, however, has abdicated its responsibilities in these matters to the church.

> But if the church by its education should have got to the point where it has either totally suppressed understanding and reason in matters of religious reflection or at least filled the imagination with such terror that reason and understanding cannot and may not dare to become conscious of their freedom . . . then the church would have . . . violated the natural right of the children to a free development of their capacities, and it would have educated slaves instead of free citizens.

In the next sentence the hypothetical phrasing is dropped, and Hegel concludes that "the state, for all its good intentions, has become a traitor to the rights of children" (pp. 186 f.).

It is quite extraordinary how far the reluctance to admit plain facts can go even among highly competent scholars. After quoting Lessing's *Nathan* once again, Hegel says on the following page:

> There is much more hope that a man who has been accustomed from his childhood to the duty of believing may later be converted to the faith of another

> church, than that a man whose imagination is free of its images and whose understanding is free of its fetters may ever be brought to such faith and such obedience to opinions as a church requires.

Now consider the most detailed treatment of the early Hegel: Theodor Haering's *Hegel, Sein Wollen und Sein Werk,* a chronological history of Hegel's development up to his first book, in two volumes of 785 and 525 pages, published in 1929 and 1938. Here is Haering's paraphrase of the second part of the sentence quoted: ". . . than to convert a man who has been brought up without any religion to a faith without which, after all, according to Hegel's opinion, a real member of a people can never be and persist" (p. 241). The young Hegel's sarcastic opposition to "obedience to opinions" and to the "fetters" of faith is transmuted into its opposite.

Such misunderstandings have been facilitated by the fact that Hegel's bitterly ironical and often picturesque criticisms are not accompanied by any positive proposals. He does not proceed, for example, to recommend that children should be brought up without any knowledge of religion. He writes as a historian with a special interest in all kinds of ironies. He has no platform of his own but is following the historical development in search of one. This distinguishes him even now from many exponents of the Enlightenment; but he himself is preoccupied with his differences with all churches.

Each church claims that nothing is

> as easy as finding the truth: one only has to memorize one of its catechisms. And it does not accept [Schiller's verse, from "Das Ideal und Das Leben":]
>
> Only seriousness paled by no toil
> Finds the deeply hidden fount of truth.

> The church holds open market with it: the river of churchly truth roars noisily through every street, and everybody can fill his brains with its water [p. 204].

Some German writers would, no doubt, prefer to level a similar criticism against the Enlightenment; but Hegel attacked the churches, and his criticism also applies to spiritualistic sectarians who claimed some sort of inspiration. Later, Hegel developed this theme, first in his critique of the romantic cult of intuition, in the preface to his *Phenomenology,* and then, in the *Philosophy of Right,* in his polemics against Fries' philosophy of feeling.

In his early essay, Hegel specifically deplores the effect of "the spread of Christianity" on ethics:

> In the moral system of the church it is crucial that morals are based on religion and on our dependence on the deity: the foundation on which morality is here developed is not a fact of our spirit, not a proposition which could be developed out of our consciousness, but something that is learnt.

In other words, ethics "is not founded on freedom, not on autonomy of the will" (p. 205). This sounds Kantian, but it also points in the direction of Hegel's *Phenomenology:* here is a hint of his later program to begin with a fact of man's spirit and then to develop out of our consciousness what the church teaches from outside.

10

Moses Mendelssohn. Ultimately Hegel finds in Christianity the loss of the very gain that Jesus represented to begin with: man is again subjected to a form of heteronomy: "the state of mind of the Christian is prescribed to him in detail," much as conduct was prescribed in detail to the Jews. When Hegel goes on to say that "in the Christian church there is also the contradictory addition that feelings are commanded, while in Judaism it was after all only actions," and that "the necessary consequence" of this had to be "self-deception" (p. 209), he shows the influence of Moses Mendelssohn, who had found the superiority of Judaism in its freedom from all dogma.

Hegel's relation to Mendelssohn is curious. Lessing's friend was the one great Jewish representative of the German Enlightenment and had tried to show that Judaism, which left the mind free and unfettered, was especially enlightened. Hegel, however, took an exceptionally dim view of Judaism and blamed the Jews' unenlightened attitude for the fateful "positivity," or authoritarianism, of Jesus. Even so, the German editor informs us in a note that Hegel's discussions of the relation of church and state in his essay on *The Positivity of the Christian Religion* "are based primarily on Mendelssohn's *Jerusalem*"; and Haering shows in detail how Mendelssohn's influence on Hegel was probably "the greatest stimulus which he received from the outside during this time" (p. 158).

The state must not allow any dominant church. "The fundamental error which lies at the bottom of the whole system of a church is its failure to recognize the rights of every capacity of the human spirit, and especially the first among these—reason." Hence "the system of the church can be nothing but a system of contempt for human beings" (p. 211).

> And if it is counter to the right of reason in every human being that he should be subjected to such a foreign code, then the whole power of the church is unrightful. The right to give his law to himself . . . no human being can renounce; for with such a renunciation he would cease to be a human being [p. 212].

This same conception of inalienable rights is still encountered a quarter of a century later in Hegel's *Philosophy of Right.*

11

Christianity as a misfortune. In an addition to his essay on *The Positivity of the Christian Religion,* Hegel attacks Christianity in still more general terms.

> Christianity has depopulated Walhalla, chopped down the holy groves, and eradicated the popular imagination as so much shameful superstition and devilish poison. Instead it has given us the imagination of a people whose climate, legislation, culture, and interests are foreign to us, and whose history is quite unrelated to us [p. 215].

Shakespeare, says Hegel, has given his people "its own sphere of imaginative representations" (p. 216); but the Germans have neither a religion of their own nor a Shakespeare.

At the same time, Hegel specifically repudiates the course to which the romantics were soon to resort and which Richard Wagner later pursued to its climax: "To reconstruct the lost imagination of a nation has always been to no avail" (p. 217). Toward the end of his career, in his Berlin lectures on aesthetics, he made the same point even more emphatically, coupled with an explicit polemic against the work done meanwhile by the German romantics (III, 348 f.).

Instead of finding some special greatness in the German past, Hegel, like Goethe, tried to encompass the best the world could offer, notably including the offerings of the Greeks, and then to add to this great heritage in turn, hoping that his own contribution might be worthy of its predecessors and deserve attention outside his own country. He did not pine for a lost past or wish he might have been allowed to live in a brighter future: he accepted the present as his opportunity to accomplish work that he vastly preferred to anything he could have done in any other age.

In his early writings, however, Hegel does accuse Christianity of having destroyed what is now, unfortunately, lost. And he adds a section on "The Difference Between the Greek Religion of Imagination and the Christian Positive Religion" in which he sarcastically repudiates the customary contrast between the Christians' alleged "happiness and science with the unhappiness and gloom of the pagans" (p. 219). How, then, were the pagans converted?

"The customary answer" seems absurd to Hegel:

> That the attention of these peoples was called to the wretchedness and misery of their religion, that their understanding came to see the absurdity and ridiculousness of the fables of their mythology . . . and that they accepted Christianity as a religion that satisfies all the needs of man's spirit and heart, that answers all questions of the human reason adequately, and that proved its divine origins by means of miracles.

In fact, these pagans "are our models today in all that is great, beautiful, noble, and free." Clearly, "the spread of the Christian religion was accomplished by anything rather than reason and understanding." Rather, "the Greek and Roman religion was only a religion for free peoples, and with the loss of freedom . . . its adequacy for human beings had to be lost, too" (p. 221).

Like Nietzsche almost a century later, Hegel considers Christianity a religion adequate for slaves:

> The despotism of the Roman princes had hounded the spirit of man from the face of the earth. Deprived of freedom, man was forced to let that in him which was eternal, his absolute, flee into the deity; and the spread of misery forced him to seek and expect blessedness in heaven. The objectification of the deity went hand in hand with the corruption and slavery of man and is really only a revelation and manifestation of this spirit of the age [pp. 227 f.].

12

Hegel, Marx, and Lukács. The last quotation may bring to mind not only Nietzsche but Marx, too. Spiritual developments are here explained in terms of sociological and economic developments: the spread of Christianity was based on the spread of misery and slavery. Yet Hegel is concerned, even in this early essay, with the human spirit only, and political and economic conditions interest him only from this point of view. If his interest is "practical" in the Kantian sense, it is wholly impractical from the Marxian point of view: Hegel's indictment of Christianity is based on moral considerations. What concerns him is not the standard of living to which the mass of men have been reduced but the heteronomy that, partly under Kantian influence, he views as a form of spiritual slavery.

These differences between the young Hegel and Marx are underestimated by Georg Lukács in his work of over 700 pages on *Der junge Hegel* (1948). Like most of Lukács' many books, this study is most erudite but constantly cites Marx, Engels, and Lenin as authoritative dogma. The author realizes that Hegel's early theological phase is a fiction, but in his polemics he substitutes invective for demonstration and supplants this legend with a myth of his own when he claims, for example, that the conception of Hegel's early theological period is "a historic legend circulated by reactionary apologists of imperialism" (p. 45).

Six years later, in 1954, a few months after I had first voiced this criticism of Lukács in *The Philosophical Review,* he published a book on the destruction of reason (*Die Zerstörung der Vernunft*), in which I, too, am classified in similar fashion. Referring to my book on Nietzsche, Lukács explains its purpose thus: "After Nietzsche has come to seem compromised by the enthusiasm of the Hitlerites, he is to be 'denazified' for the purposes of American imperialism, together with Hjalmar Schacht and General Guderian" (p. 273). Such ingenious parallels are Lukács' forte:

> Even as Truman or Eisenhower do not want to appear in public as the heirs of Hitler, but rather as the men who are continuing the lifework of Washington or Lincoln, so the direct apologetics of our time, though at heart irrationalistic, has a preference for finding its ancestors in the Enlightenment. . . . It is no different in philosophy. Kaufmann, for example, wants to turn Nietzsche into a worthy successor of the great men of the Enlightenment, and it is extraordinarily characteristic that this contemporary "renaissance of the Enlightenment" has brought us as a great discovery and revaluation, a revival of the Marquis de Sade, etc., etc. [p. 619].

Truman, Eisenhower, and the Marquis de Sade are not mentioned in my *Nietzsche;* but what *is* said in support of my interpretation of Nietzsche is ignored by Lukács. He attempts to establish guilt by association, and he appeals to prejudice and to authority, not to evidence.

Indeed, Lukács does not hesitate to base his criticisms on outright falsifications of the facts.

> In the interpretation of a contemporary American,

> like Kaufmann, Nietzsche's agreement with Christianity outweighs the differences [p. 290]. Here is the social basis for the fact that Elisabeth Förster-Nietzsche and Jaspers and Kaufmann are all so zealously concerned to find threads that link Nietzsche with Christianity and the Christian church. Socially, they are quite justified because the ethic of Nietzsche, as we [G.L.] have sketched it, agrees completely with the political practice of the pope, of Cardinal Spellman, etc. [p. 291].

In fact, no previous study of Nietzsche's thought had presented such a thorough indictment of Nietzsche's sister Elisabeth, or differed with Jaspers' reading in such detail, or given such a fully documented analysis of Nietzsche's critique of Christianity, as my own. The reader may judge for himself to what extent the argument of the present volume, or of my *Critique,* is dictated by agreement with the pope or Cardinal Spellman.

Lukács is probably the leading Marxist luminary in the whole field of intellectual history since World War II, and his prolific productions are printed and reprinted in huge editions, and respected for their erudition by many non-Marxists, too. Of course, Karl Marx was a man of incomparably greater originality than Lukács and did not toe any party line or pay periodic homage to canonical scriptures; yet in his polemics Marx, like Lukács, relied on vituperation and prejudice, and this whole tradition of which Lukács is a relatively high-level representative is by no means as enlightened and as scientific as it claims to be. The weaknesses here claimed are not only found in the writings of the hacks who crowd the lower echelons.

Marx's and Engels' essays in the *Deutsche Ideologie* are all but unreadable because they systematically preferred invective to reasons and substituted outright profanity for argument. Although they certainly did not want to stop "scientific and intellectual progress," as Popper claims of Hegel, Marx did write much of the time like a man who "wants to stop rational argument" (p. 235). To this extent at least, one may find the seeds of the positivity of the Marxist religion in the person and the teachings of the founder—in line with Hegel's parallel treatment of Christianity.

In his attack on Hegel, Karl Popper uses methods very similar to Lukács', as was shown in chapter II; but Popper's critique of Marx is extraordinarily sympathetic—especially if one compares it with his unfair treatment of Plato, Aristotle, and Hegel. But his Marx, too, differs from the real Marx. A single crucial illustration may suffice.

Popper devotes an important and long chapter to his thesis that Marx's greatness lies in part in his refusal to rely on a view of human nature and in his discovery of "The Autonomy of Sociology." What Popper has to say in this connection is interesting, but the fact remains that Marx made crucial predictions that have been proved wrong by the event—and that they have proved wrong in part because they depended on a false view of human nature.

Marx believed man's nature to be such that, under the strains of a capitalistic system, he is bound to act in accordance with the most myopic notion of his own self-interest. Like Freud in the next century, he developed a theory of human nature of which he himself was in some ways a living refutation.[2]

According to Marx, nonindustrial Russia and China should not have turned Communist when they did; but such highly industrialized countries as the United States, England, and those of western Europe ought to have developed increasingly large and desperate proletariats that, long before now, should have had no other recourse but a revolution, followed by the dic-

[2] Cf. my *Critique,* section 97, for Freud.

tatorship of the proletariat. In fact, Marx's writings helped to arouse a widespread humanitarian concern with the plight of the working class; and in some men this concern was coupled with the insight that, as it were, charity is the best policy.

In time, many members of the best families of England and the United States followed the example set by Marx and Engels to the modest extent of becoming "traitors to their class"; and, without a revolution, peaceful reforms were effected that have raised the standard of living of the working classes in the United States, for example, to a level of which Marx had scarcely dreamed.

When we try to understand Marx's mistaken view of man, we are less helped by economic facts than we are by knowing Hegel, against whom Marx was revolting. A knowledge of Hegel helps us in two ways. First, because Hegel taught us to understand the history of ideas in terms of a dialectical development in which men react against the views held by their predecessors and correct any one-sidedness in these views by going to the opposite extreme that, alas, is equally one-sided. Secondly, because it was against Hegel's one-sided emphasis on spiritual factors that Karl Marx rebelled with his materialism.

Hegel's philosophy of history illuminates Marx's philosophy of history far better than does Marx's own. The reason: Hegel's philosophy of history is at its best when applied to philosophies and things spiritual but is hardly helpful for economic analysis, while Marx's philosophy of history is at its worst when it is used—as it often is—to deal with philosophy, religion, art, and literature. To cover up its failure at that point, Marx and the Marxists since his time resort to name-calling and allegations of fantastic motives.

There is one further factor that should not be underestimated: Lukács, like hundreds of lesser Marxists, simply cannot conceive any more of scholarship that is oblivious of the politics of the hour. It would be a mistake to assume that his thirty-five books represent a tireless translation into print of his spontaneous stream of class consciousness. In a serialized "Intellectual Biography" of Lukács, Morris Watnick has shown that in 1923 Lukács' deviationist Hegelianism made him the target of a Communist campaign of "personal vilification" that had "established something of a record for calculated ferocity," and Communists had been warned against "the dangers of studying Hegel." So Lukács learned that his arguments must be "disingenuously brought into line with the structure of orthodox doctrine to make them less obtrusive." After Hitler came to power and he sought refuge in the Soviet Union, he performed "one of the most abject acts of self-degradation on record," and he filled his books with "unfailing panegyrics to Stalinism." Finally, in *Der junge Hegel,* he tried to redeem his early deviation by showing that the young Hegel had really been a good Marxist and "by appealing *ad nauseam* to the authority of Lenin's post-1914 Hegelianism, even to the point of falsifying the record where his own work was involved. But all to no avail, judging by the orthodox Communist reaction." In *Die Zerstörung der Vernunft* (1954), Watnick finds Lukács troubled by "recalling that he shared the same teachers with many of the spokesmen for Nazism, and by a frantic compulsion, therefore, to disavow them." Lukács cannot afford—and cannot understand any more how anybody else can afford—to ignore slight changes in the political weather. And it is a tribute to his astuteness, though it makes ridiculous his scientific pretensions, that he has survived all kinds of changes. Although he participated in the Nagy government in Hungary and was subsequently deported to Rumania, "where he spent some four months under house arrest . . . five months after the suppression of the Hungarian uprising he was back in Budapest, seemingly none the worse off for the experience and, at that, appointed co-editor of a new philosophical journal. . . . Of those who figured prominently in the uprising, then, he is apparently the only leader thus far to have made his peace with the Kadar regime and to resume something of his former work." This is the man whom Herbert Read and Thomas Mann have called, quite rightly, too, "the most intelligent Marxist critic of our times." Here the Twentieth Century has produced realities beyond Hegel's and Marx's imagination, and when it comes to tracing such developments, neither Hegel's nor Marx's philosophy of history provides any adequate framework of explanation.

13

The Spirit of Christianity and Its Fate. This longish piece is the last of Hegel's so-called theological essays. It was probably written in 1799, and here we encounter the first major turning point in his development; but even here he becomes neither theological nor romantic.

He begins with an account of what he considers the spirit of Judaism, and the ridiculous anti-Semitism of these pages makes it doubly remarkable that the mature Hegel, in the *Philosophy of Right,* used his considerable influence on behalf of equal rights for the Jews. Both an incredibly distorted picture of Judaism and the belief in inalienable human rights were common at the time and are found conjoined in some of the most celebrated men of the Enlightenment, including even Jefferson. Neither the young Hegel nor the mature Jefferson published his anti-Semitic remarks; and they played no part in the vast Nazi literature about the Jews.

It is in his discussion of Jesus that Hegel turns against Kant and enters a new phase.

> A man who wished to restore the human being again in his totality could not possibly choose such a path [as Kant's] which only adds a rigid conceit to the human being's division against himself. Acting in the spirit of the laws could not mean for him acting from respect for duty and in contradiction to the inclinations; for in that case both parts of the spirit (of this division of the mind against itself one cannot speak in any other way) would no longer act *in* the spirit of the laws but against it . . . [p. 266].

Kant's dichotomy of reason and inclination characterizes merely one phase in man's development. Kant was a man divided against himself, and for him morality consisted in obedience to law. According to Hegel, the Jewish religion represents the same type, though less nobly so. But any such division within the spirit makes man a slave of the law, even if it is a law he gives to himself.

To give an example, not found in Hegel: The man who must interrupt this and cannot do that because it would interfere with his self-imposed regimen is a slave of his schedule even though there is no outside authority to hold him to it. Any morality that resembles such a pattern corresponds to a stage of the spirit that must be surpassed. "Jesus' spirit, which was sublimely above morality, shows itself turned directly against the law in the Sermon on the Mount" (p. 266). What Hegel turns against, however, is not all morality but only one type of morality. Both here and in his later works, Hegel calls the type that he repudiates *Moralität,* while he calls the higher type, represented by Jesus in the present essay, *Sittlichkeit.*

Kroner thinks that Hegel here becomes "a Christian mystic" and that "it is of profound significance that he discovered his own soul by discovering the soul of Jesus" (pp. 8 f.). In fact, Hegel, who had previously put Kant's *Moralität* into the mouth of Jesus, now makes Jesus the prophet of the *Sittlichkeit* represented by Goethe's *Iphigenia.*

It is to German classicism, not to the romantic protest against it, that Hegel here owes his greatest debt. While Hölderlin, his close friend, pined away with longing for ancient Greece, Hegel found in Goethe a present embodiment of what he admired in the past. Goethe saved him from Kant and presented him, in the flesh as well as in his works, with the superior type of humanity that Hegel now exalts above *Moralität.* Here was the whole man whom Nietzsche still celebrated almost a century later: "Goethe—. . . what he wanted was *totality;* he fought the mutual extraneousness of reason, sense, feeling, and will (preached . . . by Kant, the antipodes of Goethe)."

What Hegel now calls *Sittlichkeit* is close to Aristotle's ethics. According to Aristotle, only boors must overcome temptation while the civilized man acts in accordance with his civilized inclinations. Nothing could be more at variance with his ethics, or with Hegel's *Sittlichkeit,* than Jesus' counsel. "If your hand causes you to sin, cut it off; it is better for you to enter life maimed than with two hands to go to hell, to the unquenchable fire" (Mark 9:43; cf. Sermon on the Mount, Matt. 5:30).

Hegel returns to Aristotle rather than to Jesus when he writes, in his discussion of the Sermon on the Mount: "The agreement of inclination with the law is of such a nature that law and inclination are no longer different; and the expression 'agreement of inclination and law' therefore becomes quite unsuitable" (p. 268).[3]

[3] My own views of the ethics of the New Testament may be found in my *Critique.*

When Hegel calls the state of mind that characterizes the undivided man "love," it is easy to see how this would remind a theologian of Jesus, Paul, and mysticism. But Hegel has no place at all in his scheme for a transcendent faith. He speaks of faith, to be sure, but is yet much closer to Goethe than he is to any church. In those who had faith, Jesus "recognized kindred spirits"; for "with such complete trust in another human being, with such devotion to him, with such love which holds back nothing, only a pure or purified soul can throw itself into the arms of one equally pure." And again: "Faith is the spirit's recognition of spirit; and only equal spirits can recognize and understand each other" (p. 289).

Hegel understands faith, not as the recognition of one's own impotence, not as the response to the wholly other, not as throwing oneself on the mercy of an omnipotent God whom one cannot hope to please by any works, but—and it would be hard to stray farther from Luther and Calvin, Barth and Niebuhr, not to speak of Catholicism—as the love and trust between two free spirits. He voices the essentially humanistic faith of Goethe's *Iphigenia.* Indeed, the quotations in the last paragraph describe exactly Iphigenia's attitude toward the King of Tauris, which lifts the curse of Tantalus. Hegel is also close to Goethe's later poem, *Wär' nicht das Auge sonnenhaft:*

> *Were not the eye so like the sun,*
> *It never could behold the sun:*
> *If the god's own power did not lie in us,*
> *How could that which is godlike delight us?*

In Hegel's words: "Faith in what is godlike is possible only because the person who has faith contains in himself what is godlike—what recognizes in that in which it has faith, itself, its very own nature" (p. 313).

These positive statements are best rounded out by a reference to what Hegel repudiates:

> Miracles represent what is least godlike because they are least natural and contain the harshest opposition of spirit and body in its full and overwhelming brutality. Godlike activity is the re-establishment and representation of unity; miracles represent the deepest rent [p. 339].

From here Hegel proceeds to a final unfavorable contrast of Christianity with classical Greece, and on the last page he once more names both the Catholic and the Protestant church as falling below his standard: "It is their destiny that church and state, divine service and life, piety and virtue, spiritual and mundane activity can never be fused into one." That is how the essay ends.

Much of the last part of the essay deals rather opaquely with fate and its conciliation through love; it is strikingly similar to certain sections in the *Phenomenology* and seems an elaboration of the motto that Goethe later gave his *Iphigenia:*

> *Every failing that is human*
> *Pure humanity atones.*

For the central theme of Goethe's drama is that Orestes can be reconciled with fate and liberated from the furies of his conscience without any divine intervention, simply by the pure humanity of his sister.

Goethe's *Iphigenia* is also an important source for Hegel's extraordinary exaltation, in the *Phenomenology,* of the relationship between brother and sister. Commentators have long noted that Hegel was alluding to Sophocles' *Antigone;* but Hegel's whole development was decisively determined by the fact that in his own time he found a drama of comparable stature, and a poet and human being like Goethe.

14

Revolt against the Enlightenment. In the end, Hegel turns against the Enlightenment in one important respect. Consider these lines from his discussion of the spirit of Judaism—surely applicable to the writers of the Enlightenment, too: "An image of a god was for them mere stone or wood: it does not see nor hear, etc. With this litany they consider themselves marvelously wise . . . and have no conception of the deification of such images in the vision of love and the enjoyment of beauty" (p. 250).

Does it not follow that any approach to history that depicts it merely as the record of superstition and stupidity is superficial, and that one ought to penetrate the state of mind that finds expression in each stage? This is precisely the consequence that Hegel drew a year later when, in 1800, he tried to rewrite his essay on *The Positivity of the Christian Religion.* He did not get beyond writing a new introduction, which is utterly at odds with the essay as he left it:

> The following essay does not have the purpose of inquiring whether there are positive doctrines and commandments in the Christian religion. . . . The horrible blabbering in this vein with its endless extent and inward emptiness has become too boring and has altogether lost interest—so much so that it would rather be a need of our time to hear the proof of the opposite of this enlightening application of universal concepts. Of course, the proof of the opposite must not be conducted with the principles and methods with which the education of the times fa-

> vored the old dogmatics. Rather, one would have to deduce this now repudiated dogmatics out of what we now consider the needs of human nature and thus show its naturalness and its necessity [!]. Such an attempt would presuppose the faith that the convictions of many centuries, that which the millions who, during these centuries, lived by them and died for them considered their duty and holy truth—that this was not bare nonsense or immorality . . . [p. 143].

In this fragment of 1800 we see Hegel coming around to his later attitude toward history, and at this point we can understand it. We may still feel that a historian should expose the superstitions and the evil deeds of men and institutions canonized today. But Hegel did not begin with the perverse determination to ignore all crimes and follies. Gradually he became convinced of the blindness and futility involved in seeing nothing but this. Like Goethe and Schiller, he was not long satisfied with any purely negative endeavor. He did not want to remain at the level of negation. Nor was he satisfied to leave his own standards outside the flux of history, unrelated to the past.

15

Two fateful errors. As he moved from this fragment to the *Phenomenology,* Hegel took two most unfortunate steps. The first concerns a confusion about "necessity" (see the last long quotation) and mars not only the *Phenomenology* but Hegel's later system, too. He used "necessary" as a synonym of "natural" and an antonym of "arbitrary" or "utterly capricious." Hegel failed to distinguish between giving some reasons for a development and demonstrating its necessity.

The pervasive chronological confusion of the illustrations in the *Phenomenology,* which exasperates most readers, is due to the fact that in Hegel's mind Kant's attitude toward the moral law harks back to the Jews' morality; and Goethe is close to Sophocles. This would not introduce any difficulty into an ordinary typology; but Hegel's types correspond to various levels of maturity and are represented by him as developing out of each other. Because some of the ancients were more mature than most moderns, he frequently selects his illustrations without regard for the actual historical sequence. This is surely legitimate and in keeping with the earliest fragments: the "child into whom the theological leaven has been beaten with the catechism" is not superior to Socrates; for "any consciousness gained through experience is lacking" (see section 3 above).

It is Goethe who leads us to think of Storm and Stress, classicism, and romanticism not as so many alternatives but as so many stages in a single development toward maturity. And Goethe's development probably helped to suggest to Hegel the interesting, but surely untenable, idea that *all* styles, outlooks, religions, and philosophies can be arranged in a single sequence of increasing maturity. This was the second great error which affects not only the *Phenomenology* but also the later works.

16

The logic of passion. A quotation from Goethe's *Wilhelm Meister* (VII, 9), published in 1796, gives us another clue for the understanding of the *Phenomenology*.

> Not to keep from error, is the duty of the educator of men, but to guide the erring one, even to let him swill his error out of full cups—that is the wisdom of teachers. Whoever merely tastes of his error, will keep house with it for a long time . . . but whoever

drains it completely will have to get to know it unless he be insane.

Those who merely nibble at a philosophic position may never get beyond it, while those who take it even more seriously than its creator did and push it to its final consequences will get to know it and pass through it to a more mature position, propelled higher and higher by their very seriousness. This is the sense in which the dialectic of Hegel's *Phenomenology* is a *logic of passion.*

Far from pitting reason against passion, or academic pedantry against deep experience, Hegel charges the romantics, whom he attacks in the Preface of his *Phenomenology,* with a lack of seriousness. As Goethe did, too, he considered them essentially weak spirits who tried to hide their lack of disciplined strength in a mist of emotion—or perhaps nibbling connoisseurs.

Hegel's own development illustrates the logic of passion. He embraced his puzzling faith in the essential rationality of tradition and his assumption that the great philosophies of the past are all partially true only after he had gone through the very opposite attitude and, in Goethe's phrase, swilled it out of full cups.

Hegel always remained faithful to some elements of the Enlightenment, such as the belief in inalienable human rights and the faith in reason, but he reacted violently against other aspects. Where he had previously condemned Christianity for its irrationality, he later celebrated Christian dogmas as ultimate philosophic truths in religious form.

Instead of achieving a crowning synthesis, he unwittingly illustrated his own dialectic by overreacting against the views of his youth and by going to the opposite extreme. Yet he did not atone for his early opposition to Christianity by submitting to it, as some of the romantics did. Though the tone of his later remarks about Christianity is approving, he approves of Christianity only as an admirable but inadequate anticipation of his own philosophy, at a subphilosophic level. Although many Protestants were grateful, Kierkegaard never tired of denouncing the blasphemous presumption of any such step "beyond" obedient faith.

Hegel always remained the heir of the Enlightenment, opposed to romanticisms and theology alike, insofar as he maintained until the end that there is one pursuit that is far superior even to art and religion: philosophy.

IV. HEGEL: A NON-METAPHYSICAL VIEW

Klaus Hartmann

Introduction

In spite of the so-called breakdown of the Hegelian system shortly after Hegel's death, this system has held its own as an important body of thought. Admittedly, it has suffered a setback under the impact of neopositivism and language-oriented philosophy, particularly in the Anglo-American countries; Hegel's philosophy has been branded dubious metaphysics, and indeed it counts as its worst specimen. But then again, Hegel's philosophy has stayed very much alive, if largely through the derivative uses made of it in Marxism and existentialism. In either case, credit devolves on the precursor, which furnished the theoretical means employed in more-recent doctrine.

However, discounting such derivative uses of Hegel's philosophy, do we know what to make of Hegel, do we have a convincing line of approach and appreciation? In fact, we find a somewhat disconcerting picture: Some think of Hegel's philosophy much in the way of philosophers extolling a certain principle or dominant feature. Hegel ranks as the philosopher of spirit, with spirit standing for the real purged of all unreality. This view may have had its refined exponents, such as F. H. Bradley, and yet we balk at the suggestion that, for Hegel, the real is something different from what we

This essay was written especially for this volume.

think it is. It may be argued that Hegel's way of persuading us of a dominant, if out-of-the-way, feature or principle of the real is logical, and so it may seem that his supposed relegation of reality to spirit is correct. And yet, on this view, Hegel becomes an idealist in the sense of "spiritualist," a metaphysician of a one-sided persuasion. He appears as a reductionist of a curious sort, espousing a richness of spirit rather than an impoverishment. Obviously, the opposite kind of metaphysics, materialism, is not far to seek, counterpointing the one one-sidedness by another. Feuerbach, Marx, and especially Engels and Lenin were quick to propose precisely such a metaphysical counterpart to Hegel's philosophy.

Another recent expounder of Hegel, J. N. Findlay (in his *Hegel: A Re-examination,* London and New York, 1958), is more wary in matters of metaphysics: inspired by language-oriented philosophy, he claims that in Hegel we have a system of affinities or of non-strict, loose, probabilistic implications between concepts.[1] Hegel appears first and foremost as a discerning connoisseur of the real in its manifold aspects; as for theory, his device is one of linking his finds in terms of probable conceptual connections or relationships of affinity, in short, a device affording a plausible perusal of world content. The difficulty is, however, that on this view Hegel's theoretical achievement, the dialectic, hinges on an irrationality, on likelihood and affinity rather than on strictness; nor can the ground of such affinity be stated. Findlay's view is apprecia-

[1] See op. cit. pp. 23 f., 79; *Values and Intentions* (London and New York, 1961), pp. 25, 32, 44, 55, 106, 422; *The Discipline of the Cave* (London and New York, 1966), pp. 14, 76, 81. [But see Findlay's restatement in *Language, Mind and Value,* reprinted in this volume—Editor].

tive and accommodating, and yet unsatisfactory because it underplays the theoretical claims made by Hegel.

I. Preliminary Considerations

If the two conflicting views mentioned can count as representative, we are faced with the need for another proposal to make sense of Hegel. Such a third view may take its clue from the realization that what Hegel wishes to give is an account of the determinations of the real, or of what is. If we follow his final and considered attempt at providing an introduction to his philosophy, in the Introduction to the *Encyclopedia*, of 1827, revised in 1830, his aim is to transform what is "found," what is "experienced fact," into a "presentation and reconstruction" (*Nachbildung*) of thought in terms of thought (*Enc.* §12). Thought, or reason, has a claim to "satisfaction in point of form" (*Enc.* §9): it is the said transformation of what is found, or granted as a fact or as a deliverance of science or naïve philosophy, into a reconstruction in the form of rational necessity, or in *a priori* form.

For this to be possible, there has to be a vehicle—items of thought, appropriations of the real by thought—and a procedure for relating these items. The vehicle of reconstruction will be concepts or categories;[2] the procedure will be the dialectic. It is a procedure to link up categories so as to let them result in a system that satisfies reason, i.e., which integrates any major determination of the real in a reconstructive scheme.

It is essential to realize in this context that "cate-

[2] Hegel seems to have used the latter term only for part of the concepts perused, those of "objective" logic. See *Propaedeutic*, Third Course, Part I, §1. Cf., ibid., Second Course, Part II, §6.

gory" or "concept" will be implicitly defined as such determination as permits of inclusion in an integrative, or reconstructive, scheme. On the other hand, the aim will be to accommodate all major determinations hitherto regarded as "being the case," i.e., all categories discovered or claimed by philosophy, with some more of Hegel's own proposing thrown into the bargain. Hegel wishes to "present" the finds of experience, science, and philosophy as "digests" of thought and to devise their reconstruction in terms of thought. Thought, the big eater of what other purveyors of knowledge have contributed, can escape the dietetic restrictions of observation or picturing; once in possession of content in the form of thought, it can follow its own ways of connecting the various items with one another with a view to achieving rational satisfaction.

Conversely, the procedure permitting of such reconstruction will be implicitly defined as that compound relation of affinity which categories or concepts bear to one another. Thus, Hegel's philosophy is a *theory of categories* or of such determinations of the real as permit of reconstruction and are thus borne out as categories. These, in turn, have to coincide with what must be granted in view of experience, science, and philosophy. So far, then, we are in close rapport with Findlay's account.

II. The Categorial Program as a Systemic Program

But how does the said reconstruction work in fine? What sort of reconstruction does satisfy reason? And how is such a reconstruction possible? Let us consider some requirements: The reconstruction has to be presuppositionless, since otherwise certain categorial items would be left unaccounted for. This commits the reconstruction to a linear development, to a sequence or genealogy of categories, such that each item can be regarded as "justified" in view of its antecedents. But, clearly, the sequential forward reading cannot be the whole story. How could a presuppositionless beginning lead to anything; how could the absence of determination lead to richness? Thus there must be operative a contrary consideration, pointing from the ordered richness of granted content back to its antecedents. The linear progression cannot be deduction, it can only be reconstruction; what it is heading for is granted. The question merely is how to dispose categorial items in a sequence that could be considered an "explanation" of categories, regressively, and a disclosure, or "presentation," of further categories, progressively.

And yet, progression and regression do not suffice: we cannot imagine a sequence traversing all manner of categorial content without further support. Such necessary support is afforded by the architectonic. The progression will have to begin with the presuppositionless, the zero case of categorization (being); it will lead to the fulfilled case of categorization, where thought categorizes itself as having enclosed all determination (concept). In between, there will be an area where being is regarded as on the way to such selfhood or closure, the area of essence. The architectonic thus provides for a basic ordering of material at large, but it also permits of application in any one sphere or area, such that categories will be arranged both by their subservience to being, essence, or concept, and within each sphere or area by relative proximity to immediacy or closure. Being may be categorized as comparatively immediate or closed, and similarly in the other cases. Or, to use Hegel's terms, the guiding perspectives are being-in-itself and being-for-itself, both in the over-all arrangement and in each sphere or area. Indeed, each locus exhibits in-itself potential changing over to for-itself potential, thereby giving way to another category. Or, to put it in yet another way: the concepts being-in-itself and being-for-itself have a substantive application to ontological areas at large and a formal or methodological application, both being governed by the architectonic.

With this complex unity of linearity, progression and regression, and architectonic, we have the basic structure of Hegel's *Logic*, a work that can be called an "ontology."[3] The *Logic* provides an ordered sequence or genealogy such that, in view of its antecedents, the result (thought or Idea) appears as an explanandum capable of a rational explanation. The result, in turn, is the sum-total of its genealogy making the genealogy possible, for, in order for this to be established, thought, the presumption of a unity of thought and being, has to be operative all along. Thus thought is the ground established as a ground.

The point easily lost sight of is that the said methodological structure provides a new meaning to categories that already have meaning; something is reconstructed as the zero case of thought: being or immediacy. We have a new meaning wedded to a known one. In the initial or zero case, the *Logic* has to undercut determinacy in order to provide explanatory antecedents of determinacy. This is why, in this case, it has to propose a sequence that points to, rather than determines, distinctions as determinations determinate in view of their opposites, which would pre-empt determinacy, the very thing to be explained in the first place. Similarly, being appears under the new guise of indifference: it is seen to enter into

[3] As in the case of the term "category," Hegel seems to have reserved the term "ontology" to the first and second ("objective") parts of the *Logic*. See *Propaedeutic*, Third Course, Part II, §15. *Science of Logic*, tr. by Johnston & Struthers (London and New York, 1961), p. 75.

relations external to, or not conceptually ingredient in, it; it is permissive of plural instantiation. Or, to take another case, that of essence: essence is reconstructed as unity of relation, as being in unity with a vantage point *for* which it is. We have a "pattern," a "structure," halfway between being and concept, which is instanced in each essence, though it is not itself any particular essence, in the manner of Aristotelian essences. The final stance, concept, or thought or Idea, stands for complete integration, for non-difference and non-indifference, for closure or all-inclusion; i.e., all these are the meaning of the terminal category. In it, rationality has come full circle.

What is important to realize is that the new meaning given to categories, in what may be called a "hermeneutic" of rationality, is due to systemic considerations. Meaning is enhanced by systemic meaning; systemic considerations constitute the explanans of categorial meaning. A category is "understood," explained, or justified in terms of its function with respect to making ontology—the satisfaction of reason—possible; in such a context it is immediate, determinate, or inclusive of otherness, and therefore infinite, whatever the case may be.

In other words, the systemic program—to give a reconstruction of the real in a manner satisfactory to reason—provides for the successful execution of the categorial program. It constitutes an immanence of thought, an over-all sphere in which determinations are viewed as from within, from the stance of thought, and placed with respect to their "ontological" potential.

III. The Dialectic as Implementing Procedure

But is the execution of the program not a mere play of thought with itself, as Feuerbach suggests when he says that the Idea "plays a game"? The notion of "category" will provide the answer to the question. A category is the claim that being matches what thought thinks of it. We could not account for being in terms other than those of thought. Thus thought, to set up its own genealogy, or the justification of its match with reality, has to regard its antecedent determinations as stances of grasped being, or of being grasped in various degrees of coincidence with thought. There are categories for comparatively incomprehensible things, such as being; for comparatively comprehensible ones, such as essence; and for altogether comprehensible ones, such as thought itself. Thus the categorial claim is that being, to the extent that it is categorized, enters into thought and makes a difference to thought *pro tanto;* and yet it is thought that has to provide the means for establishing such ingredience of being into thought. What is a "match" of being and thought, has to be considered a coincidence, an identity of being and thought.

The procedure to establish the ingredience of being into thought, or to establish the rationality of being in a series of categorial determinations, is accordingly to consider the otherness of being with respect to thought as a negation, and the difference such otherness makes to thought as "determinate negation." The negative and the overcoming of the negative are constitutive of the movement of understanding. In his effort to point to antecedents of determinacy, Hegel introduces the negative at the very beginning of the *Logic* as the account thought gives of being prior to any determination. All incumbent determinations are developed from this conflict of being and negation which, in the zero case, in the absence of any determination, is the indifference of the two. Hegel, in developing determinations from such a conflict of being and negation, is not guilty of mistaking negation for otherness or irreducible novelty, as some scholars of neo-Kantian persuasion have charged. Rather, we should say that, in order to rationalize otherness, Hegel has to transform it into the negation of what is already appropriated by thought. This replacement of otherness or novelty by negation in the service of comprehension is what is called the dialectic. In a dialectical framework, being appears as the complement to thought, exhaustible in moves of negation and in determinate, or double, negation. Clearly, this is possible only if the explanatory sequence is not deduction, but only reconstruction, granting categorial content. And yet we truly "understand" content only by construing it in terms of negation and double negation, by placing content in an immanence of thought. We grant not only content, but that such content can be viewed as the synthetic result of a construction moving in a forward direction. Negation and double negation are the artificial means of regarding the synthesis of a granted content as established in a forward reading. Obviously, for this to be possible, systemic requirements have to be granted.

It appears from the above that the question that haunted Bradley, namely whether everything in the real stands in internal relations to everything else, has to be dismissed. This would be a metaphysical way of raising an issue that, with greater pertinence, is discussed in terms of intracategorial systemic requirements. And yet the position adopted by Hegel is not an "as if" position; on the contrary, it asserts established rationality. Again, this rationality is not omniscience: we do not come to "know" things we did not know when we read through Hegel's categorial arrangement; we merely learn about the rational explanation of categories. From this angle, Hegel's position in the *Logic* is an innocuous one, as it cannot possibly conflict with knowledge.

With this interpretation—so far addressed to Hegel's *Logic* only—the issue between the above views of Hegel in terms of one-sided metaphysics and in terms of non-strict logical implications between concepts, has been decided by invoking a third view. Over against the metaphysical reading, Hegel's philosophy appears to us as categorial theory, i.e., as non-metaphysical philosophy, or as a philosophy devoid of existence claims and innocent of a reductionism opting for certain existences to the detriment of others. The only claim is that the categories granted for reconstruction be not empty or without instantiation. Over against the other reading in terms of conceptual affinity, the present interpretation remains in close rapport, but it can answer the case for strictness in the affirmative. Hegel's philosophy is a highly theoretical edifice exhibiting strictness of construction. To say that the implications are non-strict, as Findlay does, means to apply an external standard, that of formal logic. The dialectic is strict, however, if viewed in systemic terms. In it, the philosopher is free to devise and maintain strictness, since he legislates in the interests of rationality. Quite in keeping with this contention, Hegel identifies the *a priori* with freedom (*Enc.* §12), so why should reason not be free to be strict?

One may, of course, ask whether the dialectic, with its aspects of linearity and architectonic, is "regular," whether there is a pattern it has to conform to, serving as a criterion for its strictness. Such a paradigmatic pattern, however, has to be repudiated, since the dialectic is simply the result of reconstructing a given set of categories, thereby creating its own pattern. Similarly, if one says that the architectonic is an imposition on pre-existing material, such criticism is mistaken, since the architectonic can be taken as an innocuous ordering in the interest of rationality. But what about the "*single* line of reasoning" Findlay objects to?[4] Indeed, what seems strained about the dia-

[4] *Hegel: A Re-examination,* p. 81.

lectic is the single-file perusal of categories; many transitions, especially where they connect one area with another rather than one category with another within an area, may seem unpersuasive. Quite generally the sequential or linear aspect of the dialectic invites puzzlement; by itself, it seems inconclusive. But all that this puzzlement means is that the linear movement is not, by itself, a complete description of the dialectic. If the linear forward reading were, by itself, conclusive, we would have the impossible case of deduction. The linear scheme is an essential aspect, since, otherwise, presuppositionlessness would be violated, explanation would lapse. But, to be complete, the dialectic requires the regressive reading and the architectonic.

By the same token, the dialectic is not the traversal of the genus-and-species pyramid from bottom to top. Although incompatible species are compatible in their genus, so that a movement from species to genus would be one of avoiding contradiction by escaping to the next higher concept, a movement from species to genus is merely a movement to higher abstractions, unsupported by the architectonic. Accordingly, such a movement, though superficially similar to Hegel's dialectic, cannot be an ontology of thought as the ground for categories.

Incidentally, precisely for the reason that the dialectic constitutes a systemic ordering, we need not insist on each transition or on each categorial item included in Hegel's philosophy. One might, for example, discard parts of the philosophy of nature: the richness of natural phenomena is such that no convincing single-file perusal can be offered. Accordingly, a charitable reading of this part of Hegel's philosophy would surrender detail and retreat to a higher level of abstraction while maintaining the basic program of ordering phenomena in a systemic fashion. Hegel sometimes lapses into mere catalogue, but this does not mean that the dialectic has no strictness to it. It may simply be overextended.

IV. Solutions

As may have become clear, attention to categorial and systemic features in Hegel's philosophy, or a categorial and sytemic approach to it on our part, affords a full appreciation of Hegelian solutions to problems and provides us with an organon to rule on certain problems irksome to Hegel scholarship. Turning to solutions first, we see a major achievement on the part of Hegel in the fact that he tells us—or, rather, retells us in an explanatory fashion—what such and such is. Outstanding examples in this connection are all avatars of subjectivity. Only a dialectical stance, so it emerges, is able to say what a subject, what concept or spirit, is. Such felicities of Hegel's, simply in terms of enlightenment, are coincident with his extending the notion of category beyond the Aristotelian scope of substance and accident to all manner of unity structures, including, as prime cases, subjectivity and essence. If we consider the inability of Aristotle, in *Metaphysics* Z, to grasp "ontologically," in the spirit of his *Categories*, the relation of essence and matter resulting in a substance, we see the progress achieved by Hegel. He succeeds in supplying "ontological" meaning to all manner of content.

A similar achievement lies in the categorization of what, for Kant, had remained a case apart, namely, space and time. The categorial accounts Hegel gives seem perfectly successful, especially in the case of time. We must not, it is true, expect of categories such as these, or of any category for that matter, a panacea for all problems. Categories are not the sumtotal of axioms necessary for disciplines such as geometry or mathematics, and *mutatis mutandis* for other disciplines, to get on their feet. Categorial theory answers only the peculiar questions a philosopher may have as to what it is that a certain discipline is about. Categorial questions are luxury questions.

The categorial and systemic approach may also persuade us of the felicity, in Hegel, of dividing philosophy into a *Logic* and a "Realphilosophie" or philosophy of nature and of spirit. The *Logic* contains all ontological distinctions of note on a comparatively abstract plane, discounting the difference externality might make categorially. If there are to be more categories, or if the categorial scheme is to be extended to externality, this project would mean to regard such more- "concrete" determinations as "principled" by the categorial corpus of the *Logic*. Or, the other way around: to show that the *Logic* gives instances of categorial unity, or successfully establishes unities of thought and being, one has to show that this claim of the *Logic*, which is by itself a proposal made in immediacy, constituting the beginning of Hegel's philosophy, has consequences that legitimate the *Logic*. The philosophy of the real proves the point of the *Logic* by devising further determinations within the categorial scheme. The pertinence of the categories of the *Logic* is proved intracategorially, by showing that they give rise to further categories that we already know. (The pertinence of those further categories of "Realphilosophie" cannot, in turn, be confirmed by a third "cycle" or, what this boils down to, by a "realization of philosophy." The Young Hegelians, among them Cieszkowski and the early Marx, advocated such a further stage to Hegelianism. However, a practical realization of categories to prove their pertinence, or the pertinence of reason, transcends categorial philosophy altogether and, as will be seen presently, leads to paradox.) In this context, another remark on transitions may be appropriate. With our systemic understanding we realize that the notorious transition from Idea to Nature, or from the *Logic* to "Realphilosophie," can only be a metaphor. The rationale is systemic, or on a second-order level, not one of the first-order relatedness of concepts bearing an affinity to one another. Clearly, the systemic approach can back up Hegel.

Another virtue of Hegel's is the richness of his categories in the domain of "Realphilosophie" (discounting the philosophy of nature, which requires a charitable reading). One need only consider what it means to be offered an ontological account of what society or the state is. One may have to disagree where Hegel extends his categorial account of either in the direction of substantive theory, since it is indebted to more than the categories in question would provide for. Still, the achievement in understanding is supreme. Taking everything together, the virtue of Hegel's philosophy is that it offers a comprehensive scheme of explanation for the world's "what," the limitation being that such "what" can claim to be categorial, i.e., reconstructible.

Turning to solutions inherent in Hegel's position as a whole, we note that categorial and systemic analysis can settle the issue of idealism in Hegel. If Hegel's aim is seen to be the reconstruction of categories, then it is obvious that such an effort can take only the form of an intracategorial relating of concepts, with the dialectic as the theoretical procedure providing for the desired rationalization. It is not, for this reason, that Hegel neglects reality. The categorial stance adopted means, in fine, that the Feuerbachian and Marxian criticism is mistaken; namely, that Hegel's system forms a totality set over against another totality, the world,[5] or that a Hegelian category disregards that of which it is the category. Under the Marxian program, the integration of philosophy and

[5] See *Writings of the Young Marx on Philosophy and Society*, ed. & tr. by Easton and Guddat (New York, 1967), pp. 52, 62.

the world, or the practical realization of philosophy, would only be brought about if the higher categories proposed by Hegel in the philosophy of spirit or, more concretely, in the *Philosophy of Right*, were instanced by each individual co-constituting the entity in question; i.e., if those categories were realized in what, for Hegel, would be totality of a lower categorial order, namely, that of "species life" or "association." Hegel's categorial theory, on the other hand, can "place" Marx's counterrecipe and show it to be a category mistake, namely, the mistake of regarding an abstract categorial level as a concrete level that, to add to the paradox, is supposed to be the realization of the concrete categorial level.

Another virtue of Hegel's, given the modern philosophical scene, may be seen in the position he would take with respect to problems besetting modern, language-oriented philosophy. We hardly need modern phenomenology, which analyzes the problem of reference in thought and intuition, to remind us of the problem that arises if, as happens in language-oriented philosophy today, reference is discounted in favor of intralinguistic immanence. Apparently, intralinguistic talk can render all the information needed for defensible philosophical discourse. Reference is indeed granted, but relegated to oblivion, if only to avoid paradox. Hegel's solution, so we might say, stands between modern phenomenology and language-oriented philosophy, in that he opts for reference *and* immanence. According to his approach, the mind's reference to being can be discussed, this side of being, only in thought. We seem to remain entrenched on the side of the mind and therefore isolated from any referent of mental acts. However, for Hegel, we can accommodate reference in a notion of thought such that reference to being is already a constitutive feature of its being thought. Restriction to the conceptual or categorial level will work, but only if concepts are taken dialectically. This position, however, is not available to language-oriented philosophy; this philosophy cannot theorize about the relationship of language and the world on pain of paradox (of which paradox Wittgenstein's map theory in the *Tractatus* is an early statement). The dialectical approach will always be superior where questions of comprehensibility, i.e., transcendental or speculative questions, are asked. Answers to such questions can, as in the case of the problem of reference, be provided to the extent that the question is couched in categorial, and this means, for Hegel, dialectical and systemic, terms.

The present plea for a categorial and systemic view of Hegel's philosophy is not new; it has an exponent in R. Kroner, who gave a systemic analysis of the *Logic* and of the relation of the *Phenomenology of Spirit* and the *Logic* in his incomparable *Von Kant bis Hegel.* Similarly, other scholars have been aware of Hegel's systemic and foundational project.[6] However, the emphasis of systemic analysts is often rather different from ours: granting Hegel's intentions and presumptions, they wonder whether his theory does not suffer from facile solutions to problems requiring for their solution an anchorage in irreducible, intuitive, finite, or, if we like, Kantian, stances, however conjoined with Hegelian devices. We cannot here enter into this area of criticism;[7] all we can say here is that Hegel's philosophy, as a pure categorial theory—cate-

[6] See H. Wagner, *Philosophie und Reflexion* (Munich, 1959). See also W. Flach, *Negation und Andersheit* (Munich, 1959), and D. Henrich *et. al.* in *Hegel-Studien,* Beiheft No. 1 (Bonn, 1964). We may give pride of place to Feuerbach's article titled "Kritik der Hegelschen Philosophie" of 1839. Sämtliche Werke (Stuttgart, 1959), II, pp. 158–204.

[7] A worked-out philosophy on the lines of such criticism is available in the writings of R. Hönigswald and, latterly, in those of W. Cramer.

gorizing and "placing" even irreducibles such as intuition and the finite ego—has the advantage purity carries with it: no elements of picturing (*Vorstellung*) of how knowledge comes about are necessary. The price is, of course, circularity in the reconstruction of what is granted. But reason is only satisfied if it can accept things on its own terms, within the immanence of thought. Categories are the vehicle of such satisfaction, since they do not pretend knowledge of existences or individual items, which knowledge would have to be knowledge as to how such existences affect or fail to affect the validity of knowledge—an impossibility. Hegel does not "know" more than Kant when he "places" the thing-in-itself in a hermeneutical context while Kant denies knowing anything about it and yet talks about it. There need be no anchorage in existences by-passing categorization or understanding, in order to make ontology possible. Or, there need be no metaphysics; and if we are correct, there is a defensible reading of Hegel's philosophy as a non-metaphysical philosophy.

V. *Problems*

Turning now to difficulties, we have to distinguish those incurred by Hegel in view of his categorial and systemic stance (if, that is, we are correct in imputing this to him) and those incurred by us when we see Hegel from this angle. Let us take the first set of problems first.

It may be argued, as, for example, the later Schelling did and, in our time, E. Gilson (in *Existence and Some Philosophers*), that existence is misconstrued if it is treated in Hegelian fashion. If Schelling extended his speculative craving for an account of what is, to the problem of why something exists, and, in answer to this desire to know, introduced a surd, or God, as an existential principle, Gilson is similarly dissatisfied with the Hegelian position because it does not provide for an existential ground as *a* being. Or, Schelling and Gilson are concerned about the fate of metaphysics in the sense of a discipline making existential statements or, what comes to the same thing, in the sense of special metaphysics.

This problem has already been discussed in connection with neo-Kantian system analysis protesting against Hegel. To repeat what was said in a somewhat different context: one may have metaphysical cravings, and these are not ruled out by Hegel. Only, on our view, Hegel's philosophy does not commit one to having them. His position on God and religion, for example, is one that "places" God and the religious congregation; it offers as their categorial account that unity of spirit which, as absolute, is not subject to plural (external, indifferent) instantiation and thus transcends the real. The ontologist need not claim that God exists apart from the congregation forming a unity with him. The category would be sufficiently instanced by "religion," a concrete universal leading up to, and surpassed by, philosophy. The solution, subtle though it is, is non-committal metaphysically, if not misread in the fashion of picturing (or "*Vorstellung*"), which asks for an existence apart from thought.

More important may be an appraisal of Hegel's most concrete "real" category or concrete universal, that of the state. The problems are well known: Hegel opts for a state of "estates," for constitutional monarchy, against democracy in any real sense, against separation of powers, etc. Is all this justified categorially, or is it the miscarriage of categorial thought, exposing it as a failure? Is Hegel's account a consequence, or a function, of his categorial and systemic orientation so that this is what makes a difference to what we are used to grant when we speak about the state?

The problem can be tackled in this way: the fault of Hegel's may be not so much that his is categorial thought, but that he makes concessions to existential considerations. In a purely categorial scheme, one would expect logically related accounts of society and the state, the one motivating a move to the other. Or the state would be shown to solve the problems of society (divisiveness and atomization). But Hegel wants to discuss also the real relationship society bears to the state: he connects societal classes (or "estates") with political bodies (or "estates"), thus creating existential bonds between society and the state. This move is understandable, in the sense of "forgivable," in view of historical precedent and even language, but cannot be defended in theory. The state of "estates" is a consequence of concessions, within a categorial scheme, to non-categorial matters. If we thought these flaws away, the account of the state would be more abstract, but also more correct.

And yet, we see a serious problem in the area of society and the state, or in a concrete plural real, precisely if the flaws of Hegel's theory are removed: the coexistence of entities of various categorizations—family, society, corporation, the state—cannot be grasped, except illegitimately, as the example of the "estates" shows. Once Hegel moves to the next category, the previous one has been left behind. We are also conceptually interested in such an appraisal of concreteness—let us call it the state, which is what it is—in view of coexistent entities within it and of coexisting entities without it. Another example of this problem is Hegel's account of the state in external relationships. The consideration of this predicament leads him to introduce the military as a necessity. This may be perfectly sound, but, as a consequence of the sequential scheme of categories, the relationship of the state and the military, their subordination or non-subordination under civilian authorities, cannot be discussed, because that topic has been relinquished by the time Hegel comes to the military. Thus, concrete circumstances cannot be considered as making a difference to the thing categorized, and that failure to make a difference precisely makes a difference to the things categorized. Also, Hegel imposes a restriction: states commune only on state level, irrespective of whatever other interrelationships—for example, intersocietal and society-state relations—may make the state what it is.

To put things more generally: the problem of Hegel's categorial scheme is the linearity of exposition or reconstruction in plural realms. Categories of the social realm—where plurality matters in as much as such categories stand for plural entities and in as much as entities of diverse categorization coexist, such as families, society, and corporations in a state—seem to turn out differently from what we are used to grant because of the linear arrangement. At least this seems to be the case with the terminal category, that of the state. This is to that extent a "function" of that arrangement. (The problem in Hegel, so it emerges, is exactly the opposite of the one exercising Bradley, that of internal relations. There is too little allowance for them in Hegel.) We should not say that the terminal category—that of the state—is vitiated by this arrangement: it is not a function of the abstraction and untruth of its antecedents (the sequence leads to an affirmative conclusion), and yet, conclusions as to its legitimate content have to be revised in the light of concreteness. We need the categories that can be set up the Hegelian way, but at the same time we realize the shortcomings of the procedure used. The problem is clearly not identical with Findlay's problem when he objects to the "*single* line of reasoning," and yet it has to do with linearity. In a similar way, the linearity problem makes itself felt in derivatives of Hegel's philosophy such as Marx's *Capital,* in which the sequential scheme, placed at the service of a critique, does seem to vitiate the result as one due to the abstraction of the antecedents, or in Sartre's *Critique de la raison dialectique,* in which, again, the same conclusion may be drawn.[8] The issue is too complex to be adequately dealt with here; but it is important to realize that we may have here a touchstone for determining the limitations of the Hegelian scheme and the systemic requirements for any theory promising to be more successful than his. Analysis of the problem might afford an insight into what speculative or transcendental theory can or cannot do. It is true that the difficulty pointed out for Hegel's *Philosophy of Right* does not seem to affect the program of the *Logic;* it attaches to the extension of the method of the *Logic* to "Realphilosophie," or to the social domain. (We may be spared here a comment on the philosophy of nature from this angle.)

VI. Problems Continued

Turning now to difficulties incurred by us if we view Hegel in the categorial and systemic manner, the main problem is that of misrepresentation. Are we not doing Hegel an injustice by presenting him as a categorial philosopher? On our view, are we not losing sight of the richness of Hegel, which includes metaphysics? In order to see clearly in this issue, let us take up one representative problem, that of history. Is not Hegel's stand on history ample proof that all we seem to be doing is picking out certain palatable bits from his philosophy at the expense of the concrete whole?

[8] See the author's *Die Marxsche Theorie* (Berlin, 1970) and *Sartres Sozialphilosophie* (Berlin and Evanston, Ill., 1966).

Hegel is often regarded as a thinker who gave history its due to a point where the distinction between systematic thought and historical thought collapses. This somewhat popular notion can be disputed even if our categorial and systemic interpretation is not adopted. An appeal to inspection is all that will be needed: the *Logic* simply is not historical thought, it is systematic thought, and so is the *Encyclopedia*. However, in the philosophy of spirit, and in its close-up, the *Philosophy of Right*, Hegel gives detail, or illustrates from detail, that is historical. Thus he reconstructs a state that fits the description of the Prussian state, or a religion that fits the Protestantism of his day. Hegel thinks that a full-fledged philosophy is only possible in a developed period, and such a philosophy accordingly grants these developments and reconstructs their results. In this sense, philosophy is "its own time apprehended in thoughts" (*Philosophy of Right*, ed. & tr. by T. M. Knox, Preface, p. 11). In this same sense, philosophy is a late-comer, rationalizing what it finds, hoping to have before it an entelechy of concrete development. Philosophy cannot predict, nor can a philosophy reconstructive of an entelechy present to it be extended to cover, or usher in, future developments (as the Young Hegelians believed). The Hegelian consequence would rather be that if there is occasion to assume that things have changed significantly, then a new philosophy, a new reconstruction, would be called for. This seems to be the meaning of Hegel's sayings about putting up with the present ("hic Rhodus, hic saltus"), about the "owl of Minerva," and about philosophy's being "its own time apprehended in thoughts." Philosophy is historical in that it reconstructs a richness that is historical, and it is historical in that it is transient, provided that history changes so as to demand a new philosophy. And yet, in all this, philosophy is systematic.

Hegel has, in addition, devised a *Philosophy of History* and introduced history in a constitutive function in his lecture courses on *Aesthetics* and on *Religion.* The problem attending our view of Hegel is whether or not these treatments of history square with Hegel's systematic philosophy, or whether or not we are wrong in making such a distinction. In this case, our categorial and systemic outlook is prescriptive and bids us draw a line: in order to show that history had to be the way it was so as to produce an entelechy permitting of systematic reconstruction, we need more than systematic philosophy. We need an extension of the dialectic to existence and contingency (e.g., the divine incarnation).[9] On our view, this "maximal" claim of Hegel's philosophy is not defensible. But since Hegel, at least in certain works, makes it, the corresponding "maximal" interpretation of his philosophy is defensible. One should realize, however, that as an over-all interpretation, it involves an encumbrance. With our categorial and systemic interpretation, we feel we have to discriminate between the various levels Hegel meant to encompass —that of world history and divine revelation, on the one hand, and that of a fully developed civilization capable of systematic treatment, on the other. We feel free to single out that systematic core of Hegel's philosophy which exhibits strictness. In that sense, the interpretation presented here can stand for a "minimal" interpretation, or for a non-metaphysical interpretation, of Hegel. In its light, Hegel can be censured to the extent that he embraces history in the third of the three senses indicated or otherwise engages in metaphysics.

[9] An interpretation including this latter stance among Hegel's aims is that of K. Löwith (in *From Hegel to Nietzsche*). Lately, E. Fackenheim (in *The Religious Dimension in Hegel's Thought*) has proposed a similar view.

Conclusion

From the above, it appears that the categorial and systemic interpretation of Hegel can go a long way toward accommodating his philosophy, while, at the same time, it erects signposts where trespassing into metaphysics can be seen to be such. Conversely, the present interpretation can claim Hegel's philosophy as a possession for philosophy, as something that has come to stay, but for metaphysical extensions. In ontology in a narrower sense, in that of the *Logic*, Hegel's thought can be assessed as strict and indispensable; in fact, on the present interpretation, Hegel's claim appears, contrary to a metaphysical interpretation of his philosophy, as a very modest one. His achievement is seen to lie in a hermeneutic of categories. Admittedly, such a pursuit is a luxury in philosophy. In the concrete domain of ontology, in the philosophy of spirit, Hegel's thought appears as equally fruitful and indispensable, and yet as subject to criticism, not in terms of insufficient strictness, but of deficiencies that may be inherent in the speculative or transcendental method as such. Still, it may well be worth the effort to explore questions of foundational philosophy in general in the light of a categorial and systemic reading of Hegel and to apply insights from such reading to concrete problem areas that without them must be relinquished to uncomprehending positivism. A study of Hegel along the lines proposed can reopen discussion and offer solutions in the theory of theory construction not surmised by those who read Hegel metaphysically or who too easily discount his theoretical rigor.

V. HEGEL'S CONCEPT OF "GEIST"

R. C. Solomon

"*Geist*"[1] is a central conception of Hegel's mature philosophy, and much of the misunderstanding and hostility toward his "system" is due in part to the obscurity and quasi-mystical haze surrounding his employment of this concept. Concepts translatable as "spirit" have been part of philosophy since ancient times, but Hegel's ambitious attempt to introduce an immanent God and World-Spirit into Christianity and philosophy has all but driven the term out of circulation. If we cannot understand "*Geist*," then we cannot understand Hegel's philosophy: the "philosophy of spirit" is only as comprehensible as the concept of "spirit."

What clearly emerges from Hegel's writings is that "*Geist*" refers to some sort of *general consciousness, a single "mind" common to all men.* The entire sweep of the *Phenomenology of Spirit* is away from the "disharmonious" conceptions of men as individuals, to the "absolute" conception of all men as one. In the *Phenomenology,* we are first concerned with the inadequacy of conceptions of oneself as an individual in opposition to others (in the "master-slave relationship") and in opposition to God (e.g., in "contrite consciousness"). This opposition is first resolved in

A shorter version of this paper was presented at the American Philosophical Association meetings, Eastern division, in Washington, D.C., December 1968. I wish to thank Herold Westphal for his helpful comments. This paper is reprinted by permission of the author and *The Review of Metaphysics.*

[1] "*Geist*" is usually translated as either *spirit* or *mind.* I shall use both English terms interchangeably with "*Geist.*"

ethics, in the conception of oneself as a member of a family, of a community, of Kant's kingdom of ends; as a citizen of the state; and then in religion, in which one conceives of oneself as "part" of God and of a religious community. Absolute consciousness is the explicit recognition of one's identity as universal spirit. The concept of "*Geist*" is the hallmark of a theory of self-identity—a theory in which *I* am something other than a *person.*

Of course, this theory of superpersonal identity is not all there is to the notion of "*Geist*" in Hegel's writings. "*Geist*" is fundamentally a religious concept, and Hegel's central purpose in employing "*Geist*" is to resolve the "disharmonies" of traditional Christianity which he had discussed in his earlier "theological" writings. Because Hegel's conception of "immanent God" is dependent upon the peculiar theory of identity embodied in "*Geist*," we shall be indirectly, but only indirectly, concerned with Hegel's philosophy of religion. "*Geist*" also represents an ambitious attempt to resolve certain far-reaching epistemological problems, characterized as the "disharmony between subject and object." However, this aspect of Hegel's notion of "*Geist*" goes far beyond the problem of superpersonal self-identity, with which we shall be concerned.

1. Most interpreters have accepted the notion of "universal consciousness" without serious criticism. It is often pointed out that *Geist* is one more in a long history of such concepts, particularly common in certain mystical traditions in Christianity and Eastern religions, and more recently adopted by Fichte and Schelling as the "Absolute Ego" or simply "the Absolute." But does the notion of a universal mind make sense? If two persons' minds are identical, then it would seem to follow that whatever would be experienced or known by one would be experienced or known by the other: in Sartre's terminology, con-

sciousness is *translucent*—it has no "parts," and nothing can be "hidden" in it. Conversely, two minds would seem to be distinct if what is experienced or known by the one is not experienced or known by the other. In a very different language, *privacy* is the defining trait of minds: one mind is distinguished from another by the "private access" each has to its own "contents." The fact that different persons have different memories, experiences, and knowledge has been used often enough as a criterion for personal identity (e.g., Locke). How, then, can we make sense of the claim that *we* are all one consciousness-*Geist*, when the evidence so overwhelmingly proves that different persons have different ideas, thoughts, and feelings, and *ipso facto*, different minds. I cannot remember what Julius Caesar was thinking as he crossed into Britain; I cannot speak Polish in spite of the fact that there are persons who can; I feel pains that you do not: therefore, I do not have the same mind as Julius Caesar, the same mind as any Pole, nor the same mind as you. Now, this is all so obvious that Hegel surely cannot be denying the privacy and individuality of the minds of persons. "Universal spirit" cannot be the claim that we are all one consciousness in this sense.

A more-plausible account of Hegel's *Geist* would not deny individual mental differences, but it could *ignore* them. Thus we might reject "*Geist*" as a name for a single universal mind, but maintain that *Geist* is the name of an *abstract entity* such as "the average American housewife." "*Geist*" abstracts from the peculiarities of individuals and focuses attention on their similarities: "*Geist*" is a convenient way of talking about the common properties of a society, of a people, or of *all* people, while ignoring, but not denying, their differences. This sympathetic account of "*Geist*" eliminates the absurdity of talking about some actual mind common to all people. *Geist* is universal only in that it is the name of those properties had by every human consciousness; it is *not* universal in the sense that it is the name of a single entity (mind) common to every individual. Thus, "the spirit of the proletariat" or the "mind of middle-class America" does not refer to a single spirit or a single mind shared respectively by all proletarians or all middle-class Americans. It refers to a set of concerns, goals, beliefs, and feelings that each of (or most of) the members of those groups share. Similarly, we may sympathetically interpret Hegel's *Geist* as an abstraction ranging over all human beings, an attempt to talk about humanity as a whole without being concerned with particular individuals, an attempt to talk about human consciousness without being concerned with the minds of any particular individuals.

This interpretation is reasonable, of course, and it does make perfectly good sense out of Hegel's very difficult notion of "*Geist.*" But what a bad joke Hegel's philosophy becomes on this interpretation! The aim of the entire *Phenomenology* is to give us a realization of *Geist,* and eight hundred tedious pages are solely directed to the demonstration of "absolute knowledge," "the goal [of] which is Spirit knowing itself as Spirit" (PG, last page, Baillie trans., 808). But according to this interpretation, this grand effort is an attempt to prove only the humble and obvious thesis that we can talk abstractly about people without referring to individuals. Are we to believe that the philosopher who has been called the "Aristotle of our Renaissance world" spent his entire philosophical effort proving to us only that we can make abstractions and that in philosophical reflection we need to make abstractions? Are we to take seriously an interpretation that reduces a discovery Hegel himself equated to Divine revelation to the simple-minded claim that philosophers are not specifically concerned with people as individuals? However digestible the interpretation of *Geist* as an abstract entity might be, it can do no credit to Hegel's philosophy. Moreover, it is clearly contrary to Hegel's own insistence that "Spirit, of all things, must be looked at in its *concrete actuality*" (*LL*, sec. 34; italics mine). The *Phenomenology of Spirit* is a study of *something* called "*Geist*": it is not the invention of abstraction.

If "*Geist*" refers neither to a literally general consciousness nor to an abstraction from all men, what else might it be? We might reasonably suppose that *Geist* refers to some sort of consciousness apart from the particular manifestations of consciousness, so that sense can be made of "universal mind" without denying the obvious fact that different people have different experiences, knowledge, and the like. Traditional doctrines of *soul* would give us such a theory. If we distinguish "empirical psychology" from "rational psychology," as both Kant and Hegel have done, then we may say that "*Geist*" is a conception of rational psychology only, and that the identity thesis embodied in the concept of "*Geist*" is a claim about *souls*, not about *minds* with their particular experiences, beliefs, and so on. The soul is that which *underlies* particular mental states and events, and the notion of *Geist* embodies the claim that all individuals share the same *soul*. This interpretation at least offers us a specific and significant rendering of Hegel's notion of "*Geist*": the concept of "*Geist*" is then as clear as the concept of "soul." However, Hegel sharply distinguishes between *Geist* and *soul*,[2] ". . . soul being as it were the middle term between body and spirit, or the bond between the two" (*LL* 69). Furthermore, Hegel insists that the traditional doctrine of soul as a stable *thing* underlying all the more-particular manifestations of mind, is wrong as an analysis of *Geist*. *Geist* cannot

[2] E.g., *Lesser Logic*, Sec. 34, Wallace 2 ed., p. 69. All quotes in brackets, *LL*, Clarendon Press, 1892.

be separated from its manifestations, is not a thing, is not stable, and therefore not soul:

> One word on the relation of rational to empirical psychology. The former, because it sets itself to apply thought to cognize mind and even to demonstrate the result of such thinking, is the higher; whereas empirical psychology starts from perception, and only recounts and describes what perception supplies. But if we propose to think the mind [*Geist*], we must not be so shy of its special phenomena. . . . It is wrong therefore to take the mind for a processless *ens*, as did the old metaphysic which divided the processless inward life of the mind from its outward life [*LL* 69].

An all-too-common interpretation of "*Geist*" relates it to the traditional doctrine of the soul but avoids the traditional metaphysical arguments concerning this soul by rejecting argument and appealing to mystical (or "intellectual") insight. Accordingly, Hegel is traced to Meister Eckhart, and *Geist* is identified with immanent God-soul discoverable through special experience; Hegel the archrationalist is interpreted as a mystic. However, regardless of what Hegel's "*Geist*" and Meister Eckhart's "God" have in common, Hegel discovers his *Geist* by strictly *rational* procedures. *Geist* is not "seen" in a single experience or set of experiences; it is a *conception* of mind that can be defended only through careful *thinking* about mind. We need only remind ourselves of Hegel's various attacks on Schelling's mystical tendencies (one of which occupies several pages of the Preface to the *Phenomenology*) to see how very distant he is from this mystical tradition.

We have said that "*Geist*" is not the name of an abstract entity, that it cannot refer to the soul of traditional theology, and that it cannot refer to individual minds with their peculiar thoughts, feelings, and such. Yet it also seems that "*Geist*" cannot ignore these peculiar manifestations of individual minds either, and it appears that "*Geist*," although it is "concrete," can be discovered not through experience alone but only through "scientific" philosophical thought. But if *Geist* is neither soul nor abstraction from particular minds, what sort of thing can *Geist* be?

It has been remarked that Hegel's conception of *Geist* has its philosophical origins in Kant's *transcendental ego.*[3] However, the transition from Kant's talk of "consciousness in general" and the "synthetic unity of consciousness" to Hegel's conception of a *literally* general consciousness has been understandably challenged as one of the most confused and notoriously invalid moves in the history of philosophy. Against the influential picture of Hegel as misinterpreting and abusing Kant, however, we shall argue that this transition is neither confused nor invalid, and that the notion of *Geist* embodies an important attempt to resolve an important problem in Kant's philosophy.

How is Hegel's *Geist* related to Kant's *ego*? Kant's *ego* serves a function in his epistemology: Hegel's *Geist* functions primarily as an ethical-religious conception. But both authors are concerned with the possibility of "absolute knowledge," and Hegel was deeply dissatisfied with the Kantian critique of reason. His dissatisfaction is not given full hearing until the *Science of Logic*, but the too-often neglected Introduction to the *Phenomenology* is clearly a complaint against Kant's theory of knowledge as well. For both Kant and Hegel, self-consciousness is the key to all knowledge, and both the *Critique of Pure Reason* and the *Phenomenology of Spirit* must be considered treatises on self-knowledge. Thus, for both Kant and

[3] One recent source of such a remark is J. N. Findlay's *Hegel: A Re-examination* (New York and London, 1958), Ch. 2.

Hegel, the nature of the knowing subject is the key to all philosophical understanding, and *Geist,* I shall argue, plays the same role as subject that the *transcendental ego* plays in Kant's philosophy.

2. If Hegel's *Geist* is a reinterpretation of and improvement over Kant's *transcendental ego,* where in Hegel can we locate a critique of Kant's *ego,* and where are the arguments to show that *Geist* is an improvement over the *ego?* Although there are a few passages in Hegelian texts to indicate that Hegel did consider *Geist* as a reinterpretation and improvement of Kant's *ego* (e.g., *LL,* Sect. 20), the comparison between *Geist* and *ego* is not to be found in Hegel's writings. What, then, can we use to defend our interpretation that will argue that the two concepts are intimately related?

A nagging problem in the study of Hegel is his tendency to discuss a very specific problem without identifying it—to pluck an idea out of its specific context and display it as a problem for every philosopher. In the *Phenomenology,* for example, we are accustomed to seeing obvious references to Kant, Locke, Schelling, that conscientiously avoid any mention of Kant, Locke, or Schelling. Similarly, theses are often advanced in answer to a long-standing philosophical problem with no mention of the problem itself: in fact, the "system" as a whole is an attempt to answer philosophical problems that are never stated in Hegel's mature works. This troublesome philosophical style cannot help but create despair for the student of Hegel. We can piece together what references we can find and attempt to formulate a commentary on Hegel, adding what insights we have to the difficult text. And we can do meticulous biographical research, attempting to use Hegel's more-personal remarks in letters, and influences that he obviously felt, as clues for the construction of a hypothetical structure that might explain what is going on. But all this produces shoddy philosophy, for we cannot possibly understand a philosopher if we do not understand what he is trying to do. The first step in understanding Hegel, therefore, is to reject his classic opening line of the *Phenomenology:*

> In the case of a philosophical work it seems not only superfluous, but, in view of the nature of philosophy, even inappropriate and misleading to begin, as writers usually do in a preface, by explaining the end the author had in mind, the circumstances which gave rise to the work, and the relation in which the writer takes it to stand to other treatises on the same subject, written by his predecessors or his contemporaries.

Can we understand Hegel when we violate his own instructions? The object of this paper is in direct opposition to the two most central Hegelian methodological dictates—to try to understand Hegel by seeking out just those historical influences and unstated intentions which Hegel claims are irrelevant, and, what is worse, by plucking a single concept out of the context of his philosophy as a whole and attempting to analyze it. Hegel repeatedly warns us against considering philosophical concepts in isolation from the systems in which they are given significance. But what if, instead of focusing on these statements of method which have had such disastrous effects on Hegel scholarship, we look at Hegel's own treatment of the history of philosophy? Hegel did not restrict himself to textual analysis, and when considering the writings of others he surely did not consider it inappropriate to question an author's intentions or to relate a work to its predecessors and contemporaries. Hegel's historical technique, perhaps his most valuable contribution to philosophy, is his attempt to see historical trends and developments in a philosophy that even its author did not see, to find advances in philosophy that had not been seen as advances, to see influences on thought of which not even the thinker was aware. What we must do for Hegel, therefore, is to read his work not as he insists that we read it, but as he reads the work of his predecessors. Whether or not Hegel saw the important relationships between *Geist* and Kant's *ego,* we shall find ourselves able to better appreciate Hegel's philosophy when we see what perhaps even Hegel did not fully appreciate in his own work.

If *Geist* is an answer to a problem that is never stated, then what reason do we have to accept it as an answer to that problem *for Hegel?* Hegel nowhere argues for the interpretation that we are about to present, and he nowhere indicates that *Geist* is introduced to solve a problem derived from Kant. What Hegel does is simply present us with a "system" of philosophy in which *Geist* is the featured concept. But this sort of philosophy has been often attacked—for example by Kierkegaard and Nietzsche, by Husserl and J. L. Austin—as a sort of philosophical dishonesty, a mode of presentation of philosophical prejudices which are thereby protected from all criticism. Hegel's lack of argument for his system is taken as a ground for dismissing his system as indefensible. But all this is a profound misunderstanding of Hegel and his attempts to do philosophy. It is true that a philosophical system is well insulated from attack from the outside, but this does not mean it cannot be attacked, even if it is internally consistent. A system is not an arbitrary body of propositions; it is not even a coherent and consistent arbitrary body of propositions. A philosophical system is a super theory that attempts to resolve certain perplexities which bring us into philosophy in the first place. A system is successful in so far as it is adequate to eliminate those perplexities; it fails in so far as it leaves those perplexities intact or substitutes for them new problems of equal difficulty. Therefore, when we read Hegel, we must ask questions such as, "What problem(s) is he attempting to solve?" and "How well does this system attempt to solve those problems?" When we are investigating a single concept in Hegel's philosophy, we must ask why Hegel included "X" in his system rather than "Y" and what perplexities "X" is supposed to help resolve. Specifically, we must ask why the special concept of "(universal) spirit" is introduced instead of the traditional concept of "soul" or "consciousness" or "transcendental ego." In thus examining an individual concept, we must notice that we are not really taking it out of the system itself in examining it, even though we are examining it without thereby examining the system as a whole. In other words, it is possible to examine individual Hegelian concepts without at the same time examining the system as a whole. Hegel commentators often neglect examination of crucial concepts, particularly *"Geist,"* because they confuse Hegel's insistence that concepts be investigated within a particular system of thought with the reasonable demand that we should examine particular concepts within a system by asking how this particular concept aids our resolution of extra systemic perplexities.

We may thus restate the argument of this essay as an attempt to show that *Geist* replaces Kant's *ego* in Hegel's philosophy because it removes certain philosophical perplexities that Kant's *ego* is incapable of resolving. Enough said about the uncommon historical method that we shall employ in this paper. We are not arguing so much *from* Hegel's philosophy as *for* his philosophy.

3. The concept of *"Geist"* is a successor to both Kant's

transcendental ego, or *"I think,"* and Descartes's celebrated *Cogito.* For both Descartes and Kant, the *Cogito,* or *"I think,"* holds a precious place in philosophy: It is not merely one self-evident truth among others, but the highest principle in the whole sphere of human knowledge (B 134).[4] The *Cogito,* or *"I think,"* is the first principle of a philosophical methodology and a criterion for philosophical truth as well as a philosophical truth itself. Were it not for the very specific significance now given to the notion of "phenomenology," we might call this philosophical method the "phenomenological method." Instead, we shall utilize a less popularized but more descriptive name in current employment and call it *"methodological solipsism."*

Methodological solipsism requires that every philosophical proposition be justified from a first-person standpoint. If I wish to know what an *X* is, I must ask, "How can I and must I come to regard any *X*?" If I wish to know whether there could be any *X*'s, I must ask, "Could I come to know any such?" The methodological-solipsist view is forcefully expressed by one of its most important advocates, Edmund Husserl:

> Anyone who seriously intends to become a philosopher must "once in his life" withdraw into himself and attempt, within himself, to overthrow and build anew all the sciences that, up to then, he has been accepting. Philosophy—wisdom—is the philosopher's quite personal affair. It must arise as *his* wisdom, as his self-acquired knowledge tending toward universality, a knowledge for which he can answer from the beginning, and at each step, by virtue of his own absolute insights. . . . All various inferences pro-

[4] Kant, *Critique of Pure Reason,* tr. Kemp Smith (Macmillan Co., 1929). All references to Kant are to the second edition and are included in the text in brackets.

ceed, as they must, according to guiding principles that are immanent, or "innate," in the pure Ego.

(Husserl, *Cartesian Meditations,* tr. D. Cairns, Nijhoff, The Hague, 1960, pp. 2, 3)

According to the methodological-solipsist starting point, every philosophical problem must be construed as *my* problem: I must determine whether it is justifiable for me to believe in any theory that attempts to answer that problem, and I can justify my acceptance of this theory only by appealing to evidence that I have, and treating this evidence according to methods I am also able to justify. To this solipsist demand is often coupled the insistence that only propositions of which we are certain may be allowed into our philosophical inquiry. Together, the demands for self-evidence and certainty require that philosophical inquiry restrict itself to an examination of the necessary features of the "first-person situation." For Descartes, the resultant method limits its appeals to the clarity and distinctness of ideas and the natural light of reason. One could not appeal to natural science or the teachings of religion or "common sense," for these were not self-evident. Similarly, one could not appeal to his own beliefs unless these were self-evident, so that my believing that *X*, is not sufficient to ascertain *X*. In Kant, the dual restrictions of certainty and appeal only to the first-person case yield a "transcendental method" whose aim is to provide me with these features of (self-)consciousness which are necessary.

According to the methodological solipsist, my mind is not one mind among others, and I am not one person among others. Every philosophical proposition (and therefore every proposition) depends upon *my* mind for its justification, but every other mind can only be a philosophical problem. I know the existence of my own mind without doubt: if I can know of the existence of other minds at all, it must be the result of a calculation derivative of certain facts about my own consciousness. This is not to say that the methodological solipsist openly accepts solipsism as a philosophical truth, of course; it is only his starting point. Solipsism is an initially given problem to be resolved, and one of the central efforts of all who have adopted this method has been to show that solipsism is false in spite of the method. This is obvious for Descartes and for Kant (in the "Refutation of Idealism"); it is not always understood in discussions of Hegel (and Husserl).

The supreme test of methodological solipsism turns out to be the analysis of the basic concepts of the method itself (as Husserl never tires of telling us). Thus we should not be surprised to find Descartes, Kant, and Hegel very much concerned to analyze the concepts of "first person" and "self-consciousness," which lie at its foundation. Before philosophy can insist upon "appeal to the first-person case," we must understand what this first-person case is. Thus the epistemology of Descartes is dominated by the *Cogito;* and the transcendental analytic of Kant's *Critique of Pure Reason* rests upon the necessity of the "possibility for the 'I think' to accompany all my representations" (B 131). For Descartes and Kant, methodological solipsism is a position that must be explained and defended; for Hegel, it is simply there to be used. As a result, we do not get from Hegel an elegant expression of his starting point; he simply starts. Yet it is clear that his "phenomenology" does accept this beginning:

> A self having knowledge purely of itself in the absolute antithesis of itself. . . . The beginning of phi-

> losophy presupposes or demands from consciousness that it should feel at home in this element.
>
> Preface to the *Phenomenology of Spirit;* Baillie 86

4. How can an analysis of "self-consciousness" be carried out from a methodological-solipsist position? We cannot appeal to a scientific study of consciousness or even other philosophical analyses of "self-consciousness"; we cannot appeal to other persons, to be sure, or to other persons' experiences of themselves, or to the language *we* use to communicate about ourselves. I cannot even appeal to myself as a *person,* for persons have *bodies,* and the existence of my body or of any connection between that body and my mind is still being held in philosophical suspension. According to methodological solipsism, I must ask, "How can I and must I come to be conscious of myself?"

For Descartes, the "I" of the *Cogito* is clearly not dependent upon other persons and not itself a person. But its exact nature is a matter of great concern for him; in the second of his *Meditations on First Philosophy,* he thinks:

> I do not yet understand what is this "I" that necessarily exists. I must take care, then, that I do not rashly take something else for the "I" and thus go wrong even in the knowledge that I am maintaining to be most certain and evident of all.

Descartes concludes (in the sixth *Meditation*) that the "I" is neither person nor human body, but the thinking mind:

> I recognized I was a substance whose whole essence or nature is to think and whose being requires no place and depends on no material thing.

In Kant, the "I think" is a *formal* necessity, a unifying principle that constitutes a necessary precondition for any consciousness:

> Only in so far as I can unite a manifold of given representations in *one consciousness* is it possible for me to represent to myself the identity of the consciousness in these representations [B 133].

The formal principle of this unity, "all my representations are mine," is analytic, but, according to Kant, the unifying principle of consciousness is itself not analytic:

> . . . the *analytic* unity of apperception is possible only under the presupposition of a certain *synthetic* unity [B 133].

The introduction of the "I think" as the "vehicle of all concepts" (B 399) must be carefully distinguished from two other concepts of "self" with which it is naturally confused. First, this "I" that thinks is not equivalent to a *person* but only to that non-material conception of the "I" that thinks which is transcendentally necessary for there to be consciousness at all. Second, and more dangerously, this transcendental "I," which "can have no special designation because it serves only to introduce all our thought as belonging to consciousness" (B 399–400), is naturally but mistakenly spoken of as a "thing," as a *substance,* as a *soul* (cf. Descartes).

The inference from the necessity of the "I think" to the existence of the "I" as a thing, Kant argues, is the result of a paralogism—an invalid syllogism—that mistakenly argues from the formal conditions for consciousness to a conclusion about super sensible objects: in this case, the soul or the "self-in-itself." But no such doctrine about the "I" as object can be established by appeal to the necessity of the "I think," the "bare consciousness that accompanies all concepts," because

> . . . consciousness in itself is not a representation distinguishing a particular object (the soul) but a form of representation in general [B 404].

The analysis of the "I think" will admit only inferences that state necessary conditions for employment of the understanding. The argument against the paralogisms,[5] therefore, proceeds by demonstrating that all talk of the "I" as substance does not state such necessary conditions. The "I" that thinks and is necessary to consciousness is only the subject of experience, not an object of experience. Because the "I," by its very nature, cannot be an object of experience, the categories of the understanding cannot be applied to it, which means that this subject cannot be considered as unit or plurality of substance(s), cannot be exhibited in causal relationships with anything else, and, in summary, cannot be *known:*

> The unity of consciousness . . . is only unity in thought by which alone no object is given. . . . Consequently, this subject cannot be known [B 421–22].

Thus, on Kant's account, the substantial "I think" postulated by Descartes is necessarily unknowable, for it corresponds to no intuition, and thought alone can proceed to it only fallaciously.

5. With this analysis of the "I think" Hegel is in general

[5] In this brief discussion, I have avoided discussing the various doctrines of rational psychology individually, as Kant does in the first edition. It is the first three theses, that the soul is substance, is simple, and remains identical in time, that would be relevant to a more detailed discussion of the relation of the paralogisms to Hegel's *Geist.*

agreement, and the concept of *Geist* reflects much of the Kantian transcendental "I." *Geist,* like the "I," is the subject of all possible experiences and is not itself a "thing" to which the categories can be applied. *Geist,* like the "I think," is an activity and not a "soul-thing" lying "behind" our thoughts. *Geist* is the "universal in action," as the "I think" is the unifying activity of employing universal concepts (or reason and of the understanding). The only sense in which the "I think" exists is the sense in which it knows of itself or is "reference-to-self." *Geist* is "being-for-itself," and its existence and its knowledge of its existence are the same.[6] Finally, Hegel speaks mysteriously of *Geist* as "infinite and negative" (*LL* 179) and as "infinite negativity."[7] But these obscure phrases can be unpacked as an equivalent of what Kant says of "negative" or "limiting" concepts, "the function of which is to curb the pretensions of sensibility" [B 311]. The concept of the thinking "I," considered as an object, is just such a concept, for it represents a thought for which there can be no corresponding intuitions. *Geist,* like the "I think," is indicated in every experience, but it is not itself experienced in any of these.

Most importantly, considering the frequent charges that Hegel ignored Kant's critique of metaphysics, Hegel accepted Kant's rejection of the paralogisms for their "confounding of one kind of truth for another" and the "replacing of empirical attributes by categories" (*LL* 95). He commends Kant for

> . . . emancipating mental philosophy from the "soul-thing," from the categories and consequently from

[6] Hegel's general thesis, so often attacked, that essence and existence, thought and being, are one and the same, clearly makes perfectly good sense in this particular context.

[7] *Phenomenology,* Preface, part 3, tr. Baillie, p. 96.

> questions about the simplicity, complexity, materiality, etc., of the soul [*LL* 95].
>
> By his polemic against the metaphysics of the past Kant discarded those predicates from the soul or mind. He did well, but when he came to his reasons, his failure was apparent [*LL* 97].

Hegel does qualify his commendation, however, with a criticism of some of Kant's arguments, most notably his argument that to get rid of the soul as a supersensible thing was to get rid of it as an object of knowledge altogether. For Hegel,

> This style of abstract terms [the categories of the understanding] is not *good enough* for the soul which is very much *more* than a mere unchangeable sort of thing [*LL* 97, italics mine].

But Hegel's refusal to return to the metaphysics against which Kant argued is clear, and the concept of *Geist* does not refer to the supersensible or the unknowable. Hegel is neither a metaphysician in the old sense, nor a mystic, and *Geist* is neither metaphysical nor mystical.

The disagreement between Kant and Hegel was not, however, a simple dispute over the correct reasons for accepting a mutually agreeable thesis. They did concur on the non-substantiality of the "I think," but Hegel charged that Kant ignored his own prohibitions and inadvertently reintroduced to philosophy just those notions that his most brilliant doctrines sought to eliminate. Kant recognized the importance of the differences between the transcendental "I think" and the empirical self or person and the metaphysical notion of the soul, but, complained Hegel, he "never went into the details of this."

6. The *Critique of Pure Reason* is notably obscure on

the relationship between the "I think" and personal identity. As two recent commentators, Bennett and Strawson, have pointed out, Kant pays so little attention to the problematic connections between the thinking subject and his body, and the "I" that thinks and the person, that questions concerning the attribution of mental predicates to other persons, or even questions concerning ourselves as persons, remain unanswerable. Yet Kant's free use of the pronouns "my" and "mine" throughout the *Critique* makes it quite clear that the "I think" is a *personal* "I think": there is one such subject *per person.* In the *Critique of Practical Reason,* however, it becomes evident that the noumenal acting ego there discussed is the same ego presupposed by the "I think" in the first *Critique:*

> We should become aware that in the consciousness of our existence there is contained a something *a priori,* which can serve to determine our existence . . . as being related, in respect of a certain inner faculty, to a non-sensible intelligible world [B 430–31].

And this ego, whether applying concepts in the employment of the understanding, or reason, or willing in the employment of practical reason, is a *personal* ego. For every *person,* there is an "I" that both thinks and wills.

Now, this almost tautological thesis raises immense problems for Kant's doctrine of the transcendental ego within the demands of his methodological solipsism. First, there is the question of how I can know whether there are any other subjects or "I thinks"—or, if you like, whether there are any other *persons*—by arguing from my own case. From Kant's own characterization of the "I think," it is clear that the existence of other subjects can never be established as an *a priori* truth. If it is to be established at all, it must be by some form of inductive argument—by analogy, or as an inference to the best explanation or theory about the "behavior" of certain objects. Within Kant's first *Critique* we are forced to adopt a provisional behaviorism with respect to other persons. But this is not a moot point here—first because it is not a problem unique to methodological solipsists of Kantian persuasion, but mainly because it is not a problem that seriously seemed to confront Hegel. It is only in the second *Critique* that recognition of other persons becomes a matter for *practical* concern (it cannot, therefore, become an object of *knowledge*). For Hegel, first recognition of others arises in the conflict of the master-slave confrontation. (But, for Hegel, who does not distinguish between theory and practice, this recognition does constitute knowledge, but knowledge of a relatively unsophisticated sort.) However, the problem with which we must be concerned here is not this problem of *other* minds so much as the problem of identifying *our own mind.*

According to Kant, the nature of the "I think" is such that it abstracts from all empirical content, or, in his terms, there are no true empirical propositions applicable to it. This means, foremost, that any statement about human bodies cannot be a statement about the "I think," for Kant clearly states the independence of all talk about bodies as part of the empirical ego which has no place in transcendental deduction of necessary states of consciousness. We have already seen that Kant, like Descartes, considers the relationship between "me" and my body a strictly empirical relationship, albeit a very special empirical relationship. But neither can any statements about what Kant calls the *content* of consciousness, e.g., particular thoughts, be statements about the "I think," for the fact that a consciousness "contains" any particular thought or set of thoughts is again strictly empirical, but also again, as exemplified by, e.g., memories of childhood, these facts might be very special facts indeed.

But what this means is that any criterion that we would normally use to identify *persons* does not suffice to help us identify the "I think." Thus the "I" that thinks is not a person, and, moreover, considerations about the "I think" are quite independent—logically and causally independent—of considerations about myself as a person. This independence results in a most embarrassing consequence for Kant's thesis of the *transcendental ego.* Because "I thinks" cannot be individuated by individuating persons, it is possible, on Kant's analysis, that I share a transcendental ego with others, or that there are several subjects occupying "my" body, or that there are several of us, though not knowing of each other, who are sharing the same thoughts, memories, feelings, and the like. The almost trivial thesis that human "I thinks" are commensurate with persons turns out to be no more defensible on Kant's theory than the bizarre thesis that my body is "inhabited" by two "I thinks," one of which my body shares with an automobile. If we have no way to identify and individuate "I thinks," then any thesis about the number or distribution of (transcendental) subjects is as defensible as any other.

This argument may be further reinforced when we consider the privileged status of the "I think" in Kant's philosophy which leads him to reject the paralogisms. The categories cannot be applied to this "I," says Kant, because the categories presuppose the "I"—thus the errors of rational psychologists who do attempt to categorize the "I think" as soul. But what Kant evidently fails to notice, as Hegel's system brings out, the individuation of the "I think" as a personal "I think" presupposes the categories just as surely as do the paralogisms. Individuation requires the discussion of the quantitative categories of unity and plurality just as surely as do Kant's rejected theses that the "I" is non-composite, simple, and so on. Furthermore, any talk of the "I think" as being *in* space and time embodies the same confusion, for it is the "I think" that imposes these forms on any possible experience. (This, of course, is how Kant himself manages to introduce his own doctrine of immortality of the soul in the second *Critique.*) But this means, again, that we have no way of individuating instances of "I"; in fact, we are not even justified in talking as if subjects (transcendental subjects) can be individuated at all. We must, as Kant argues, attribute all thoughts and experiences to a subject, but we cannot, by Kant's own insistence, identify or individuate subjects as we individuate persons.

7. Why does Hegel use the concept of *Geist* instead of the concept of the *transcendental ego?* The traditional use of *ego* carries with it the more or less explicit stipulation that there is one such ego for each *person.* Similarly, "I" and "I think" are used to refer to individual persons. But any attempt to use these concepts in transcendental philosophy constitutes a serious confusion. The subject of transcendental philosophy does not individuate individual persons, and it is therefore nothing like the "ego" or "I" of traditional philosophical and everyday discourse.

We might interestingly compare Hegel's rejection of the traditional concepts of self-reference to Peter Geach's rejection of Descartes's *Cogito.* In *Mental Acts,*[8] he argues that Descartes uses "I" to refer to a self not seen by others, whereas "I," in so far as it has any intelligible use in our language, is

> . . . used to draw attention to the speaker. . . . "I" can refer only to a human being; "I" in this special [transcendental] context is idle and superfluous.

[8] Cornell University Press, 1956, p. 117.

In other words, the "I" of the *Cogito* is no more than a confused parasitic use of our ordinary grammar of self-reference. But in philosophical discussions of the transcendental "I," there can be no reference to persons and therefore no intelligible use of "I" to denote at all. If we wish to talk, as the methodological solipsist supposes we must, of the transcendental subject in philosophy, it cannot be through this traditionally misleading use of the *personal* pronoun "I." The subject of philosophy is not a person, is not an individual, but must be referred to *simpliciter* as *subject,* without any pretense toward identification or individuation with persons. But this notion of *subject* is precisely Hegel's notion of *Geist.* For Hegel, the transcendental ego, as *Geist,* is a literally general or universal consciousness, as it *ought* to have been for Kant. Hegel's *Geist* is Kant's ego without the unwarranted claim that there is one ego per person. *Geist* is simply the underlying unifying principle of consciousness and, at the same time, the underlying rational will "behind" all practical reason and action. Hegel does sometimes speak as if there is only *one Geist,* particularly in the Preface to the *Phenomenology,* where he attempts to personify *Geist* as the divine subject. But these mostly grammatical attempts at individuation are not frequent, and the movement of the *Phenomenology* as a whole seems to indicate clearly that the transition from Kent's *ego* to Hegel's *Geist* is a transition from a personal subject to a universal subject. Kant's "consciousness in general," with its necessary "I think," is forced to become universal *Geist,* no longer stating the laws necessary for any consciousness but also stating that every consciousness is *transcendentally* indistinguishable from every other.

8. One cannot help but mention here a fascinating modern analogue to this contest between Kant and Hegel. In Wittgenstein's notes after *Tractatus Logico-Philosophicus,* we also find a brilliant philosopher who,

through his commitment to a methodological-solipsist approach to philosophical truth, is forced into a position of admitting that he cannot explain our accepted correlation between persons and subjects. This leads him into hesitantly admitting what Strawson, in *Persons,* characterizes as a "no-ownership theory of consciousness," not very far from Hegel's universal-ownership-of-consciousness theory. One striking difference, of course, is that Strawson and the later Wittgenstein took this conclusion as a *reductio ad absurdum* argument against any such first-person-oriented theory of persons, while Hegel took the argument to establish an interesting and true ("absolutely" true) proposition. Of course, in philosophy we are not unused to seeing what is established as uncontrovertible theory in one conceptual age later constitute a manifest absurdity. Nonetheless, if the result of Hegel's introduction of *Geist* is outrageous, it is not peculiarly Hegel's outrage. A rejection of the bizarre consequences of Hegel's *Geist* should not call for the "return to Kant" so often urged by his detractors, but rather for a renewed attack on Kant's most-treasured methodological presuppositions.

VI. THE OPENING ARGUMENTS OF THE *PHENOMENOLOGY*

Charles Taylor

IN THIS PAPER I'd like to look at the first three chapters of the *Phenomenology of Spirit*—the section on "Consciousness"—as an essay in transcendental argument. By "transcendental arguments" I mean arguments that start from some putatively undeniable facet of our experience in order to conclude that this experience must have certain features or be of a certain type, for otherwise this undeniable facet could not be. Obviously, the best-known examples are to be found in Kant, and it is because of this pre-eminence that the "transcendental" is appropriate.

Thus the transcendental deduction in its different versions can be thought to appeal as bedrock to two basic facets of experience; its unity (reflected in the fact that the "I think" must be able to accompany all my representations) and its polarization between subject and object (which requires some form of objectivity, that is, a distinction between the way things are and the way they seem). From these facets, which seem hard to gainsay, Kant builds the proof of the necessary application of the categories by attempting to show that without their application these two undeniable characteristics could not hold of experience.

But this type of argument is not confined to Kant. It is very much part of contemporary philosophical debate. Two examples may illustrate this: Strawson, in *Individuals*, argues that the concept of a person as a being to which "*both* predicates ascribing states

This paper was written especially for this volume.

of consciousness *and* predicates ascribing corporeal characteristics, a physical situation, etc. are equally applicable . . ." (p. 104, italics in original) not only must be applicable, but must be "primitive," that is, not analyzable as a "secondary kind of entity in relation to two primary kinds, viz. a particular consciousness and a particular human body" (105). The argument for this, as for the ancillary thesis that P-predicates must "have both first- and third-person ascriptive uses" where neither is primary (108), is founded on two related facets of experience: "Why are one's states of consciousness ascribed to anything at all?" and "Why are they ascribed to the very same thing as certain corporeal characteristics, a certain physical situation, etc.?" (90) That we make such ascriptions of states of consciousness, and that we make them along with ascriptions of bodily characteristics, is fairly taken for undeniable. The argument then consists in showing that this kind of ascription could not be, unless the concept of a person were primitive. We thus have a transcendental argument. Of course, in keeping with the "linguistic turn" of contemporary Anglo-Saxon philosophy, the undeniable starting point has to do with the use of language, here the *ascription* of certain states, but the family relation to Kant's work is clear nonetheless.

Of course, it is hardly surprising that we find in Strawson's work an affinity with Kant. But this is not to say that such an affinity must be present for a philosopher to have recourse to transcendental argument. Much of Wittgenstein's argument in the *Investigations* can, I believe, be understood in the same light; except that it is clearer what Wittgenstein is arguing against than what he is arguing for. Let us take the arguments against private ostensive definition, which turn on the impossibility of a private language. In *Philosophical Investigations*, I, paras. 258 ff., Wittgenstein attempts to show that we could not succeed in operating with a truly private sign "E" for a certain sensation. His argument turns on showing that we could have no "criterion of correctness" for the use of such a sign.

The rock-bottom starting point of Wittgenstein's argument can be understood as this: that our concepts, being general, are used to reidentify fresh examples of the sort of thing that falls under them, that a distinction must thus be possible between correct and incorrect reidentification and hence right and wrong use of the term. This in turn founds the necessity of criteria, and it is the supposed incapacity of private ostensive definition to provide criteria that justifies its being swept aside as a picture of experience and its relation to language.

This argument has some interest for us because it has a degree of affinity to one of Hegel's arguments which we will examine. The plausibility of the view of experience Wittgenstein is attacking here, that it is a private realm of knowledge to which the subject has privileged access, rests on one's ignoring language in a certain sense. We focus on the preverbal experience in our imagination, and hence what we imagine to be the preverbal experience: here we are contemplating a certain "sensation" of red, or a certain inner feeling of unease or depression. Surely we have at this stage already gained some knowledge, however exiguous, viz. that this sensation or feeling is experienced. On the strength of this, we can then go on to *name* it, hence introducing language.

Put this way, the story is quite plausible. But can language thus be held at arm's length? What is involved in our claim to "know" as we confront the pure, as yet unnamed, experience? We are certainly not talking about a genuine pre- or non-verbal consciousness of things, such, for instance, as that of an infant or an animal; for these can't be said to know in any human sense. For us, knowing is inseparably bound up with being able to say, even if we can only say rather badly and inadequately, and even if we may have in desperation to have recourse to such words as "ineffable." An experience about which nothing at all could be said, not even that it was very difficult if not impossible to describe, would be below the threshold of the level of awareness which we consider essential for knowledge (in the sense relevant here, i.e. knowledge of the currently experienced). It would have been either lived unconsciously, or else have been so peripheral that we had or could recover no hold on it.

This relation of knowledge to what we can say is recognized by the theorists of experience as private knowledge, for they present a picture of the subject as being in a position to *name* the object of the experience, and hence in a position to say, even if possibly in a private language, what he had experienced. But of course to be in a position to name an object is already to have a linguistic consciousness of one's experience. Naming an object presupposes being ready to apply to it other terms which will situate this name in our discourse and identify what it names. Naming cannot take place in isolation outside of a context of linguistic capacity. We have to know what we're naming, and this means that we have to be able to say, however inadequately, what we're naming.

Thus the situation evoked above, in which we're in a position to name our experience, cannot really be preverbal. Typically, we would be able to say something like this: "There's that damn sensation again, I better find a name for it, let's say 'E'"; or "Hello, this is a new sensation, let me call it 'E.'" Naming can take place here, because we have delineated what we name by "sensation," and in each case we could probably add some other descriptive terms as well (e.g., "intermittent, throbbing, mildly painful sensation in the left shoulder").[1]

Thus we could look at a goodly part of Wittgenstein's argument in the *Investigations* as a transcendental one with the following starting point: to know, we must be able to say (in the sense in which admitting indescribability is also a form of "saying"). This gives the wherewithal to destroy the picture of preverbal consciousness which lends the notion of experience as private knowledge its plausibility. But more, by exploring the nature of language and showing that it cannot be constituted by the introduction of names independently of each other, but rather that each term has meaning only through a skein of relations to others, Wittgenstein hopes to put paid to the idea that we can have a private language (that is, descriptive terms that wouldn't derive their meaning from their relations to the words of our common language) and hence an experience-world of private knowledge. He tries to show, in other words, that a putative descriptive term of a private language, unless situated through the words of the common language, is nothing more than an "inarticulate sound" (op. cit., I, para. 261), that emitting it doesn't amount to saying anything, so that if this is all that can be "said" about an experience, it can hardly be considered an object of knowledge. So that irreducibly private experience (experience not shaped through common language) could only be if it were not the case that to know is to be able to say; or in other words, a necessary condition of this seemingly undeniable facet of our conscious experience, that we be capable of speaking about it, is that there be no irreducibly private experience.

[1] Cf. Wittgenstein, op. cit., I, para. 261: "What reason have we for calling 'E' the sign for a *sensation*? For 'sensation' is a word of our common language, not of one intelligible to me alone" (italics in original).

This argument, as I mentioned above, is of special interest to the purpose at hand because it parallels Hegel's opening argument in the first chapter of the *Phenomenology,* which also turns on the basic starting point that to know is to be able to say. But before getting on to this, perhaps a word should be said about the principle of reading these passages of Hegel as transcendental arguments.

A first point of rapprochement springs to mind immediately. The examples we have been looking at of transcendental argument have a certain bent in common; they are all directed against one or other aspect of the dualist picture of experience developed and handed down to us by Cartesianism and empiricism. This impression of common bent would be strengthened if we cited other prominent cases of transcendental argument in our day, those of philosophers of the phenomenological school. For indeed, one of the uses of phenomenological "description" with a writer such as Merleau-Ponty is to provide such starting points of transcendental argument whose conclusions were meant to be a refutation of empiricist and "intellectualist" notions of experience.

We may perhaps understand the background to this correlation in the following way: both Cartesianism and empiricism present us with a picture of experience that is derived mainly from a certain notion of the human epistemological predicament. Those who opposed them, either because they had a different notion of epistemology or because they disliked the picture of human nature that resulted, have thus been tempted to attack, at the weakest spot, the very schematic and implausible notion of experience. And this terrain lends itself to transcendental arguments, since it is at least tempting to believe that we can delineate facets of experience that are basic and pervasive enough to be undeniable, and these can be the starting points for our arguments. Kant's first *Critique* thus opened a two-century-long hunting season on empiricism, in the course of which a great many philosophers have joined in.

In terms of bent, Hegel is undoubtedly of that company, not only in general, but in particular in the passages we propose to examine here; for Hegel starts off in the first chapter of the *Phenomenology* examining "sensible certainty," a notion of experience as simply receptive (*aufnehmend*) and as preconceptual. But this affinity of bent is hardly enough to justify our classing Hegel's arguments together with the others as transcendental, the more so in that Hegel's ultimate goal, to show that "consciousness" (consciousness of an object) is ultimately one with "self-consciousness," is an ambition shared by none of the other philosophers mentioned. Of course, the fact that the ultimate goal is different doesn't in any way rule out the possibility of substantial similarity in argument on the way there; and as we shall see later, much of what Hegel attempts to prove as steps toward his ultimate goal resembles the conclusions of contemporary philosophers. But transcendental arguments are not identified by their bent but by their structure as argument, and this is the parallel we have to show to Hegel's work.

This will come out in one way as we look at the argument itself. But this is not really enough, since Hegel purports to be very clear and explicit about his own way of proceeding, and it is this notion of the dialectic that we must confront as well with the structure of a transcendental argument.

Hegel's aim in the *Phenomenology* is to move from the "natural," i.e. commonsense, view of consciousness to his own. He makes clear in the Introduction that he intends to take nothing for granted, that he does not intend to present his way of thinking over against that of "natural consciousness" and let his case rest on assurances that it is better founded. His method will be to start with ordinary, "natural" consciousness and show that on examination it transforms itself into another "figure" (*Gestaltung*). But how transform itself? Because, says Hegel, "natural consciousness," or the ordinary commonsense notion of consciousness, comes to see its own untruth or inadequacy.

But how can natural consciousness come to see its own inadequacy? Our ordinary notion of experience is that of a knowing subject who has a certain vision of things; the notion of experience is characterized by the notion we have of what is experienced, sense-data (sensible qualities), particulate data (fields), and so on. Now, it is no use going outside this notion of experience and judging it by what we know (or think we know) to be effectively there in the world. For this would be introducing a "yardstick" (*Maszstab*) from outside this notion of experience; and moreover, it would be irrelevant, since experience is not just a function of what is there in the world to be experienced.

But how, then, can a false notion of experience be shown to be wrong from the inside? It can, Hegel claims, because a notion of experience contains its own "yardstick"; it contains, that is, an idea of what it is to know an object. Now, with this we can compare experience as it effectively is, and see if they agree; if effective experience fits the model projected for it.[2]

In other words, natural consciousness can be transformed from within, because it is not just a given effective experience but an effective experience shaped by a certain *idea* of what experience is. Conscious-

[2] "An dem also was das Bewusstsein innerhalb seiner für das *Ansich* oder das *Wahre* erklärt, haben wir den Maszstab, den es selbst aufstellt, sein Wissen daran zu messen" (71, italics in original).

ness is not just any object, it is an object that lives in relation to a model of itself: "das Bewusstsein . . . ist für sich selbst sein *Begriff*, dadurch unmittelbar das Hinausgehen über das Beschränkte und, da ihm dies Beschränkte angehört, über sich selbst" (p. 69). Hence it has the kind of duality that can enable it to be in contradiction with itself, where what it is effectively when it attempts to realize a given model violates that model.

The change that results from this kind of contradiction Hegel calls dialectical movement. And of course it is a real change and not simply a disappearance of a model thus smitten with contradiction; for the contradiction between model and reality is a determinate (*bestimmt*) one; as such, it calls for a particular transformation to overcome it; and of course, the transformation must be in the model or yardstick, for it is this which is at the root of the contradiction, that in trying to realize it, effective experience violates it.[3]

Hence, any inadequate notion of consciousness will transform itself from within in the following way: as a notion of consciousness, it must contain an idea of experience, of what it is to know an object. Let us try to experience in this way, to have this kind of knowledge. If it turns out that effective experience guided by this model contradicts it, that we cannot attain knowledge along this path without violating the model in some way, then it will be shown to be impossible and will have to be changed. We will make the changes that the contradiction revealed by this particular experience has shown to be necessary, and this will yield us another notion of consciousness with which to start another test.

But this procedure presupposes that we can characterize effective experience in terms independent of

[3] "Die Prüfung ist nicht nur eine Prüfung des Wissens, sondern auch ihres Maszstabes" (73).

the model of experience we are working with. Moreover, if we are to show that the model is not just unrealized in a given case, but cannot be realized, we have to be able to identify some basic and pervasive facets of experience independently of our model (they must be independent, i.e. not derivable from the model itself, if they are to contradict it and show it to be impossible). Hence the method that Hegel outlines in the Introduction to the *Phenomenology* can only be applied if such basic facets can be picked out, and his arguments will stand only to the extent that they can be shown as beyond question.

Hegel's argument will thus have to start from undeniable characteristics of experience; and since it will go on from there to show that the various inadequate models of consciousness are incompatible with these characteristics, which on the contrary require other conceptions if they are to hold, his argument, to the extent that it follows the plan of the Introduction, has many affinities to transcendental arguments. Now, this claim could not be made for the whole book, but the argument of the first three chapters of the *Phenomenology* does conform to the method laid out in the Introduction, and hence, as we shall see, Hegel's arguments can easily and convincingly be presented in transcendental form, and this section of his work can be mined as the source of interesting transcendental arguments.[4]

The arguments here, of course, are closely related to others in the rest of his work, notably the *Logic*.

[4] Reciprocally, we could construe Wittgenstein's argument mentioned above along the lines of Hegel's dialectic. In order to show the impossibility of the kind of experience that could be the basis of a private language, we attempt to realize this model in imagination with our sensation "E." The conditions of successfully identifying "E" violate the terms of the model, for they require that we link "E" up with the public language. The model is shown in Hegel's sense to be contradictory.

But since the *Phenomenology* is designedly a dialectic of forms of consciousness (however much or little later parts of the work conform to this description), it is obviously here that one finds the arguments that are closest to recognizable transcendental form. In fact, however, many arguments in the *Logic* are also of the transcendental type, but it would take us too far afield to explore this at the moment.

II

The notion of consciousness with which Hegel starts his dialectical critique is one he calls "sensible certainty." This is a view of our awareness of the world according to which it is at its fullest and richest when we simply open our senses, as it were, to the world and receive whatever impressions come our way, prior to any activity of the mind, in particular conceptual activity. "Wir haben uns ebenso *unmittelbar* oder *aufnehmend* zu verhalten, also nichts an ihm (sc. dem Seienden), wie es sich darbietet, zu verändern und von dem Auffassen das Begreifen abzuhalten" (79). Now, according to the view called sensible certainty, this pure receptivity is supposed to give us the richest knowledge, as well as the truest, and both these for the same reason, viz. that "sie hat von dem Gegenstande noch nichts weggelassen, sondern ihn in seiner ganzen Vollständigkeit vor sich" (loc. cit.).

This view has evidently a certain resemblance to empiricism. It is not identical with empiricism, since it is not by any means as fully specified: it lacks, for instance, the definition of what is received in terms of "sense data" (or "ideas," "impressions," as they were variously called in the classical version). But the idea of consciousness as primordially receptivity, prior to any intellectual (i.e. conceptual) activity, and the view that a greater degree of certainty attaches to the deliverances of this receptivity than to any judgments we might make on the basis of it, these are recognizably empiricist themes.

Now Hegel's *démarche* in face of this conception is very similar to Wittgenstein's: he challenges sensible certainty to *say* what it experiences. The underlying principle is the same, viz. that if this is really knowledge, then one must be able to say what it is,[5] and this is (here as with Wittgenstein) the starting point of what we called above a transcendental argument. But in Hegel's presentation, it is seen primarily as the application of his method. Sensible certainty claims knowledge by pure receptivity; very well, let us try to see what knowledge can be effectively attained in this way, or what is the same thing, let us try to say what we know in this way. As we shall see, the attempt to say will contradict the basic requirements of sensible certainty, will take us beyond its defining limits, and hence it will stand self-refuted in the way outlined by the dialectical method of the Introduction.

There are two main ways in which the attempt to say takes us beyond the limits of sensible certainty. The first is a minor theme in this first chapter, although it is the major one in the opening passages of the *Logic:* the great richness of this form of consciousness is purely apparent; as we "take in" the scene before us, we might mistakenly believe that we are taking in an inexhaustible richness of detail, because in fact an inexhaustible number of detailed things could be said about this scene. But the requirement that we say what we know shows that what we are really aware of is a selection from this inexhaustible fund, for in grasping things under some descriptions, we exclude (for the present) being aware of them under others. Looking at the objects in my study under their ordinary descriptions as use objects (type-

[5] "Die Sprache . . . ist . . . das Wahrhaftere" (82).

writer, desk, chairs, etc.), I cannot see them as pure shapes; or looking at them as pure shapes, I cannot see them as the juxtaposition of different materials, and so on.

Thus, says Hegel, this form of consciousness, far from being the richest, would in fact be the poorest, for its very lack of selectivity condemns it to emptiness. To go beyond selection in the attempt to "take in everything" can only be to fall over into unconsciousness, a trancelike stare. The references to "pure Being" (80) evoke parallel arguments of the *Logic.*

But the main theme of this first chapter is a refutation of the claim of sensible certainty to be in immediate contact with sensible particulars, without the mediation of general terms, which not only introduce selectivity, as we have just seen, but involve grasping the objects before us through aspects that they have in common or could have in common with other things, rather than in their own particularity. Sensible certainty is rich and true because it is (supposedly) in touch with the particular thing itself, and not simply with it in so far as it is an instance of a given class.

The thrust of Hegel's argument is therefore quite close to that of Wittgenstein mentioned above: they both focus on the inescapable role of the concept or descriptive expression; only while Wittgenstein's main interest is to go on to show how the concept only has meaning within a skein of relations to others, and hence to the common language and ultimately life-forms, Hegel's principal point here is the impossibility of bare knowledge of the particular.

Hegel's argument for the necessary mediation of knowledge through a concept or universal has basically two stages: In the first, he imagines the protagonist of sensible certainty answering the request to say by pure demonstratives ("this" or "here" or "now"). Hegel could argue at this point that these must be inadequate expressions of what I am aware of, that the object must be more determinate than this if I am to be said to be aware at all. But instead he takes another tack, that of claiming that a term such as "this" or "now," applying as it can indifferently to many different contents, itself functions as a universal, and hence shows that there can be no immediate knowledge of the particular–knowledge, that is, unmediated by general terms. As a matter of fact, in Hegel's particular usage of the term, this likeness of function is enough to class these demonstratives as universals (as he will also class the "I"). "Ein solches Einfaches, das durch Negation ist, weder Dieses noch Jenes, ein *Nichtdieses,* und ebenso gleichgültig, auch Dieses wie Jenes zu sein, nennen wir ein *Allgemeines* (82, italics in original).

This stage continues with a consideration of the possible riposte on behalf of sensible certainty: that we can identify the particular time and place meant by "here" and "now" by adding that they are the here and now that *I* am contemplating. But "I" in this context, as Hegel points out, is as much a "universal" as "this." I *mean,* of course, one particular person, but I succeed as little in saying which particular person in saying "I," as I do in saying what particular thing in saying "this."

But of course this will not satisfy the protagonist of sensible certainty. And Hegel's assimilation of "I" to the demonstrative terms discussed earlier just brings the malaise to a head. I cannot say who is meant by "I" or "this" or "now" in a way that will be available to anyone regardless of context; and, for the same reason, sentences containing such words cannot be just transplanted from their context and retain the same truth value. But when I say "I" or "this," *I* know what I mean, and I can *show* you, if you will just place yourself in the same context.

Here we come to the real idea underlying the notion of sensible certainty. As a pure contact with the particular, it is of course only available in context, and as a knowledge unmediated by concepts, it can of course only be shown. In this second stage of his argument, Hegel is getting down to the real issue:

> *Zeigen* müssen wir es uns lassen; denn die Wahrheit dieser unmittelbaren Beziehung ist die Wahrheit *dieses* Ich, der sich auf ein Jetzt oder ein *Hier* einscränkt. Würden wir *nachher* diese Wahrheit vornehmen oder *entfernt* davon stehen, so hätte sie gar keine Bedeutung; denn wir höben die Unmittelbarkeit auf, die ihr wesentlich ist (85, italics in original).

We come across here, in another form, the familiar theme of ostensive definition. This is the nub of the argument.

Hegel's answer is similar to Wittgenstein's, as we have seen. *I* cannot know even what I mean in this context if all I can say is "this" or "here." For what do these terms embrace? Take "now": does it mean this punctual instant, this hour, this day, this decade, this epoch? It can mean all of these, and others in different contexts. But, for it to mean something for me, and not just be an empty word, there must be something else I could say to give a shape, a scope, to this "now"; let it be a term for a time period, such as "day" or "hour," or some description of the event or process or action that is holding my attention and hence defining the dimensions of my present.

And so, Hegel concludes, there is no unmediated knowledge of the particular. Sensible certainty ends up saying the opposite of what it means (88), and this is the proof of its contradictory nature. Any attempt at effective awareness of the particular can only succeed by making use of descriptive, i.e. general, terms. The purely particular is "unreachable." What remains beyond description as the "unexpressible . . . is nothing other than the untrue, irrational, simply pointed to" (das Unwahre, Unvernünftige, bloss Gemeinte, 88). And by the same token, the particular is the subject of potentially endless description; for at any point, descriptions in general terms will not have captured its particularity, and yet there is nothing further to be done in order to express this particularity other than mere description in general terms.

The thesis as here presented will not seem strange, or even wrong, to many contemporary philosophers. But the argument and its conclusion are presented by Hegel in a way that reflects certain major themes particular to his philosophy. Thus the unavailability of the bare particular is not just an epistemological truth; it reflects the ontological one that the particular is doomed by its very nature to disappear, that it is in principle mortal. What is permanent is the concept. So the unsayability of the particular is simply the expression of its ontological status, as that which cannot remain, that which must pass. And reciprocally, external particular existence is impermanent because it cannot be expressed in concepts.

That is why it is astounding, says Hegel, how some philosophers can continue to hold to the sensible reality of the particular as the final ground of knowledge. Even the beasts are wiser than this:

> . . . denn sie bleiben nicht vor den sinnlichen Dingen als an sich seienden stehen, sondern, versweifelnd an dieser Realität und in der völligen Gewissheit ihrer Nichtigkeit langen sie ohne weiteres zu und zehren sie auf (87).

But, in Hegel's ontology, if it is true that the particular is mortal, it is also true that it exists of necessity, that the concept, the Idea cannot be outside of its embodiment in (a series of) particulars. The concept reveals itself in the procession of particulars, their coming to be and passing away. The particular can only be understood as a passing vehicle for the concept.

This background of theory makes Hegel present the argument for the unsayability of the particular in a fashion peculiar to himself. The argument reflects not just the impossibility of bare unmediated knowledge of the particular, but also the movement underlying experience itself. As particular sensuous beings, we encounter particular things, we come across them, as it were, with our senses. But as soon as we try to grasp them, they disappear, so to speak; we can hold onto them only by subsuming them under a concept. In Hegelian language, our attempt to grasp things in knowledge first negates them as particulars; then, negating this negation, we recover them by grasping them through mediated conceptual consciousness. The immediate is negated, but it is retained in mediated form.

The term in connection with which Hegel presents this argument is "now"; and although there are some respects in which this particular example is unrepresentative, the point is plainly meant to be general. The "now" of sensible certainty could be understood in its most immediate sense as designating the punctual present. But this is no sooner designated than it is past, hence gone, "negated"; but when we fall back on a description that gives the scope of our present, say "today" or "this hour," the immediately fleeting present is recuperated and reintegrated into this larger "now"; the first negation is negated.

This example is less illuminating than it might be, because the particular fleetingness of time, whose punctual instants vanish in becoming past, cannot be matched easily in the discussion of "here" or "this." But the general point seems to be this: in experience we meet particulars; we can grasp these particular things only by in some sense "pointing," either literally or by focusing on a thing in a way we could only convey through the use of some demonstrative or related word. But the experience itself of pointing (*Aufzeigen*) is that, in trying to grasp the thing, we show the fleeting, unseizable nature of the particular, and we can recover it and hold it before our gaze, as it were, only by subsuming it under a universal.

In other words, "das Aufzeigen ist das Erfahren, dass Jetzt *Allgemeines* ist" (86, italics in original). And by that terminal "ist" Hegel means to convey the point that this experience brings us to the ontological truth of the matter, that the particular only is, as a vehicle for the concept. But what is germane from our point of view here is that Hegel has not just argued to the impossibility of unmediated knowledge of particulars and the necessary role of concepts, but wants to present the idea that the argument, as the depiction of an attempt to grasp the particular that fails, reflects our experience itself, as we encounter and reach out for particulars and discover that we can only really hold them through the mediating instruments of universal concepts.

III

This notion—that the argument reflects the movement of experience itself—sets the stage for another pair of transcendental arguments, which occupy the second chapter and the transition to the third.

The movement of experience is the attempt to grasp a particular that issues in an awareness of the object as falling under certain descriptions. The particular can never itself be grasped in language; an attempt to do so can issue only in a potentially endless list of descriptive terms being applied to it. But just because it is potentially endless, no list of properties can ever exhaust the thing and hence overcome the duality between the particular thing and the descriptions found true of it.

These latter are what we call "properties," and hence the new notion of the object of experience that emerges out of the dialectic of the first chapter is that of a thing with properties (*das Ding und seine Eigenschaften*). The notion of experience as consisting in knowledge of this object, Hegel calls "perception" (*Wahrnehmung*).

This is the starting point for a new dialectic in which Hegel tries to show that experience defined in terms of this object reveals itself once more as contradictory, for the object itself suffers an inner contradiction. Common sense will try to avoid this conclusion by attributing the inconsistencies to the process of perception itself. But, Hegel argues, all these attempts to save the thing are doomed to failure. We will have to conclude at the end of the chapter that the conflict and movement that we attribute to perception are in the thing itself.

But how can we say that the thing is contradictory? Hegel's argument attempts to establish this by showing that there is a conflict between the two dimensions of the thing—as particular, and as ensemble of properties; and yet that each is necessarily linked with the other. These two theses are the conclusions respectively of the two interesting transcendental arguments mentioned above. Let us take the latter first.

The idea is that there is a kind of mutual dependency here, that we couldn't logically have our property concepts if we didn't operate with particulars, and reciprocally that we couldn't identify particulars without property concepts.

If we thought of properties as just "matters" (Hegel takes up here a concept connected with one of the false starts of physics of the late-eighteenth century, e.g. in the attempt to account for heat by "calorific matter") existing alongside each other in the universe but not bound together in particulars, then we would not be able to derive our property concepts. For our predicates can be given meaning only through contrast with other predicates. We could, for instance, have no notion of red if this were our only color concept; we have the concept we have only because of the range of contrasts available; another society with another range of contrasts would be said to have a different concept. Hegel is here, of course, returning to one of his central themes, which can be expressed in a slogan borrowed from Spinoza: *omnis determinatio est negatio.*

It is thus true of all properties that they are opposed to some others, and it is this contrast, essential to the very meaning of the terms, that lies behind necessary truths of the kind: "nothing can be red and green all over." But of course, without the notion of a particular or something closely resembling a particular, such a phrase would be meaningless; for it is only of particulars, of things that can bear properties, that one can say that they cannot be both red and green.

But, it might be objected, we cannot argue from this that the idea of a particular is essential to such a contrast, or that the contrast wouldn't appear to a consciousness that didn't distinguish particulars. Imagine a static visual field, i.e. one on which there were no changes of color; surely one can imagine a subject whose perception was restricted to this distinguishing different colors, even though he might have no use for the idea of a something that might have now this color, now another.

But, even here, there would nevertheless be an ineradicable role for the notion of thing. For there could be no contrast between colors without there being boundaries, however vague, between parts of the field that are differently colored. But then our most exiguous primitive consciousness of colors would be distinguishing particulars, viz. parts or patches of the field, that would "bear" a color property and also others (e.g. shape, size, position, saliency) in indefinite number.

The general point underlying this is that for there to be consciousness of contrast between two properties, they must somehow be presented over against each other. But, in being presented in contrast, these two percepts obviously must differ in more than the qualities concerned; they must differ in place or time, or in "position" in some space analogue; in short they must differ in some respect having to do with the mode of presentation. And this is what must open a place for the concept of a particular, i.e. something that bears the property and at least those others which are related to its "position" in the mode of presentation concerned, and there is no way in which these can be limited to a finite list. The relevance of the principle that nothing can be both "A" and "B" (where "A" and "B" are contrasted properties) should be seen in a new light. We can now see it as a way of saying: for A and B to be contrasted, they must somehow be presented in contrast, and that means that they must belong to different "things."

But we cannot have the concepts "A" and "B" unless they are contrasted; and so these property notions require a consciousness that identifies particulars.

How about the other way around? Can we identify particulars only by contrasting properties? The answer is clearly affirmative if we accept the principle of the identity of indiscernibles, which Hegel does. But we don't need to go into this dispute here. It hangs on whether we want to call the space-time coordinates of an object "properties" or not. But, in the context of the argument here, there is no reason not to do so. If we think of its properties as facts about the object that we can pick out in descriptions and a list of which, however long, fails to exhaust what can be said, then we can perfectly well think of its position in space and time as a property (and if this is still shocking, then we can reformulate the argument using the long periphrasis above, for this is what is essential to Hegel's purpose).

We can then say, along with Hegel, that without appeal to one or some properties in this extended sense, we cannot distinguish particulars. The dependency is thus reciprocal. We cannot operate with property concepts without attributing them to particulars,[6] and we cannot operate with particulars without

[6] Of course, the above argument is compatible with there being only particulars whose properties are perceptible by one sense alone, such as the example above. Hegel's argument throughout, however, is in terms of the intersensorial particular, and this will be important at a later stage. But there are various ways in which one can close the gap by showing these latter to be necessary as well.

To start with, even in the example above, many of the other properties cited besides color–shape, position, saliency, for instance–are not simply visual, but available to more than one sense, and this enters into their very appearance to sight (which is why the penny on its side does *not* look elliptical, as so many classical discussions seemed to assume). So that as far as the actual properties are concerned by which we describe our experience, many could be distinguished only by being related to intersensorial particulars.

More fundamentally, we could take a line similar to Kant's and argue that the condition of a notion of objectivity, and hence the ability to draw a distinction between things and the way they appear to us, when this is appropriate, is that experience be at least partly of things that are in principle accessible to more than one sense, even if we might have been so constituted that we could experience the world through only one sense; just as our present world, accessible to our five senses, is such that we could not rule out its being perceived quite differently by an Alpha Centaurian who was sensitive, say, to electromagnetic waves. For in a world *in principle* accessible

applying some property concepts to them. Perception requires that we use both of these in tandem.

But why should this make any trouble for the notion of experience Hegel calls "perception"? Because, thinks Hegel, these two dimensions of a thing, as particular (*ausschliessendes Eins*) and as ensemble of properties, are somehow incommensurable; they cannot be combined coherently into a single consistent notion of the object.

But why should this be so? It is hard at first blush to identify the problem here. Hegel seems to feel that there is some conflict between the diversity of the object as an ensemble of properties, and its unity as a particular. We today would shrug this off as two ways of presenting the same object that have no need to be considered as opposed. But perhaps when we see what underlies our sense that there is no problem here, and look at what Hegel tried to extract out of this supposed contradiction, some of his argument may become clearer.

To take the latter first: Hegel's conclusion is that we cannot combine these two dimensions in order to form a stable static image of the thing. Rather, we can only move back and forth between a notion of it as particular unity and a notion of it as deployed in diverse properties. One of these refers us to the other,

---

to only one sense, there would be no way of making the distinction between what is and the distortions it may from time to time undergo in experience, i.e. between what is and how it looks. And without this distinction there is no notion of objectivity. (This difficulty faces even the ingeniously devised auditory world of Strawson in *Individuals,* ch. 2, sec. 3. He achieves one of the conditions of objectivity—reidentification—but fails of the one discussed here.)

Hegel, however, does not face this difficulty. For the rest of this paper, I propose to follow him in taking it as met, and continue the discussion as he does in terms of the intersensorial particular.

and vice versa. But we can solve the problem by seeing that this reciprocal movement is not just in the perceiving mind, but is essential to the object itself.

But this yields a quite new model of the object, a dynamic one, in which the various features that we describe in our predicates are seen as emanations of a power implicit in the underlying unity, which are at the same time held together by this same power. This is the concept of the thing that is based on Hegel's notion of "force" (*Kraft*), the analysis of which occupies the opening pages of the third chapter. In stepping from the thing to the object of force, we move from a one-tiered to a two-tiered concept, rather like the step from being to essence in the *Logic*. For we are now looking on objects as on two levels, as it were, as external manifestations of underlying powers. Hegel is saying in effect that we can resolve the contradiction of the thing only by admitting that it is more complex than we allowed and seeing it as two-leveled in this way. Attempts to put together the unity and the diversity on the same level are bound to fail.

This is thus the burden of the second transcendental argument that can be found in this chapter, an argument whose conclusion I should like to reformulate in the following way: we couldn't have the experience we have, i.e. of objects with properties, unless these objects were grasped as the locus of causal properties and relations.

This requirement can be further spelled out in two related theses: 1) that particulars can only be the bearers of many properties because they are the locus of the causal background of these properties; that is, when we attribute a property to a thing, we generally see that feature as at least partly grounded in a causal background involving other properties of the thing, a background with which we would have to come to grips to alter the thing in this respect; 2) that particulars as the locus of such causal backgrounds must be identified at least in part by causal properties, that is, by their mode of interaction with others.

Obviously the key notion that I am introducing here in order to explicate Hegel's conclusion is that of the thing as the "locus of causal background." Now, a thing plays this role relative to one of its properties when an explanation of this property involves reference, *inter alia,* to other factors within the thing (which can be thought of, within the language of this chapter, as other "properties" of the thing), and, hence, altering this property involves acting on the thing not just in respect of this property.

But we are dealing here, of course, as throughout this first section of the *Phenomenology,* with epistemological theses. Hegel's conclusion, as I am trying to interpret it, is that our experience, in this sense, is of the thing as the locus of causal backgrounds. For this, it is not enough that the subject discover "correlations" between two properties A and B such that he can come to explain B's occurrence by A; this could occur even if experience were simply a flow of sensed properties, and not of *things* at all. Thinghood would be a status conferred by the subject on groups of properties that experience showed to be in repeated concatenation, but it would not be an inescapable structure of experience itself.

Hegel's conclusion here requires, rather, that our most primitive experience of properties be a perception of these as properties of things that 1) are not identical with any concatenation of properties, because they cannot be exhaustively characterized by any list of properties however long, and 2) are perceived, in however schematic, unspecified, and implicit a fashion, as containing the causal background to these properties. And Hegel's proof will be, in effect, as we shall see, that we cannot have 1) without 2).

I have unpacked Hegel's thesis here considerably

more than he does, but I believe that this is what he is driving at in this chapter. And if this is what he is trying to prove, and if he holds this conclusion to be somehow the refutation of the model of experience he calls "perception," then this latter model must be understood by him as lacking this causal dimension.

Now, the epistemological view that is ultimately inhospitable to phenomenal causality is the contemplative notion of perception that comes to us from the empiricist (and to some extent also the Cartesian) tradition. "Contemplative" here refers to a notion of experience as consisting of the passive reception of sense data, so that the nature of experience itself is not bound up with the way we interact and deal with the world (although *what* particular experience we have will obviously depend partly on how we move, where we look, etc.). This view, as Hume amply demonstrated, cannot help but make causality problematical. For, as he eloquently argued, there is no room within a contemplative account of perception for an impression of natural necessity, of "power." Only if our experience of things is essentially linked to our interaction with them, can we speak of causal properties and relations as objects of experience.

Thus we have some grounds for interpreting Hegel's "perception" here within the terms of the essentially contemplative view of knowledge of the empiricist-Cartesian tradition, so that his transcendental arguments have a bent similar to that of all other authors mentioned, in that they are specifically aimed at this epistemologically grounded deformation of experience.

Now, if this is so, we can better understand and appreciate Hegel's claim that the object of perception is contradictory. For empiricism notoriously encountered great difficulty in accounting for our perception of things with properties. As long as knowledge was essentially seen as the reception of impressions, it was possible to understand observing properties—red, hard, round, etc.—but the linking of all these in an object was essentially mysterious. The object became the underlying substrate, the *je ne sais quoi,* or even outright fiction. In any case it was essentially imperceptible. But if it is really true that we cannot perceive properties without perceiving things as well, then this notion of perception is in contradiction with itself.

This interpretation is strengthened when we look at the detail of Hegel's argument. It is true that Hegel refers, toward the end of the chapter, to the protagonist of "perception" as a model of experience as "der . . . oft sogenannte gesunde Menschenverstand." But any temptation we might have to identify this protagonist with the plain man disappears when we examine the arguments Hegel puts in his mouth. Hegel paints him as seeking by all means to avoid the conclusion that his object is contradictory. To this end, he distinguishes between appearance and reality, or else between the thing in itself and the thing for us. The contradiction can then be resolved by attributing one of the terms to the object and the other only to our perception of it. We can hold, for instance, that the thing is really one and only appears multiple; or else that a real multiplicity is unified by our understanding. Or else we can try to distinguish the thing "für sich" from the thing "für ein anderes," i.e. in its relation to others.

But these are all dodges of the traditional epistemology. For they all presuppose that the particular thing, bearer or locus of many properties, is somehow beyond *perception;* it is either an unseen substrate or a creation of the mind. And this accurately reflects the difficulty specific to a contemplative epistemology, that it can't give an adequate account of the perception of things. Hegel's argument here thus strengthens the interpretation that his target under the title "perception" is the contemplative view of experience.

Hegel's strategy is simple, and it is evident from the foregoing. He takes the thesis that we described above as the conclusion of the first transcendental argument of the chapter, that we cannot separate property concepts from particulars, and uses it to destroy all the dodges of the traditional epistemology and hence this epistemology itself. Thus any attempt to separate the unity of the thing from its multiple properties, taking it as either a substrate or a creation of the mind, must make unintelligible our perception of these properties. And any attempt to distinguish the thing "for itself" from the thing in relation to others encounters the crucial objection that things can be distinguished from each other only by (in the broad sense above, which includes spatiotemporal position) their properties, and that these can be identified only by contrast.[7]

The nub of Hegel's argument thus appears to be this: if we cannot operate with property concepts without attributing these to particulars (and vice versa), then any account of perception that cannot find a place for the multipropertied thing as object of perception, or that can account for particulars only as punctual properties (this smell, this patch of red), must be wrong.

From here Hegel moves on to show that the object of perception must be the locus of force or causal properties essentially by the following argument: the object of perception is contradictory; it is both the single thing and the multiple properties that the traditional epistemology couldn't reconcile. The movement from one to the other which the subject of perception makes in thought must thus be seen as a real movement in the object. It is a movement whereby the

[7] This argument is close to the similar argument about the "thing" (*Ding*) in the *Logic;* cf. *Wissenschaft der Logik,* Book II, second section, first chapter, "Die Existenz."

unity of the thing goes over into or produces the multiplicity of its properties, and this multiplicity returns to unity. But to speak of this unity as going over into (*übergehen*) external multiplicity, to think of the latter as emanating from unity and returning to it, is to characterize the object of perception in terms of force (*Kraft*) or causal properties.[8]

This argument may not appear very convincing to contemporaries. But the conclusion that the object of perception must be seen as the locus of causal properties and relations can be quite convincingly defended from the considerations Hegel has adduced in this second chapter. It can be shown to be implicit in the refutation of the traditional epistemology, in that what makes this latter incapable of accounting for the perception of things is precisely that it cannot account for the perception of causal relations; these two incapacities, in other words, are closely bound together.

We are trying to prove 1) that our perception must be of things that contain part at least of the causal background of their properties (this is ultimately our way of interpreting the thesis that the "unity" of the thing goes immediately over into its deployment [*Entfaltung,* sc. into its multiple properties], which then returns to unity [105]), and 2) that particulars must be identified at least in part by causal properties.

Now, as to 1), there are of course an indefinitely large number of ways in which we could carve the world up into particulars, and a great number of these are actually explored at one time or another; but generally when we see A and B as properties of the same

[8] "Die selbständig gesetzten gehen unmittelbar in ihre Einheit, und ihre Einheit unmittelbar in die Entfaltung über, und diese wieder zurück in die Reduktion. Diese Bewegung ist aber dasjenige, was *Kraft* genannt wird" (105, italics in original).

particular, the claim is that a significant part of the causal backgrounds of both A and B lie in this same thing.

Now, the ground of this claim is that we couldn't have our notion of particulars without the range of notions connected with that of causal background. We can imagine a phenomenal world, such as the purely visual color field above, where we might use particular terms without any causal concepts at all. But in our world, where we attribute properties to the same thing that are accessible to different senses, we cannot do without the notion of a thing that is not just the locus of different perceptual features, but also has certain causal properties.

We call this candy red and sweet. What kind of thing must it be for us to attribute both to it? Not simply a visual percept. On the contrary, this red is a visual property of something that can be taken and felt, has a certain consistency, and can be put in the mouth and thus tasted. Now, a thing of this kind must be one that is able to straddle these boundaries in its interactions with us, and this because the causal background of one feature takes us into another.

For instance, we may alter the color of an object by scraping off the surface, and thus altering its shape, or alter its smell by adding something to it. In altering its shape we have to come to grips with its consistency, using tools appropriate for cutting, whittling, etc. an object of this substance. These other features that we have to deal with in changing a given property are what I called above its "causal background."

What I am claiming is that we wouldn't have the notion of an object that straddles the gap between the different senses, that can bear properties accessible to different senses, unless this object were capable of the kind of interaction with us in which the causal background of some features consists of others. It is this which enables us to straddle these differences. If we were not able to turn color into shape, or shape into consistency in this way, we wouldn't even be able to have a single space linking all senses. We cannot conceive of a space common to sight and touch without objects that are perceptible by both; so far from being able to account for these common objects in terms of a congruence of properties in visual and tactile space, we can operate in this common space only by reference to intersensorially accessible objects, of which our body is not the least important. And the kind of object that can be the common bearer of these disparate properties is one that links them together by interwoven causal backgrounds.

To put the point in another way, one might ask what allows us to speak of a thing as having many properties. How can we speak of this diversity as a unity? In the simple contemplative model of the visual field, we might think that sameness of visual location is enough. But this is totally insufficient to account for any of those things access to which straddles different senses. For here the very notion of sameness of location presupposes the identification of common objects that it is meant to explain.

We can think of these as objects having many properties only because they are interwoven; and the manner of their interweaving is that the causal background of each is woven into that of the others.

So much for 1), but 2) follows from it. For if perceiving a thing with properties is perceiving in however rudimentary a way the locus of causal background to these properties, then our grasp of things is necessarily bound up with our awareness of the way they interact with others. For instance, if part of what makes an object for me an object of a certain sort is that the causal background to its weight is such that this would be reduced were a part lopped off, or the causal background to its shape is such that powerful tools would be necessary to alter it, then the object for me is characterized at least in part by the kinds of objects or events that could have certain kinds of effects on it. And this, of course, cannot be separated from an awareness of the kinds of objects on which it would have certain kinds of effects.

Hegel's second transcendental conclusion thus seems to follow from his first. If one cannot have properties without particulars that are the bearers of many properties, it is also true that one cannot have such particulars in one's experience unless they are the loci of causal backgrounds of their diverse properties and hence are partly identified by their causal properties.

But the proof of this latter thesis is bound up with the refutation of the traditional contemplative epistemology. This view was set aside because it cannot provide an account of perceiving; and it cannot do this, because by separating our perception of from our interaction with things, it cannot really allow a place to phenomenal causality. Only by recovering an understanding of perception as a consciousness of our interaction with the world, can we allow for the perception of causal relations. But it is the same contemplative view, which splits perception from interaction, that cannot allow for the perception of things. And now we can appreciate the reason for this, for there cannot be a perception of things without there being a perception of causality. Perception of objects is available only to a subject who is an embodied agent interacting with the world he experiences.

IV

Hegel continues in the third chapter, moving from the notion of the object as the locus of force, through the related notions of law and necessity, to his conception of infinity, through which consciousness of the object can be shown to be one with self-consciousness.

But, for our purposes, we can leave the dialectical

train here. What we can extract from these first chapters is an interesting chain of transcendental arguments, that is, a series in which the later ones build on the conclusions of the earlier ones; these earlier conclusions provide the undeniable starting point for the later ones.

Hence we begin with the supposedly undeniable beginning that conscious experience must be sayable; and with this we destroy the idea of a purely receptive, preconceptual experience of the particular. On the contrary, in grasping the particular we are forced to have recourse to descriptive expressions; the particular on its own remains ineffable. But this means that the object of experience is a particular that can be grasped under an undefinite number of descriptions, or in more traditional language, a thing with an indefinite number of properties.

This is, then, the starting point for a second argument: thing and properties cannot be separated in consciousness, for the identification of properties requires that they be seen as belonging to things, and the distinction between things requires that they have properties (in the broad sense mentioned above). Hence, any notion of experience that would make the thing not an object of perception, but rather an inferred substrate or a construct, must be set aside.

The thing with properties as an object of experience is thus the starting point of the third argument, in which it is shown that the object of experience must be a locus of causal backgrounds if thing and properties are to be part of the same experience. We thus come through a series of arguments to a view of experience in which, counter to the empiricist tradition, phenomenal causality recovers its place.

In this respect, then, Hegel's transcendental arguments here have the same bent as Kant's, and it would be illuminating to compare them briefly. Kant rehabilitates causality in the Second Analogy as necessary, rulelike connection. Causality is considered only in the guise of a connection between two terms already distinguished (even if one may be unknown for a time, we still know of it that it is *distinct* from its mate). The phenomenal causality that Hegel recovers in the arguments we have been considering is much broader: it includes not only experience of the explicit causal relation but also of things as the loci of causal efficacy as yet unexplicited; indeed, of an efficacy that, like the properties of the thing, could never be fully explicited without remainder.[9]

In this, Hegel is closer, I believe, to the reality of experience. But whether this is right or not, it is clear that he is closer to the picture of experience that has emerged in the middle of the present century in opposition to the empiricist tradition. (I am thinking here, of course, primarily of the phenomenological movement, although related ideas have been emerging at the same time in the Anglo-Saxon world.) In this area Hegel's doctrines have a contemporary ring that Kant's do not.

We can understand this difference better if we examine a bit closer their respective arguments for phenomenal causality. Kant sees this as connection between two terms by rule, because, it would appear, he thinks of the categories of the understanding as working on fragmentary representations, like the particulate data of empiricism. There is, of course, this enormous difference that such particulate representations are not *by themselves* experienced, but only when combined by the understanding; but Kant's constant reference to the work of the understanding as synthesis or combination (*Verbindung*) implies the fragmentary nature of the manifold. ("But the com-

[9] Cf. Hegel's distinction here between "zurückgedrängte Kraft" on one hand, and its "Äusserung" in causal relations on the other, 105–11.

bination [*conjunctio*] of a manifold in general can never come to us through the senses, and cannot, therefore, be already contained in the pure form of sensible intuition" [B 129–30].)

From this point of view, then, Kant has not entirely broken with the epistemological tradition that he overturned. At least in the Transcendental Logic, intuition, while "blind" on its own, is seen on an empiricist model (how this fits with the unity of time and space in the Aesthetic is another matter). Kant stresses that in intuition we are receptive, "affected." It is this which founds the distinction between phenomena and things in themselves, and that sets the limits to our understanding.

What separates contemporary rejections of empiricism's doctrine of experience from Kant's refutation of it is the fundamental notion mentioned a number of times in the above discussion that our experience of things is bound up with our interaction with them; that, moreover, this interaction is prior, and that what we think of as conscious human experience is an awareness that arises in a being who is already engaged with his world. (Cf. the notion of "être-au-monde" in Merleau-Ponty, and that of "geworfener Entwurf" in Heidegger.) From this point of view there is no level of experience that can be thought of, even as an abstraction, as pure receptivity. For our most original experience can only be understood by reference to a prior handling of or engagement with the world.

It is within this notion of experience that we can understand a perception of causality that is not fully explicited in causal relations, since our perception builds on a prior relation to things in which we come to grips with them. And it was the absence of this notion in Kant's conception of experience that made it inevitable that he present causality as necessary succession according to a rule.

This view of experience is linked with another fundamental notion widespread today and not admitted by Kant: the rejection of mind-body dualism. The notion that perception of things arises out of a prior interaction with the world is not compatible with a view of mind and body as separate, joined at best by purely causal relations, so that consciousness, as "mental," must be understood without reference to the bodily. Kant, on the other hand, although he did not espouse the dualism of Descartes or the empiricists, and even persuasively refuted the Cartesian proof of a thinking substance, nevertheless upheld the distinction between appearances and things in themselves, which, applied all the way around, even to myself and my own body, forces us to think of consciousness as exclusively "mental."

Now, on these two issues which divide Kant from contemporary philosophical movements of thought that directly or indirectly owe a great deal to him, Hegel stands clearly on the contemporary side. His entire philosophy is a rejection of a set of connected dualisms, of which that between mind and body is not the least important, and the polemic against the Kantian "Ding-an-sich" is one of the constantly recurrent themes of his work. At the same time, he is led in trying to bridge these oppositions to a genetic view of consciousness, in which our way of conceiving the world alters and progresses through the transformations that our ways of dealing with it undergo. Hegel initiates the theme, later developed by Marxism, that our way of grasping the world intellectually is transformed by our way of grappling with it, that is, work. Hence, the universal consciousness of the Stoic philosophy is built on the disciplined, productive work of the slave.

Thus, it is not surprising that Hegel's attempt to establish our experience of causality should be so much closer to contemporary doctrines of experience than Kant's. For Hegel is the originator of some themes that are central to much contemporary philosophy. In this section, our references have been to phenomenological writers who acknowledge the debt to Hegel. But similar themes can be discerned in the Anglo-Saxon world. The declining credence accorded to any version of mind-body dualism requires no comment. But the related theme that our consciousness of things is not primordially the reception of data, but is built on a more original engagement with them, is also in evidence.

We can see this by returning to Wittgenstein (admittedly not an Anglo-Saxon philosopher . . .). The notion that experience was to be understood by what we could say of it, and the meaning of what we say ultimately understood by reference to "forms of life," reflects the same basic preoccupation. Rather than understand experience as built out of basic data received into the mind—a "mind" that could be that of any type of body, or even of none—which data then just remain to be pointed to and named, Wittgenstein asks us to look at experience as shaped by language that in turn can be understood only as the language of a certain group of men, since it gets its meaning from the way that they deal with each other and with their world. This is the way to get the fly out of the fly bottle, the skein of insoluble puzzles that arise when we try to take seriously the picture of experience as made up of data.

But once out of the bottle, the fly is not free; he is enmeshed in another set of problems, harder if more rewarding to explore. These concern the genesis of consciousness, its origin in "forms of life." Wherever this is on the agenda, Hegel cannot really be ignored for long.

VII. NOTES ON HEGEL'S "LORDSHIP AND BONDAGE"

George Armstrong Kelly

WHAT IS LIVING in Hegel? The mid-twentieth century is prone to answer: his sense of the collective, his notion of a politically structured people as the unit of historical meaning, his grounding of right in intersubjective purpose, his penetrating explorations of psychological and sociological conflict. Both admirers and hostile critics fasten on these categories, because, as issues of debate, they are not only living in Hegel, but living in our time.

Thus Hegel's philosophy did not, as it were, merely paint "gray on gray." Not surprisingly, however, contemporary interest in this "ultimate philosophy" is due chiefly to the suggestive expansion of its insights, rather than to any desire for systematic reconstruction. In a discretionary way, Hegelian problems and patterns have gained a new lease in the fields of social and religious thought and among those for whom classical political theory is not a dead exercise. One might say that Hegel remains vital because he continues to raise polemical questions. When a giant structure of human speculation is superseded—a fate which some feel, wrongly I think, that Hegel tacitly acknowledged for his own philosophy—but survives *in membris disjectis*, anthologies tend to be compiled for partisan purposes. Karl Löwith reminds us that this was the destiny of the fragile Hegelian balance

Reprinted from *The Review of Metaphysics*, Vol. XIX, No. 4, June 1966, by permission of the author and the editor of *The Review of Metaphysics*.

in the hands of the philosopher's immediate disciples.[1] The last generation has seen a renewal of this *Kulturkampf*, but now on the far side of total war, Marxism, and religious crisis. The opposition of "What did Hegel mean?" and "What does Hegel mean for us?" is posed and reposed. I personally feel —as a historian of ideas—that some intellectual mischief is caused by the failure to raise the two questions in mutual rapport.

An important case in point would be the characteristic modern treatment of Hegel's famous scenario of "Lordship and Bondage," the account of liberation through work which so deeply affected the young Karl Marx in his 1844 manuscripts.[2] This tableau is most fully developed in the *Phänomenologie des Geistes* of 1807, but is also covered more tersely in the *Propädeutik* (1808–1816) and the *Enzyklopädie der philosophischen Wissenschaften* (editions 1817, 1827, 1830, and 1840–1845), essayed in rudimentary form in both series of Jena lectures on the philosophy of spirit (1803–1804 and 1805–1806), alluded to in

[1] See Karl Löwith, *From Hegel to Nietzsche*, trans. by David E. Green (New York, 1964), pp. 65–135.

[2] Karl Marx, *The Economic and Philosophical Manuscripts of 1844*, ed. by Dirk J. Struik (New York, 1964), esp. pp. 170–193 ("Critique of the Hegelian Dialectic and Philosophy as a Whole"). Marx writes (p. 177): "The outstanding achievement of Hegel's *Phenomenology* and of its final outcome . . . is thus first that Hegel conceives the self-creation of man as a process, conceives objectification as loss of the object, as alienation and as transcendence of this alienation; that he thus grasps the essence of *labor* and comprehends objective man . . . as the outcome of man's *own labor*." It would be appropriate here to mention that, like Hegel, I assign no particular significance of nuance to the synonyms "slavery," "bondage," and "servitude." I have also chosen to avoid taxing the patience of the reader with unnecessary dialectical vocabulary.

the *Grundlinien der Philosophie des Rechts* (1821), and, according to some interpreters, foreshadowed in the discussion of Hebrew religion in the so-called early theological essays.[3] As a form of consciousness, lordship and bondage was continuously indispensable to Hegel's dialectical deduction of the formation of subjective mind and had occupied him from his earliest attempts to construct a system. Since there can be no quarrel about the centrality of this philosophical "moment," it becomes essential to grasp its precise meaning and content.

A full précis of this much admired passage will be dispensed with here. I have no particular dispute with, for example, Hyppolite's treatment, as far as it goes.[4] However, many modern readings—inspired by Kojève's artful exegesis in his *Introduction à la lecture de Hegel*[5]—tend to distort lordship and bondage in the total Hegelian structure. Though every student of Hegel is deeply enriched by Kojève, this experience is not without its dangers. In the present case, the difficulty seems to me chiefly twofold: the subjectivity of the scenario is largely ignored, and the master-slave relationship is made an unqualified device for clarifying the progress of human history. The one tendency leads to a unilaterally "social" interpretation of the *Phenomenology*, particularly the section

[3] Cf. Jean Hyppolite, *Genèse et Structure de la Phénoménologie de l'Esprit de Hegel* (Paris, 1946), I, p. 166; and T. M. Knox (trans.), *Hegel's Early Theological Writings* (Chicago, 1948), intro. by R. Kröner, p. 13.

[4] Hyppolite, I, pp. 161–171.

[5] This remarkable study is a compilation of Alexandre Kojève's courses on the *Phenomenology* (ed. by Raymond Queneau [Paris, 1947]), given at the Sorbonne in the years 1933–1939, which exerted a powerful influence on Sartre and French Hegelianism in general.

on *"Selbstbewusstsein"*;[6] the other easily gathers in anachronistic overtones of the Marxian class struggle.

The regulative idea of lordship and bondage runs like a golden thread through much of Kojève's analysis. His general introduction stresses the point: "The Slave alone is able to transcend the World as it is (in thrall to the Master) and not perish. The Slave alone is able to transform the World that forms him and fixes him in bondage, and to create a World of his own making where he will be free."[7] In a later passage, Kojève asserts that he has given an "anthropological" reading of the *Phenomenology*, and that Hegel intends a "metaphysical" dimension as well, the two currents being necessarily syncretized in the final chapter on Absolute Knowledge.[8] A footnote here seems to clarify Kojève's resolve to treat equally of the interior and exterior relations of the consciousness (as was surely Hegel's purpose) under the anthropological notion. But, in fact, although both exterior (political) and interior (psychological) consequences are acknowledged, he sees the master-slave relation-

[6] "Awareness" is conceivably a better translation of *Bewusstsein* than is "consciousness," but there are problems with each. I have reluctantly chosen the traditional term because in Hegel's language *Bewusstsein* is an agent as well as a condition or capacity.

[7] Kojève, p. 34.

[8] *Ibid.*, pp. 308–309 and 308n. A comment on the perspective of the *Phenomenology* imposes itself at this point. I tend to agree with those who hold that the sequence and development of the *Phenomenology* are *sui generis* and related to the intention of the work, as juxtaposed, especially, to the *Encyclopedia*. Thus these differences alone do not allow us to conclude that Hegel changed his philosophical viewpoint between 1807 and 1817. In cases of disagreement between a "philosophy of mind" and a "phenomenology of mind," caution of interpretation is advised. This reservation does not seem applicable to the case of "lordship and bondage."

ship purely as an external confrontation. For Kojève this *motif* persists in various ascending forms until the Hegelian end of time. Thus: Work and Struggle = Freedom = Time = History = Transience = Nothing = Man. In more humble language, the future belongs to the once-terrorized producer, progressively liberated by the spiritualized quality of his own labor, not to the seemingly omnipotent consumer, who treats both the servant and his product as mere dead things. Effectively, the slave releases history from nature, and it is the slave's satisfaction that will bring history to a close. Thus, while retaining the Hegelian primacy of ideas over things, Kojève, like Marx, tends to regard forms of servitude as epiphenomena of the relations of production.

As students of the career of philosophical ideas know, Kojève's lectures on Hegel have had an enormous impact. To take a recent example, the British scholar, John Plamenatz, in his two volumes on European political thought, has, with full acknowledgment, provided a Kojève *cum* Hyppolite reading in his chapter on the *Phenomenology*. He casts lordship and bondage entirely at the interpersonal level, and his conclusion reflects the familiar line of argument: ". . . the future is with the slave. It is his destiny to create the community in which everyone accords recognition to everyone else, the community in which Spirit attains its end and achieves satisfaction."[9] But where did Hegel ever say this? Plamenatz's criticisms of Hegel (via the French commentaries) are grounded in the same analysis. How, he inquires, can one explore the possibilities of community in terms of one master and one slave, as Hegel appears to do? How can one refuse to see that manual toil is not the exclusively dignified form of labor; is there not also

[9] John Plamenatz, *Man and Society*, 2 Vols. (New York-San Francisco, 1963), II, p. 155.

managerial toil?[10] Although Hegel is sometimes no easier to vindicate than he is to understand, this type of question will not seem so pressing if lordship and bondage is given a more balanced, more "phenomenological" interpretation. By "phenomenological" I mean that Hegel's ego must be seen here as an ideal type, collective only in the sense of exemplary, subject to a genetic onslaught of existential moods (*Gestalten*), each of which will be cancelled but also retained as a moment of eternal significance.

I am not proposing some legerdemain that will take the "social" out of Hegel. Clearly he argues that the true ethical life (*Sittlichkeit*) of man is "concrete" and "objective," grounded in collective experience according to the immanent harmonies of a rational community where liberty and order coalesce. "The experience of what spirit is . . . ," according to the *Phenomenology,* is "the Ego that is 'we,' a plurality of Ego, and 'we' that is a single Ego."[11] Although the pages that introduce the discussion of self-consciousness announce this principle, collective mind does not become a reality until reason (*Vernunft*) achieves intersubjectivity and passes into spirit (*Geist*).[12] Lordship and bondage is a "moment" of *Selbstbewusstsein* that foreshadows society and has explicit historical ramifications. However, the view that the scenario represents a purely social phenomenon is one-sided and needs correction.

[10] *Ibid.,* II, pp. 190–192. However, neither Kojève nor, especially, Karl Marx would ask Plamenatz's second question. Cf. Marx, *Manuscripts of 1844, op. cit.,* p. 177: "The only labor which Hegel knows and recognizes is *abstractly mental labor.*"

[11] G. W. F. Hegel, *Phänomenologie des Geistes,* ed. by J. Hoffmeister (Hamburg, 1952), p. 140; *Phenomenology of Mind,* trans. by J. Baillie (London, 1927), p. 227. I have furnished Baillie's translation throughout.

[12] *Ibid.,* Hoffmeister, pp. 313 ff.; Baillie, pp. 455 ff.

What I am about to argue is that lordship and bondage is properly seen from three angles that are equally valid and interpenetrable. One of these angles is necessarily the social, of which Kojève has given such a dazzling reading. Another regards the shifting pattern of psychological domination and servitude within the individual ego. The third then becomes a fusion of the other two processes: the interior consequences wrought by the external confrontation of the Self and the Other, the Other and the Self, which has commenced in the struggle for recognition (*Kampf des Anerkennens*).[13] On the overtly social plane there are, at a given point in history, slaves and masters. In the interior of consciousness, each man possesses faculties of slavery and mastery in his own regard that he struggles to bring into harmony; the question arises whenever the will encounters a resistant "otherness" that goes beyond mere physical opposition to its activity. In turn, the social and personal oppositions are mediated by the fact that man has the capacity to enslave others and be enslaved by them. Because of the omnipresence of spirit the continuum is not broken by the distinction between world and self.[14]

In brief, man remits the tensions of his being upon the world of fellow beings and is himself changed in the process. This relationship should be stressed, since

[13] Among the various classical and Biblical resonances of this image (e.g. Eteocles and Polynices, Cain and Abel), one detects the motif of Jacob's struggle with the angel, secularized in Hegel's hands. Cf. Genesis xxxii: 24–28: "Let me go and I will bless thee" becomes "Let me go and I will serve thee."

[14] Here, one is tempted to believe that, as in so many other sectors, Hegel begins with a characteristically Aristotelian image; cf. *Politics*, 1255b: "The part and the whole, like the body and the soul, have an identical interest; and the slave is part of the master, in the sense of being a living but separate part of his body. . . ."

it furnishes the bridge between psychology and history. Let it be added here also that Hegel's psychology is moral, not analytical: this is why experience continually causes it to shift its ground and why it is, in the deepest sense, historical, a psychology of development, a *Bildungsroman.*

On the one hand, Hegel is showing that mere political mastery or subjection cannot inaugurate the long adventure of history and freedom unless faculties of the subjective mind, necessarily present in all men, create the possibility and condition the result. On the other hand, it is clear that none of this is conceivable in a solipsistic universe. "*Es ist ein Selbstbewusstsein für ein Selbstbewusstsein*"[15] is the abrupt and dramatic prelude to the struggle for recognition out of which mastery and slavery will arise. The possibility of philosophy, morality, and right depends on the postulation of a second finite ego and, ultimately, on the assumption of a plurality of egos. Much in the same way that Fichte produces a second ego in order to ground his doctrine of natural right,[16] Hegel posits society at the dawn of self-consciousness for a still more profound purpose: the analysis of the broken ego striving to restore itself. But if the Self and the Other are, to speak bluntly, men, they also dwell within each man. They are original principles of the ego, awakened to combat by the appearance of another ego in which they are reduplicated, and thenceforward transformed by history. Without this shock,

[15] Hegel, *Enzyklopädie und Schriften aus der Heidelberger Zeit, Sämtliche Werke,* VI, ed. by H. Glockner (Stuttgart, 1927), paragraph 352, p. 253.

[16] J. G. Fichte, *Grundlage des Naturrechts, Sämmelte Werke,* III (Berlin, 1845), pp. 30 ff.; *The Science of Right,* trans. by A. E. Kroeger (Philadelphia, 1869), pp. 48 ff. "Natural right" demands a judge, a "third party" and this is precisely the facility that Hegel denies to the origin of civil society.

there would be no history, only desire (*Begierde*), man's link with the animal world, and the unproductive and repetitive cycles of biological nature.

Hegel is, to be sure, much less explicit about the internal aspects of lordship and bondage than he is about the interpersonal and historical dimensions. The most casual reading of the *Phenomenology* and other texts makes clear that Hegel intends the analysis of relations among men and a reflection on the rise of historical communities through conquest. But my elucidation in no way denies this obvious fact.

Certain other contingencies obscure the reading I am suggesting. In the first place, the "social" implications of the tableau are even more emphatic in the Jena sketches, to which a scholar will wisely refer if he wants to understand the evolution of Hegel's thought. In many passages of this early and experimental "philosophy of the spirit" Hegel is deeply concerned with the concrete formation of society, the nature of work and its elevation to spiritual substantiality, and the creation of a scheme of dialectical development. Different sequences of unfolding and different terminologies—some derivative (mainly Schellingian) and some original—are essayed in these lectures. What will later have discrete places in the treatment of subjective and objective spirit—desire, labor, love, family, *Volksgeist,* etc.—are seen struggling for systematic deployment. And admittedly in the "recognition" scenario the emphasis is on the concrete and social. In the 1803–1804 lectures, the deduction of the family precedes the struggle for recognition, indicating that Hegel is here concerned with anthropohistorical development rather than the presentation of "facts of consciousness."[17] But in the 1805–1806 lectures, in a passage corresponding to

[17] Hegel, *Jenenser Realphilosophie,* I, ed. by J. Hoffmeister (Leipzig, 1932), pp. 223 ff.

what Hegel will later call "anthropology" (the forms of the human soul before the awakening of consciousness), the Other is evoked as a Schellingian "dark principle": "The Other [is] Evil, a being-in-itself, the subterranean principle, the thing which knows what lies in daylight and witnesses how it purposively [brings about] its own decline, or is in such active opposition that, on the contrary, it substitutes negativity for its own being, for its own self-preservation."[18] The *Encyclopedia* will clarify for us how the preconscious being is bifurcated even before it gains awareness of its own selfhood, and how lordship and bondage will display an analogous autoalienation at the higher conscious level.

A second factor which might mislead is the characteristic Hegelian insistence, against Kant, that the properties of the mind are integral and not the derivations of separate faculties or principles, like theoretical and practical reason (cognition and will),[19] or like the Fichtean dichotomy of finite Ego and pure Ego resolved only by an *ought.*[20] Of course, this is the "standpoint of reason," the goal of the Hegelian philosophy. But one obviously cannot jump from here to the conclusion that lower forms of consciousness apprehend themselves monistically. In fact the opposite is true, whether the Other is felt as impulse, as a hostile stranger, or as a transcendent God. Since Hegelian philosophy is process, even though its apotheosis is unity, it has mostly to do with the logical, genetic, or historical oppositions that have come about in the progress of the spirit.

Mr. G. R. G. Mure, in his excellent study of Hegel's

[18] *Jenenser Realphilosophie,* II, ed. by J. Hoffmeister (Leipzig, 1931), p. 200.

[19] See for example, Hegel, *Philosophy of Right,* trans. and ed. by T. M. Knox (Oxford, 1945), *Zusatz* to paragraph 4, p. 227.

[20] *Enzyklopädie,* in Glockner, VI, paragraph 332, p. 246.

Logic, has called particular attention to the dualistic tread of "higher" and "lower" principles in Hegel and has doubted their effective resolution.[21] I share this feeling. One cannot of course gather in the depths of the *Phenomenology* by looking at it through post-Enlightenment spectacles alone. In the background always and at the surface much of the time Hegel is wrestling with the problems of Greek antiquity and seeking both to overcome and to eternalize them in an alien climate. The Platonic parallel between the struggles in the state and the struggles in the soul is never far distant. I will permit myself the liberty of saying that the great figures of Aristotle, Plato, and Sophocles bestride, respectively, the sections on *Bewusstsein, Selbstbewusstsein,* and *Geist*. The problem of lordship and bondage is essentially Platonic in foundation, because the primal cleavage in both the history of society and the history of the ego is at stake. The two primordial egos in the struggle that will lead to mastery and slavery are also locked in battle with themselves.

A third deterrent to a balanced reading of lordship and bondage is the temptation to treat the *Phenomenology* as an enigmatic philosophy of history. Sometimes this is done so that its "progressive" implications can be favorably compared with the conclusions of Hegel's later lectures. But the schematic arrangement of Hegel's finished system, given by the *Encyclopedia*, should warn us away from this adventure: history belongs to objective spirit and phenomenology to subjective, even though the experience of objective spirit is a fact of consciousness. Although the *Phenomenology* must necessarily utilize history to illustrate forms of consciousness, it is not to be inferred that the two genealogies are integrally parallel. He-

21 G. R. G. Mure, *A Study of Hegel's Logic* (Oxford, 1950), pp. 367–368.

gel's conscious avoidance of proper names is the best clue to his design.

This point can become confused, since Hegel in both instances is dealing with temporal process and since historical time is the condition for human thought. The evolution of mind runs along the same time scale as the fate of nations. Thus, philosophical analyses that are conceptually independent must be joined in communicative discourse and must plunder the same treasury of empirical materials. Mind as *Geist* is the integrative operator, just as temporality makes the operation possible. But the *Phenomenology* is not primarily a disquisition on political philosophy; it is the record of the spirit's efforts to attain peace in the knowledge that there is nothing outside itself.

One may question, as I do, the prestidigitatory feats of Hegel in keeping these two lines of philosophical inquiry discrete and correlative at the same time. There is more than animus in Haym's famous complaint that "etwas Anderes ist die Geschichte, und etwas Anderes ist die Psychologie."[22] In fact, we all do read the *Phenomenology* as historical and political commentary quite legitimately, since it is concerned with the external relations of mind amid a plurality of egos. But the transformations of mind within itself are equally important. Both destinies, according to Hegel, will be identical in the last analysis.

Finally, if we hypothesize that mastery and slavery contains both developments, we shall not be greatly disturbed by Hegel's leaps between the social and the solitary in his deduction of *Selbstbewusstsein*, as he delineates the forms of "otherness" (*Anderssein*) in stoicism, scepticism, and the "unhappy consciousness."

[22] Rudolf Haym, *Hegel und seine Zeit* (orig. ed. 1857; photostatic reproduction, Hildesheim, 1962), p. 241.

The clue to the whole matter is, I think, given in the following passage from the *Phenomenology:*

> The conception of this its [of self-consciousness] unity in its duplication, of infinitude realizing itself in self-consciousness, has many sides to it and encloses within it elements of varied significance. Thus its moments must on the one hand be strictly kept apart in detailed distinctiveness, and, on the other, in this distinction must, at the same time, also be taken as not distinguished, or must always be accepted and understood in their opposite sense. . . .[23]

If Hegel means what I think, he is encouraging us to draw the plenitude of associations from the Self-Other confrontation. Thus although Hegel can be only imperfectly conveyed by static formulas: Self = Other; Self = Self + Other; Self (Other) < > Other (Self); and Self + Other in Self = Self + Other in Other, etc. I regard the final formulation as most complete. In the following discussion, Hegel expands this idea:

> This process of self-consciousness in relation to another self-consciousness has . . . been represented as the action of one alone. But this action on the part of the one has itself the double significance of being at once its own action and the action of that other as well. . . . The action has then a *double entente* not only in the sense that it is an act done to itself as well as to the other, but also in the sense that the act *simpliciter* is the act of the one as well as of the other regardless of their distinction.[24]

A corresponding passage from the *Propädeutik,* be-

[23] Hoffmeister, p. 141; Baillie, p. 229.
[24] Hoffmeister, p. 142; Baillie, p. 230.

ing simpler (prepared for the instruction of pre-university students), has perhaps greater clarity:

> A self-consciousness which is for another self-consciousness is not only for it as a pure object, but *as its other self*. The ego is not an abstract universality which, as such, contains no distinction or determination. The ego being thus object for the ego, it is for it, in this view, like the same ego which it itself is. In the other, it intuits itself.[25]

One difficulty in following Hegel lies in the fact that he often tries to convey the experience of the consciousness both from its own point of view and from the high ground of the philosopher. Another is in the perpetual passage from inner to outer which is the motor of the consciousness's experience that will be dissolved in ultimate knowledge. But the awakening of opposed faculties in the ego proposed by the fact of society is the principle on which self-consciousness would seem to depend. First, the spiritualization of desire will create the basis for selfhood. Then recognition will be demanded for its authentication. The faculties of the ego must contend in order to act, since a single comprehensive faculty, in however many egos, would render them either totally static or totally destructive (which amounts to the same thing).

Correspondingly, the pattern unfolds in social life. The mutual awareness of two persons, their reciprocal need for recognition, their struggle to obtain it, and the final subjection of the one to the other—these stages idealize the primitive sources of human history, seen this time from the angle of society but still rooted in the problem of the developing consciousness. Mr. Plamenatz should have no difficulty with the fact that

[25] *Philosophische Propädeutik,* Glockner, III, paragraph 30, p. 108.

there are only two protagonists. For, from this angle, when the struggle concludes in mastery and slavery, the master will perceive but a single slave-machine that does his bidding and the slave but a single source of oppression. Hegel's formulation here establishes the mediating link between consciousness and society, serving somewhat the same purpose as the analogous device of the *homo economicus.* Indeed, it is to the famous tale of Robinson and Friday that Hegel refers us in the *Propädeutik.*[26]

Just as the Hegelian analysis demands the postulation of two egos (one man as spirit would be God, or would possess no spirit),[27] so at each of its ascending stages the consciousness must apprehend itself as two estranged principles until its goal is reached. This is most clearly seen in the *Encyclopedia,* where we can delve behind the stirrings of subjective mind or "phenomenology" proper into "anthropology," which has as its focus the notion of the "natural soul." Here spirit has emerged out of nature but not yet awakened to consciousness. In this relatively little-studied part of Hegel's work, the soul corresponds roughly to what psychoanalysis will later label the "preconscious"; here are contained many perceptive insights into neurotic anxiety, undoubtedly based on the philosopher's personal experience and the tragic deterioration of his friend Hölderlin.[28]

In *Encyclopedia,* paragraphs 318–319 (1817),[29] Hegel makes it clear that the soul is life on the margin of consciousness, that it primitively feels its bifur-

[26] *Ibid.,* paragraph 35, p. 110.

[27] Cf. *Phenomenology,* pp. 226–227: "A self-consciousness has before it a self-consciousness. Only so and only then *is* it self-consciousness in actual fact; for here first of all it comes to have the unity of itself in its otherness."

[28] See Johannes Hoffmeister, *Hölderlin und Hegel in Frankfurt* (Tübingen, 1931).

[29] Glockner, VI, pp. 236–237.

cation, its antagonism with otherness. It is subjectively anchored to its future self-conscious career and yet mired in the blind universality of nature. On the other hand (paragraph 323),[30] the opposition is productive and necessary. Here is the primary internal opposition in the genesis of the human condition.

Consciousness arises when the natural soul, by setting its instinct against nature, can affirm itself as an ego (paragraph 327).[31] The relationship to otherness is now a dichotomy between self and natural soul (paragraph 329).[32] Self-consciousness, on the other hand, will require the affirmation by the ego of its own identity, taking the immediate form of desire (paragraphs 344–346).[33] Here the "*Selbstbewusstsein*" section of the *Phenomenology* properly commences, with the inadequacy of repetitive desire, the application of desire to another ego, the struggle for recognition, and the dialectical resolution in lordship and bondage. The internal struggle which expressed itself first in the natural soul, then in the consciousness, has not been resolved or abandoned. Rather, personality can emerge only because of its need for self-recognition, a consequence of ceasing to direct desire merely upon the objects of sheer natural appetition (paragraph 351).[34] A higher, resistant otherness has been encountered; it expresses itself externally as a second ego, internally as primitive reason or self-mastery, and reciprocally as the capacity for will and freedom. But, like the original assertion of self-consciousness through the ego's becoming aware of itself, this new stage of being must in turn be authenticated. This will happen in the struggle for recognition,

[30] *Ibid.*, p. 242.
[31] *Ibid.*, p. 244.
[32] *Ibid.*, p. 245.
[33] *Ibid.*, pp. 251–252.
[34] Glockner, VI, p. 253.

where appetition and spiritual self-regard contend. They can no more destroy each other than can the social antagonists: the career of man is the proof. Thus mastery and slavery ensue, both within the ego and, as Hegel makes abundantly clear (paragraph 355), in the history of society.[35]

The parallel explanations are necessary. For, taken from a purely social point of view, there is no good reason why two identical egos, locked in combat, should not struggle to a static stalemate. To say that Hegel's resolution is good dialectics answers nothing. Instead we should discern the idea that natural inequalities arise in consequence of internal imbalances, not through the absence or presence of pure principles in single individuals. I shall return to this point in connection with theories of history.

"Where did Hegel's ideas on the relation of lord and servant originate?" inquires Dirk J. Struik in his edition of Marx's 1844 manuscripts.[36] This interesting question has a considerable bearing on the subject at hand. We can help to clarify the significance of Hegel's passage by referring to the intellectual milieu in which his philosophy took shape.

It is important to understand that this is still a world where normative psychology is seen as dominating the forms of society. Despite primitive stirrings of a social science, one still asks the question "what is man?" in order to understand the social order man has created. The strife within man's nature is a commonplace; as Montesquieu put it: "man . . . is composed of the two substances, each of which, in its flux and reflux, imposes and suffers domination [*empire*]."[37] On the

[35] *Ibid.*, p. 255.

[36] Marx, *op. cit.*, p. 232.

[37] Charles, Baron de Montesquieu et de la Brède, *Pensées*, *Œuvres Complètes* (Paris, 1949), I, p. 1015.

psychological plane we should recall Hume's striking dictum that "reason is the slave of the passions" and the consequent attempts of German idealism to restore the primacy of reason by enlarging its content. We should notice also that the reason-passion relationship gathers in a metaphorical content, which is precisely that of mastery and servitude. In essence, Kant's philosophy, grounded in the ideal of personal autonomy, is a theorization both of how the individual can acquire mastery over his content-directed interests through the exercise of morality or "pure practical reason" and of the conditions by which a legitimate social order can make this possible. The famous aphorism "man needs a master"[38] carries both public and private overtones. In fact, according to Kant, man *ought* to be his own master. But, in the words of Richard Kroner, "because he ought to master himself, man is not really free but divided against himself, half-free and half-slave. At best, he is his own slave, enslaved by his master, reason."[39]

Behind this urgent question, which burst out of speculation and into history with the coming of the French Revolution, lies the dual preoccupation of Rousseau: his assertion that there is no "right of conquest" in society, and his profound research into the warring sides of the human personality which the shock of social relations has induced. "A man thinks he is master of others, whereas he is actually more of a slave than they," writes Rousseau in *Contrat social,* I, i;[40] in his eighth *Lettre de la Montagne* he repeats:

[38] Immanuel Kant, "Idea for a Universal History from a Cosmopolitan Point of View," *Kant on History,* ed. by L. W. Beck (New York, 1963), p. 17.

[39] Kroner, introduction to Knox (trans.), *Hegel's Early Theological Writings,* p. 11.

[40] C. E. Vaughan, *The Political Writings of Jean-Jacques Rousseau,* 2 Vols. (New York, 1962), II, p. 23.

"He who is a master cannot be free."[41] As we know from the second discourse, *Émile,* and the autobiographical writings, a struggle of the human faculties underlies the social dilemma.[42]

Not only for Hegel, but for his great predecessors and his age as a whole, mastery and slavery was a multi-dimensional problem—and a paradoxical one. The paradox is this. Antiquity, which had sanctioned the institution of slavery, had nevertheless intensely researched the dilemma of man's enslavement of himself. The Enlightenment, by contrast, progressively attacked social bondage as abusive and immoral, while scratching only at the surface of its spiritual dimensions. And yet the Enlightenment, taken generally, viewed the social order from individualistic premisses. Descartes had founded the ego and, from the time of Hobbes on, the empirical school had constructed a mechanistic psychology which purported to explain the nature of society by way of its members. The revival of antiquity, in substance as well as form, by Rousseau on the one hand and the German idealists on the other—even when the battle of ancients and moderns had been seemingly won by the latter—is in part a response to this perplexity. The Enlightenment had furnished a sense of progress; it had not restored the conviction of harmony. Both the mind and the social order were implicated. If society was in process, then the mind could not be explored statically as the rationalists had taught. With Hegel there is the recognition that both elements of explanation are necessary and that they must be mediated. This becomes possible only when mind is seen to have a history of its

[41] C. E. Vaughan, II, p. 234.

[42] Cf. *Émile ou l'Éducation* (Paris, 1961), Book IV, p. 404: "O my friend, my protector, my master . . . prevent me from being the slave of my passions, and force me to be my own master by obeying my reason and not my senses."

own. The tensions that propel social history are correspondingly translated to the development of the ego (a procedure in which the works of Rousseau and Kant are way-stations). Here the profundities of Greek thought find their place and their role. The problem of mastery and slavery lies along this axis. For Hegel, however, the resolution can be only tragic or unbearably smug (one takes his pick) because history, the carrier of *Geist* and freedom, is also the perfect warrant of man's fate.

A passage from Fichte's *Contributions to the Rectification of Public Opinion Concerning the French Revolution* (1793) further illustrates the currency of the lordship-bondage metaphor. Here the youthful Fichte employs the figure of the warring personality in a coinage borrowed from the French historian Marmontel.[43] Reason (i.e., the principle of the Revolution) rhetorizes against conventional self-interest (hereditary privilege):

> From our birth, he [reason] invited us to a long and terrible duel where liberty and slavery were at stake. If you are stronger, he told us, I will be your slave. I will be a very useful servant for you; but I will always be a restless servant, and as soon as there is some slack in my yoke, I will defeat my master and conqueror. And once I throw you down, I will insult you, dishonor you, trample you under. Since you can be of no use to me, I will profit by my right of conquest to seek your total destruction.[44]

[43] Jean-François Marmontel, contributor to the *Encyclopédie,* replaced Duclos in 1771 as historiographer of France. He was elected to the *Conseil des anciens* in 1797, but was retired from public life by the *coup d'Etat* of 18 Fructidor. Fichte cites one of his poems.

[44] J. G. Fichte, *Beiträge zur Berichtigung der Urteile des Publikums über die Französische Revolution,* ed. by Stecker (Leipzig, 1922), p. 51.

We do not know whether Hegel read Fichte's incendiary tract against the German Burkeans, but it seems likely that he did, since it was, to say the least, hot copy among young intellectuals. In any case, the contemporary associations of lordship and bondage are not to be understood without the illustrations from across the Rhine.

However, when Hegel came to formulate his mature system, he was, as we know, not an unqualified admirer of the French Revolution or of the autocracy of abstract reason with its "bad infinity." The new "right of conquest" had no more appeal than the old. Like all stages of human struggle, the oppositions of the ego had to be reconciled, not concluded in a new unilateral domination.[45] In the primitive scenario of the *Phenomenology* the resolution of lordship and bondage is in "stoicism," and it is probably no accident that there are resemblances between this form of consciousness and Kant's transcendental idealism, the idea posed above the French Revolution.[46] Though I do not want to draw parallels out of context in Hegel's system, it may not be amiss to call attention to the climate of ideas in which his thoughts about

[45] See *Enzyklopädie*, Glockner, VI, paragraph 393, pp. 276–278.

[46] See especially *Philosophy of Right, introduction*, paragraphs 19–21, pp. 28–30. Cf. Hegel's early (1797) attack on Kant (re: *Religion Within the Limits of Mere Reason*, IV, 2, paragraph 3) in his essay "Der Geist des Christentums und sein Schicksal," *Hegels theologische Jugendschriften*, ed. by Herman Nohl (Tübingen, 1907), pp. 265–266: ". . . between the Tungusian Shaman, the European prelate governing Church and State, or the Mogul or Puritan, and the man obedient to the commandment of duty [the Kantian], the distinction is not to be made that the one enslaves himself while the other is free, but that the one is dominated from without, while the other, having his master within, is by that token his own slave. . . ."

lordship and bondage developed. Undoubtedly the split-personality view of contemporary European philosophy counts for much.

Another brief excursion into German intellectual history can provide a different illustration. When Hegel was developing the rudiments of the master-slave dialectic, he was associated, though not uncritically, with the philosophical ideas of his younger but more precocious friend Schelling. By the time he published the *Phenomenology* in 1807 he had struck his own highly original posture. In the meantime, the split between the philosophies of Schelling and Fichte (which Hegel himself attempted to mediate in his *Differenz des Fichte'schen und Schelling'schen Systems* of 1801) had become irreconcilable and had led to vituperative exchange. The same half-decade saw the rise of the Romantic movement, under the aegis of Novalis and the Schlegels, and the efflorescence of interest in philosophy of history, which had been heralded by Lessing and Herder in the previous century.

Schelling's philosophy, which began from the premiss of the identity of the Absolute, required a theory of history by which the descent of the Absolute into the plurality of creation and the return of created things to the Absolute could be explained. The key to this movement was to be discovered in the principle of human freedom. Schelling traced the idea grandiosely and abstractly in the *System des transzendentalen Idealismus* (1800), in the *Vorlesungen über die Methode des akademischen Studiums* (1802), and in some later writings. In reply to Schelling and, more especially, the Romantics, Fichte entered the lists with his public lectures, the *Grundzüge des gegenwärtigen Zeitalters,* delivered in 1804 and published in 1806. Fichte's scheme of philosophical history, built on purely deductive foundations and in some ways indebted to Kant, challenged his opponents on a variety of issues that do not concern this essay.[47] What is of interest is a fundamental assumption that Fichte and Schelling shared and which could scarcely have failed to draw Hegel's attention.[48]

The speculative histories of Fichte and Schelling were phased and developmental; both in effect sought to deduce the pattern whereby original man, innocent but instinctual in nature, mounted to his goal of rationality in freedom, or achieved what Schelling described as a "second nature." In order to do this, the principle of reason had to be explained at its origin. Schelling was the first to postulate that at the dawn of humanity there had been creatures of pure instinctual reason and simple barbarians. Fichte borrowed this explanation (which is not without its obvious indebtedness to mythology): ". . . out of nothing, nothing can arise; and thus Unreason can never become Reason. Hence, in one point of its existence at least, the Human Race must have been purely Reasonable in its primitive form, without either constraint or freedom. . . ."[49] However, this "*Nor-*

[47] For a full clarification of these issues, see Xavier Léon, *Fichte et son temps,* 3 Vols. (Paris, 1924), II, pp. 394–463.

[48] We know that Hegel read Fichte's excursus on philosophical history and thought little of it, as well as of the "popular philosophy" in which Fichte indulged; see Hegel's letter to Schelling, dated Jena, January 3, 1807, No. 82, *Briefe von und an Hegel,* ed. by J. Hoffmeister (Hamburg, 1952), I, p. 131. His knowledge of the *Grundzüge* was probably too late to affect the *Phenomenology;* however, he was perfectly familiar with all Schelling's ideas antecedent to 1804 because of their close collaboration at Jena.

[49] J. G. Fichte, *Grundzüge des gegenwärtigen Zeitalters,* Lecture IX (Hamburg, 1956), p. 138; *Characteristics of the Present Age, The Popular Works of Johann Gottlieb Fichte,* trans. by William Smith (London, 1884), II, p. 147. See also F. W. J. Schelling, *Vorlesungen, Sämmtliche Werke* (Stuttgart and Augsburg, 1854–1860), V, pp. 224–225.

malvolk" had no history; for them, one day was like the next, and "religion alone adorned their existence."[50] It was thus necessary to postulate a race of barbarians. The union of the two races was what made history and society possible. In the "*Normalvolk*" there was no tension to activate the spring of progress; on the other hand, they embodied the principle of human destiny. The savages, on their part, lacked this principle utterly, but they contained the force of historical propulsion. Consequently, after an interlude when Cartesian paradise and Darwinian brutishness presumably coexisted, society took form with the dispersion of the races, the subjection of the savages to "*Normalvolk*" kings, intermarriage, and the tortuous ascent of miscegenated man to freedom. Apparently, Asia was the historical location for this event; the Old Testament was a "myth of the normal people."[51]

The parallel between this historical hypothesis of Schelling and Fichte and Hegel's lordship and bondage is much more than coincidental. Either the idea was in the air, or there was direct cross-fertilization from Schelling. However, Hegel does not accept this solution.[52] He nowhere endorses any speculation concerning original "rational" men and original "savage" men. Reason is not a natural principle in his anthropology, any more than it is for Rousseau. In Hegel, as we have seen, the appearance of self and self-awareness will succeed the primitive efforts of the preconscious soul to wrest its being from nature. Consequently, although a social event, mastery and slavery will result necessarily from struggles of awareness and recognition within the ego and not from the absolute opposition

[50] *Grundzüge,* p. 139; Smith, p. 148.
[51] *Grundzüge,* p. 143; Smith, p. 152.
[52] See Hegel, *Die Vernunft in der Geschichte* (Hamburg, 1955), p. 31.

of racial principles embodied in discrete, historical individuals. Hegel is defending a doctrine of original equality which is curiously and dangerously denied by Fichte.[53]

Thus I believe that the passage in the *Phenomenology* and in other works can be justifiably interpreted, *inter alia,* as an attempt to explain inequality at the foundation of society without resorting to the dual-nature hypothesis. The alternative is to explain it from within the ego. Here, precisely, is the "phenomenological" dimension that we lack in Kojève.

Let us attempt to restore this dimension. The "master" who emerges from the struggle for recognition can be identified with the primitive notion of control or decision. Hegel tells us specifically that this act of victory is the birth of freedom (*Encyclopedia,* paragraph 355).[54] Man is the only creature which, under certain "non-natural" pressures, is willing to stake its life. This is, so to speak, the first creative act of the human personality: the slave will invent history, but only after the master has made humanity possible. The master's solution, however, is without issue. Hegel has already (in *Encyclopedia,* paragraph 323 and elsewhere)[55] pointed out the danger of imbalance between higher and lower principles. One cannot abandon nature, nor should one drown himself in it. In the master-slave situation, there is neither education, nor progress, nor history—only the repetitive fulfilment of the master's wants.

[53] Fichte is, of course, the German philosopher who, *par excellence,* stressed equality and was often attacked as a Jacobin. However, there is a nervous resemblance, across all human history, between the *"Normalvolk"* of the *Grundzüge* and the *"Urvolk"* of the *Addresses to the German Nation* (1808).

[54] Glockner, VI, p. 254.

[55] *Ibid.,* p. 242.

In this impasse, the master-principle—courage, decisiveness, idealism—is seen to pass into its opposite, becoming, as Kojève points out,[56] a new form of *Begierde.* Higher development can come only from the slave-principle, which has itself been transformed through the experience of subjection and terror into the activities of labor, conservation, and memory: the conditions of human advance. Here are manifold historical overtones which it is not difficult to exploit. I think, though, that two points must be argued against Kojève: (1) the slave-master dialectic is appropriate only to a certain stage of consciousness for Hegel, even though it is still cancelled and retained (*aufgehoben*); succeeding history will be a record of more subtle and comprehensive forms of estrangement; (2) both principles are equally vital in the progress of the spirit towards its destiny: if Marx developed one side of this dichotomy, Nietzsche seized upon the other.[57]

This is decisively clarified by Hegel himself in the *Philosophy of Right:*

> The position of the free will, with which right and the science of right begin, is already in advance of the false position at which man, as a natural entity and only the concept implicit, is for that reason capable of being enslaved. This false, *comparatively primitive* [my italics], phenomenon of slavery is one which befalls mind when mind is only at the level of consciousness. The dialectic of the concept and of the purely immediate consciousness of freedom

[56] *Lecture de Hegel*, p. 52.

[57] Though he doubted its persistency in Europe, Hegel was not loath to praise the masterly virtue (involved in a complex manner with his defense of war); cf. *Philosophy of Right*, paragraph 328A, p. 212: "To risk one's life is better than merely fearing death."

> brings about at that point the fight for recognition and the relationship of master and slave.[58]

In a corresponding *Zusatz* Hegel adds: ". . . if a man is a slave, his own will is responsible for his slavery, just as it is its will which is responsible if a people is subjugated. Hence the wrong of slavery lies at the door not simply of enslavers or conquerors but of the slaves and the conquered themselves."[59]

This should be sufficient to show that "the future belongs to the slave" is an unwarranted and romanticized refraction of Hegel's thought. Slavery cannot found the right of political communities any more than it can account for the free personality. But it is necessary for history as well as for the development of mind: both right and free personality appear in history and do not repose above it. In the *Encyclopedia* of 1845 (paragraph 435, *Zusatz*) Hegel describes the subjection of the servant as "a necessary moment in the education (*Bildung*) of every man."[60] "No man," he adds, "can, without this will-breaking discipline, become free and worthy to command." As for nations, "bondage and tyranny are necessary things in the history of peoples." This could be adapted to the Marxian view of the proletariat. But as we recall from the *Phenomenology,* the dialectical outcome is not a trans-historical class struggle but the temporary refuge of stoicism, where emperor and slave see the world with the same eyes. Even though "only through the slave's becoming free can the master be completely free,"[61] the Hegelian future will unfold out of their joint endeavors. They can no more be incessantly opposed than can the organic faculties of the ego itself.

[58] Knox (trans.), paragraph 57, p. 48.
[59] *Ibid.,* p. 239.
[60] Glockner, X (*System der Philosophie,* III), p. 288.
[61] *Ibid., Zusatz* to paragraph 436, p. 290.

My conclusion is foreshadowed. Although inner and outer, higher and lower, reason and passion are undoubtedly intended to be dissolved at the ultimate Hegelian apex, the internality of the ego cannot be disregarded in understanding the development of *Selbstbewusstsein.* The social reading, taken alone, can encourage sharp distortions. Nor is history for Hegel simply a record of the millennial efforts of the slave to overthrow the master, just as the development of spirit is not the continous attempt of a single faculty to triumph in the ego. In both cases, the aspiration is harmony and self-knowing identity, the sense of "being at home" (*zuhause sein*) so frequently evoked in Hegel, the assimilation of freedom and fate. The failure to read Hegel's texts (especially those leading up to "lordship and bondage") with close attention to levels of discourse can beget social hypotheses that do not square with Hegel's known conclusions. We can further profit by exploring the philosophical and historical issues of Hegel's own time, instead of superimposing those of an industrial epoch which he only narrowly, if shrewdly, glimpsed. That the character of the rational Hegelian society is much more Platonic than it is Marxian is already clear from the Jena lectures which antedate the *Phenomenology.*[62] Kojève's original exegesis of Hegelian themes is a profound work for our own times. But from the standpoint of historical understanding a "Marxian" *Phenomenology* does not make very good sense. This view ignores the depth and passion of Hegel's Greek attachments; it ignores, too, the complicated range of his struggle with the Kantian split vision. These are the two combatants wrestling on the soil of Christian

[62] *Jenenser Realphilosophie,* II, pp. 253–263. We must not ignore, however, that Hegel carefully draws the distinction between the Platonic (Lacedemonian) and the modern polity (p. 251).

Europe for the possession of Hegel's own ego.[63] It is to be questioned whether he resolved this struggle of the old world and the new in his higher *Sittlichkeit* of the nation-state and in his "Christianity without pictures."

[63] The Greeks for Hegel, as for Schiller, Hölderlin, and others, have developed the perfect harmony and proportion of humanity; Kant's morality, on the other hand, represents the infinity of striving and is framed not for man but for "all rational beings." In one of his most electrifying and brilliant passages, Hegel describes the impact of the infinite and the finite, always in the same metaphor of struggle and comprehension: "I am the struggle [between the extremes of infinity and finitude], for this struggle is a conflict defined not by the indifference of the two sides in their distinction, but by their being bound together in one entity. I am not one of the fighters locked in battle, but both, and I am the struggle itself. I am fire and water . . ." (*Vorlesungen über die Philosophie der Religion*, Glockner, XV, p. 80).

VIII. HEGEL ON FACES AND SKULLS

Alasdair MacIntyre

The Phenomenology of Spirit was written hastily. It is notorious that one outcome of this is that arguments are compressed, that the relation of one argument to another is often unclear, and that paragraphs of almost impenetrable obscurity recur. The commentator is therefore liable to feel a certain liberty in reconstructing Hegel's intentions; and the exercise of this liberty may always be a source of misrepresentation, perhaps especially when Hegel's arguments are relevant to present-day controversies. Nonetheless, the risk is sometimes worth taking, for although it is true that to be ignorant of the history of philosophy is to be doomed to repeat it, the joke is that we are doomed to repeat it in some measure anyway, if only because the sources of so many philosophical problems lie so close to permanent characteristics of human nature and human language. It is in this light that I want to consider Hegel's arguments about two bad sciences—physiognomy and phrenology—and their claims to lay bare and to explain human character and behavior, and the relevance of those arguments to certain contemporary issues.

This essay was written especially for this volume.

1.

PHYSIOGNOMY WAS an ancient science that in the eighteenth century enjoyed a mild revival, especially in the writings of Johann Kaspar Lavater (1741–1801). The central claim of physiognomy was that character was systematically revealed in the features of the face. Character consists of a set of determinate traits; and the face, of a set of determinate features. In some cases the cause of the face's being as it is, is the character's being as it is; but in other cases certain experiences, such as the experiences incurred in certain occupations, may leave their marks both on the character and on the face. In this latter type of case the features of the face are not effects of the traits of character, but remain revelatory of character.

In his discussion of physiognomy, Hegel begins by noting that its adherents assert that their science makes a different type of claim from that made, for example, by the adherents of astrology. Astrologers assert that types of planetary movements and types of human actions are correlated in certain regular ways; the connection is purely contingent and external. But the face is an *expression* of human character; what a man is, appears in his face. Hegel next notes the difference between this claim as it is made by the physiognomist and this claim as it is made in everyday life. Part of our ordinary human relationships is to read off from each other's faces thoughts, moods, and reactions. But we do not treat the facial expression simply as a sign of something else, the outer as a sign of something inner, any more than we treat the movement of the hand in a human action as a sign of something else, the inner meaning of what is done, the intention. We treat the expression of the face and the movement of the hand as themselves actions, or parts or aspects of actions. In this connection Hegel makes four points.

It is not what the face is, its bone structure or the way the eyes are set, that is the expression of character or action; it is what the face does that is such an expression. We are therefore not concerned with mere physical shapes, but with movements that are already interpreted. This leads on to Hegel's second point. A man's character is not something independent of his actions and accessible independently of his actions. There is nothing more to his character than the sum-total of what he does. Hegel here sides with Ryle in *The Concept of Mind* in his enmity to the notion of dispositions as causes of the actions that manifest them. The conjoint force of these two points is as follows:

When we see someone with a sad expression on his face, we do not infer to an inner sadness he feels on the basis of an observed correlation between such a physical arrangement of the facial features and inner states of sadness. We read or interpret the expression as one of sadness in the light of the conventions in our culture for interpreting facial expressions. Notice that we have to learn how to do this in alien cultures, and that no amount of correlating one observable characteristic with another in the search for regularities would assist us in the task of such learning. There is thus a difference between seeing a set of physical features and seeing that set as a face and as a face with a particular expression, just as there is a difference between seeing a string of physical shapes and seeing that string as an English sentence and as a sentence with a particular meaning. To learn how to read a face or a sentence is not to follow rules justified by observation that embody a correlation between two sets of items, one of which is the physical features or shapes.

What Hegel's argument has done so far is to show that the physiognomist's treatment of the face as expressive of character, and the physiognomist's treatment of the face as (at least sometimes) the effect of character, cannot be combined without damaging inconsistency. Hegel's two next points are still more damaging to the claim of physiognomy to go beyond the prescientific understanding of facial expression to a scientific knowledge of the causal relations allegedly underlying that expression. He points out sharply how the rules that we use in everyday life in interpreting facial expression are highly fallible. We can express Hegel's point in this way: if someone is apparently glaring at me and I accuse him of being angry with me, he has only to retort that he was thinking of something quite different and I shall have no way to rebut him by appeal to some set of rules for interpreting facial expression. Hegel quotes Lichtenberg: "If anyone said, 'Certainly you behave like an honest man, but I can see from your face that you are compelling yourself to do so and are a villain underneath,' there is no doubt that every brave fellow so greeted will reply with a box on the ear."

Finally—although Hegel makes this point earlier in the discussion—our dispositions of character, as expressed in our actions, speech, and facial expressions, are not simply given as physical features are given. My bone structure can be altered by surgery or violence, but at any given moment it is simply what it is. But my character is not determinate in the same way as my bone structure, and this in two respects: First, a disposition to behave in a particular way always has to be actualized in some particular context, and the nature and meaning of the action that manifests the disposition is in many cases unspecifiable apart from that context. If I strike a man dead when he attacks me murderously, my action does not have the same nature and meaning as when I strike a man dead in a fit of bad-tempered gratuitous aggression. Dispositions that are actualized independently of context are like tendencies to sneeze or to produce compulsive movements; their manifestations will be happenings that in virtue of their independence of context cannot be viewed as intelligible behavior, except perhaps as nervous habits. But about my action produced in a context, we can ask if it is appropriate or inappropriate in the light of the norms defining intelligible behavior in such a context; indeed this is a question that any agent can ask about his own actions. In asking this, he has to characterize his actions in such a way that he becomes self-conscious about what he is doing.

An agent, for example (my example, not Hegel's), may find himself performing a set of multifarious individual actions. Becoming conscious of the character of these, he becomes aware that his over-all conduct is jealous, let us say, or cowardly. But now he is able to place, indeed cannot but place, his conduct *qua* jealous or *qua* cowardly in relation to what Hegel calls "the given circumstances, situations, habits, customs, religion, and so forth," i.e., in relation to the relevant norms and responses of his culture. But to do this is to provide himself with reasons, perhaps decisive reasons, for altering his conduct in the light of those norms and responses and of his own goals. It is of the nature of the character traits of a rational agent that they are never simply fixed and determinate, but that for the agent to discover what they are in relation to his unity as a self-conscious agent—that is, what they are in his personal and social context—is to open up to the agent the possibility of exchanging what he is, for what he is not.

Moreover, the agent who does not change his traits may change their manifestations. Indeed, for him to become conscious that he manifests certain traits and so appears in a certain light, is to invite him to do just this. The relation of external appearance, including the facial appearance, to character is such that the discovery that any external appearance is taken to be a sign of a certain type of character is a discovery that the agent may then exploit to conceal his character. Hence, another saying of Lichtenberg, in *Über Physiognomik,* which Hegel also quotes: "Suppose the physiognomist ever did have a man in his grasp; it would merely require a courageous resolution on the man's part to make himself again incomprehensible for centuries."

2.

But who now is likely to be impressed by the claims of physiognomy? Reading Lavater's *Physiognomische Fragmente zur Beförderung der Menschenkenntniss und Menschenliebe,* with all its romantic whimsy—Lavater on the basis of a youthful acquaintance associated piercing eyes with power of memory, for instance—one might well ask, ought anyone ever to have been impressed by such claims? Part of the answer is that we ought in any case to be interested in bad sciences if only in order to illuminate the contrast with good ones. The study of astrology, physiognomy, or phrenology is justified in so far as it helps us to understand the character of chemistry and physiology. But part of the answer concerns the way in which certain issues may be raised in precisely the same way by bad sciences such as phrenology and physiognomy as by good ones such as genetics or neurophysiology.

In the case of phrenology some of the central theses actually survive in the history of physiology into the present day. It was, for instance, a central thesis of phrenology that different features of the brain were localized in different areas of the brain. This thesis is still controversial, of course, but the empirical neurophysiological and neuroanatomical evidence seems to be against it, especially if localization is understood in anything like the terms in which the phrenologists understood it. There is secondly the thesis, distinctively phrenological, that the different areas of the brain correspond to different areas of the cranial bone, and that the shapes of these areas, the famous bumps of the phrenologists, reveal the different degrees of development of each area of the brain. It is scarcely necessary to remark that this empirical contention is false. There is finally the thesis that the local activity of the brain is the sufficient cause and explanation of behavior, and that therefore the shape of the cranium allows us to predict behavior.

Buried in these dubious contentions is one that is less obviously dubious, that is indeed familiar and widely accepted. I mean of course the thesis that there are biochemical or neural states of affairs, processes, and events, the occurrence and the nature of which are the sufficient causes of human actions. This thesis wore phrenological clothing in 1807; today its clothing is as fashionable as it was then, only the fashions are not what they were. Moreover, when Hegel attempted to rebut the claims of physiognomy and phrenology, he did so in such a way that if his rebuttal is successful it would hold against the thesis that I have just stated whatever its scientific clothing.

At this point, someone may object to my metaphor. The thesis, so it may be protested, does not merely wear scientific clothing, it is itself part of science; and, being a scientific thesis, it is an empirical question, and purely an empirical question, whether it is true or false. My reply to his point, and what I take to be Hegel's reply to this point, occupies a large part of the rest of the paper. But it is worth noting initially that the thesis *has* survived the most remarkable changes in our empirically founded beliefs about the anatomy, physiology, and chemistry of the human body, and that if it is a thesis in natural science, it is certainly not a thesis at the same level as the contention that the shape of the brain is partly the same as that of the cranium or that the nucleic acids play a specific part in reproduction.

In the debate about phrenology in the early-nineteenth century, the attempt to challenge the thesis was undertaken by a number of writers very different from Hegel, and his project deserves to be sharply distinguished from theirs. The standard statement of the phrenological position was taken from the writings and lectures of Franz Joseph Gall (1758–1828) and his pupil J. C. Spurzheim, who developed Gall's doctrine, later claiming both that he had in fact originated some of the basic ideas and also that his doctrine was very different from that of Gall. Gall and Spurzheim drew maps of the cranium locating not only character traits but abilities in different parts of the brain, and their manifestations in what they took to be the corresponding parts of the skull. Examples of traits are secretiveness, combativeness, and acquisitiveness; examples of abilities are the power of speech and the power of imagination. Gall was charged by his critics with determinism, materialism, and consequently atheism. Both Gall and Spurzheim denied these charges, Spurzheim seeking to show that they held of Gall's version of phrenology but not of his. The critics in question, notably Francis Jeffrey, the editor, and Brougham, the lawyer, fastened all their attention on the alleged causes, seeking to show that the mental cannot have a physical, or more specifically a physiological, cause. To show this, they rely on a simple dualism of matter and mind, and the vapid naïveté of Gall's and Spurzheim's science is matched only by the vapid naïveté of Jeffrey's and Brougham's philosophy.

The spirit of their attack on phrenology is as alien to the spirit of Hegel's attack as any could be. Hegel's opposition to Cartesian dualism is of so thoroughgoing a kind that he would have to reject all the premises of Jeffrey's and Brougham's attacks. Nor is Hegel interested in showing that there cannot be physiological causes of the type cited by the phrenologists. His whole attention is focused not on the existence or non-existence of the alleged causes, but on the character of their alleged effects.

Hegel deploys a number of arguments that are closely allied to his arguments against physiognomy in the interests of his conclusion that "it must be regarded as a thoroughgoing denial of reason to treat a skull bone as the actuality of conscious life. . . ." What Hegel means by this is indicated by his further contention that "It is no use to say we merely draw an inference from the outer as to the inner, which is something different. . . ." Hegel wants to say that if we regard the traits of a rational agent as belonging to the type of item that can stand in a genuinely causal relation to anatomical or physiological or chemical states, then we are misconceiving the traits of a rational agent. Why does Hegel think this? We can usefully begin from a point that Hegel did not make in his discussion of physiognomy.

Traits are neither determinate nor fixed. What does it mean to say that they are not determinate? "Just as, e.g., many people complain of feeling a painful tension in the head when thinking intensely, or even when thinking at all, so it might be that stealing, committing murder, writing poetry, and so on, could each be accompanied with its own proper feeling, which would over and above be bound to have its peculiar localization." Hegel's discussion in terms of the localization of feeling has of course a specific reference to contemporary phrenology; but what he goes on to say about local feelings can easily be translated into a thesis about particular dispositions. "Feeling in general is something indeterminate, and that feeling in the head as the center might well be the general feeling that accompanies all suffering; so that mixed up with the thief's, murderer's, poet's tickling or pain in the head there would be other feelings, too, and they would permit of being distinguished from one another, or from those we may call mere bodily feelings, as little as an illness can be determined from the symptom of headache if we restrict its meaning merely to the bodily element."

What would the corresponding theses about dispositions be? Let us consider points from two of Hegel's examples—those of the murderer and of the poet. A given murderer, for instance, commits his crime because he fears his own humiliation by losing his beloved. If we are to look at the traits and other qualities manifested in his action, they do not include a disposition to commit murder, but such things perhaps as a general intolerance of suffering, a disposition to avoid specific kinds of humiliation, his love for the girl, and so on. The same dispositions might explain to precisely the same extent the same person's outbidding others in giving to a deserving cause in order to impress the same girl. But just this fact puts in question the use of the word "explain." Hegel makes this point in relation to phrenology: "And again his murderous propensity can be referred to any bump or hollow, and this in turn to any mental quality; for the murderer is not the abstraction of a murderer. . . ."

Suppose that to this the reply is made that the same given set of dispositions may well produce quite different actions, but that this is because the agent is responding to quite different situations (although in some sense, in my example, the situations are certainly the same). So that we explain the particular action by reference to a conjunction of the set of dispositions and some feature of the situation. We then explain the acts in an entirely familiar and unproblematic way by appealing to a generalization of the form "Whenever such and such a set of dispositions and such and such a type of situation are ignored, such and such an action will occur." To cite human traits in such an explanation would be precisely parallel to citing the dispositional properties of physical objects in explaining physical events.

But this is to suppose that what the agent is responding to is some conjunction of properties and not the specific historical situation. An empiricist would generally not be prepared to draw this contrast; for him, there is nothing to any specific historical situation but a set of properties, the conjunction of which may as a matter of contingent fact be unrepeated, but which is in fact repeatable. Why, then, does Hegel insist on the contrast and deny this characteristic empiricist contention?

A particular historical situation cannot on Hegel's view be dissolved into a set of properties. One reason for this is that such a situation has to be characterized in terms of relations to earlier specific events and situations. There is an internal reference to the events and situations that constitute its history. So the English revolt against Charles I not only has as key properties specific reactions to particular acts of Charles I, but responses to events and situations in the past as recent as acts of Elizabeth and as far off as Magna Charta and the Norman Conquest. Now, to respond to a particular situation, event, or state of affairs is not to respond to any situation, event, or state of affairs with the same or similar properties in some respect; it is to respond to *that* situation conceived by both the agents who respond to it and those whose actions constitute it as particular.

Suppose that to this position some empiricist were to respond as follows: that the agents treat the situation as particular and that the situation is partially constituted and defined by reference to the particular events and situations, does not show that everything relevant to explanation cannot be expressed in terms of repeatable properties. But this reply fails to notice one key point. Hegel would be the last to assert the ultimacy of unanalyzed and unanalyzable particulars (such as Russell's logical atoms). But he does assert what we may call the ultimacy of concreteness. What the ultimacy of concreteness amounts to is this: just as there are good conceptual reasons for holding that existence is not a property, so there are good conceptual reasons for holding that occurrence at some specific time and place is not a property.

By a property I mean that kind of attribute which a subject of the appropriate type (appropriate for that type of attribute) may or may not possess, which a given subject may possess at one time but not at another, and which may (although it need not) be possessed by more than one subject. On such an account of properties, existence fails to count as a property, because the appropriate type of subject cannot either possess it or fail to possess it and because the appropriate type of subject cannot possess it at one time but not at another. On the same account of properties, occurrence at some specific time and place (e.g., at 3 P.M. in the year 1776 at the point where the Greenwich meridian crosses the south bank of the Thames) fails to count as a property, because any subject of the appropriate type (events, situations, states of affairs) cannot possess any particular example of this attribute at one time but not at another and because any particular example of this type of attribute cannot be possessed by more than one subject.

It is properties about which we construct genuine empirical generalizations of such forms as $(x)\,(\phi x \supset \psi x)$ and $(x)\,(\phi x \supset \psi y)$, in which the values of variables of the type of ϕ and ψ are property-ascribing predicates. But it is on Hegel's view universals particularized in their concrete occurrence to which we respond in our actions—both those concrete particulars which we actually encounter and those which are the counterpart in the actual world to the intentional objects of our beliefs, attitudes, and emotions. A poet does not take pride in his having written some poem that has properties of such and such a kind, but in his having written *this* poem. A murderer did not strike out at anyone who happened to have such and such properties but at *this* person. Just because this concreteness is not constituted by a mere collection of properties, it evades causal generalizations and so makes causal explanation, whether phrenological or neurophysiological, inapplicable.

Note what Hegel is *not* saying. Hegel is not asserting that the movements of the murderer's hand or the poet's hand do not have causal explanations. Nor is he asserting that it is impossible that there should be agents with responses only to the abstract universal and not to the concrete. It is just that in so far as someone did respond to presentations of properties with the degree of uniformity that would warrant the construction of causal generalizations, he would not be at all like characteristic human agents as we actually know them and they actually exist. It is a contingent empirical fact about human beings that they are as they are and not otherwise, but in Hegel's philosophy there is no objection to taking notice of such contingent empirical facts. Nonetheless, Hegel is not denying that it is logically possible for some human actions to have causes, and he is not denying that some human actions do or may have physiological causes. Let me draw a parallel with another type of case.

Some Africans who believe in witchcraft point out that to explain the onset of a disease by referring to bacterial or virus infection leaves unexplained such facts as that Jones should have been afflicted by such an infection immediately after quarreling with Smith. "What is the cause of that conjunction?" they inquire, pointing out that Western science gives no answer. Now, if indeed it were true that every event had a cause, that event which is Jones-going-down-with-measles-on-the-day-after-he-quarreled-with-Smith would presumably have a cause. But no champion of natural science feels affronted by the assertion that this is not an event with a cause or an explanation, although the event that is Jones-going-down-with-measles certainly has a cause and an explanation. So also, when Hegel allows that a certain kind of causal explanation will not give us the understanding that we require of self-conscious rational activity, his argument does not require him to deny that many properties of the agents engaged in such activities will have such explanations.

I now return to Hegel's point that traits are not determinate or fixed. I have argued that the indeterminacy of traits is an indeterminacy vis-à-vis any action or given set of actions. From the fact that an agent has a given trait, we cannot *deduce* what he will do in any given situation, and the trait cannot itself be specified in terms of some determinate set of actions that it will produce. What does it mean to say that traits are not fixed? Let me reiterate the crucial fact about self-consciousness, already brought out in Hegel's discussion of physiognomy; that is, its self-negating quality: being aware of what I am is conceptually inseparable from confronting what I am not but could become. Hence, for a self-conscious agent to have a trait is for that agent to be confronted by an indefinitely large set of possibilities of developing, modifying, or abolishing that trait. Action springs not from fixed and determinate dispositions, but from the confrontation in consciousness of what I am by what I am not.

It is a failure to notice this, that on Hegel's view most of all underlies those would-be sciences that aspire to give to observation the same role in the study of human beings that it has in inquiries into nature. For what we can observe in nature is, so to speak, all that there is to discover; but what we can observe in human beings is the expression of rational activity, which cannot be understood as merely the sum of the movements that we observe. (For a Hegelian, Hume's failure to discover the character of personal identity is the result of his fidelity to the methods and criteria of observation.) From Hegel's position, a radical thesis about experimental psychology would follow.

For a large class of psychological experiments, a necessary condition for experimental success is that the stimulus that is administered or the situation with which the agent is confronted shall have its effect independently of the agent's reflection on the situation. The situation or the stimulus must be the same for all experimental subjects; so one subject's envisaging the situation in a particular way must not constitute that situation a different one from that which it is for a subject who envisages that situation in some quite different way. Now, there is a real question as to whether this requirement can ever in fact be satisfied except in experiments in which the stimulus is purely physical (for example, a variation in intensity of light) and the response purely physiological (for example, a constriction of the pupil). But this question I shall put on one side. What Hegel would assert is that even if such experiments are possible, they are so different from the key situations in which rational agents operate, that any inferences from the behavior of such experimental subjects to behavior outside the experimental situation will be liable to lead us into error.

3.

Whatever else the arguments in this paper may or may not establish, they do seem to show that between the Hegelian mode of understanding human action and the mode that has dominated modern thinking about the relevance of such sciences as neurophysiology and genetics, there is a basic incompatibility. Hence, the refutation of Hegelianism in the relevant respects would be a prerequisite for that mode of thought and not merely that frivolous, positivistic refutation to which Hegel has so often been subjected and that he himself adequately characterized. Whether a more adequate refutation is possible, I shall not discuss here. What I do want to do, in conclusion, is to try to characterize Hegel's alternative mode of understanding inquiry into human action.

Three features of Hegel's account stand out: The first is the way in which each stage in the progress of rational agents is seen as moving toward goals that are only articulated in the course of the movement itself. Human action is characteristically neither blind and goalless nor the mere implementation of means to an already decided end. Acting that is the bringing about of such an end by a calculated means certainly has a place, but a subordinate place, in human activity. That it is only in the course of the movement that the goals of the movement are articulated is the reason why we can understand human affairs only after the event. The owl of Minerva, as Hegel was later to put it, flies only at dusk. The understanding of human beings is not predictive in the way that natural science is.

The second feature of Hegel's account is the role of rational criticism of the present in the emergence of the future. Hegel did not believe that the future followed from the present simply as its rational sequel; this he denies as strongly as Voltaire does. But it is in the working out of the failure of the present to satisfy the canons of reason that the future is made. It is this which involves Hegel in seeing history as composed of sequences in which the actions that constitute later stages of the sequence involve reference to, and thus presuppose the occurrence of, actions that constituted earlier stages of the same sequences. The sequences that constitute history are themselves discrete and can stand in the same logical relation to each other as can the stages of a single sequence. But the doctrine that all the sequences of history constitute a single movement toward the goal of a consciousness of the whole that is absolute spirit and that by its consciousness of the whole of history constitutes that whole into a single rational totality, is a thesis certainly held by Hegel to be the key to his whole doctrine; yet, Hegel's other doctrines as to human history do not seem in any way to entail his doctrine about the Absolute, and to be willing to admit the truth of that doctrine ought not to be a source of prejudice against Hegel's other doctrines.

The third feature of Hegel's account relates closely to his criticism of physiognomy and phrenology. Historical narratives are for Hegel not a source of data to be cast into theoretical form by such would-be sciences. Instead, Hegel sees our understanding of contingent regularities as being always contributory to the construction of a certain kind of historical narrative. History, informed by philosophical understanding, provides a more ultimate kind of knowledge of human beings than inquiries whose theoretical structure is modeled on that of the natural sciences. It is outside the scope of this paper to develop or to assess Hegel's view on this matter, but a concluding remark may be in place.

It concerns the question: if history is not a matter of general laws and of theories, in what sense does it give us understanding at all? The Hegelian reply is that the self-knowledge of a self-conscious rational agent has always to be cast in a historical form. The past is present in the self in so many and so important ways that, lacking historical knowledge, our self-knowledge will be fatally limited. Moreover, this type of self-knowledge could never be yielded by theoretical sciences that aspire to explain behavior in terms of physiological structures and processes. It is in fact just because our history constitutes us as what we are to so great an extent, that any explanation that omits reference to that history, as did and do the explanations of phrenology and neurophysiology, may explain the aptitudes and conditions of the human body, but not those of the human spirit.

IX. THE FORMALIZATION OF HEGEL'S DIALECTICAL LOGIC

Its Formal Structure, Logical Interpretation and Intuitive Foundation

Michael Kosok

The moving Finger writes, and having writ,
Moves on; nor all thy piety nor Wit
Shall lure it back to cancel half a line,
Nor all thy tears wash out a word of it.

Rubaiyat, LI

1. *Dialectic as Reflection*

THE FORMALIZATION of Hegel's dialectic logic rests upon the contention that Hegel's intuitively generated system can be represented as a meta-language structure in which a given set of elements on one level are capable of being analyzed from a meta-level which refers to the original elements from a perspective of *reflection*, thereby bringing out and expressing properties *about* that level not capable of being formulated *within* the original level itself. This analysis leads to an inverted pyramid of relations, which increases the complexity and concreteness present by each successive meta-level analysis, instead of contracting a set of given elements into an abstract absolute or unity. By explicating the activity of reflection, it is possible to develop a *formalized* structure representing the unfolding of a unique dialectic *logic*

Reprinted from *International Philosophical Quarterly*, Vol. VI, No. 4, December 1966, by permission of the author and the editor of *International Philosophical Quarterly*.

which I believe is inherent in Hegel's *Phenomenology* and *Encyclopedia* as the basic "generating" principle governing the *intuitive* movements of his structure as it evolves increasingly complex levels of interrelation. The usefulness of such an inquiry into dialectic logic lies in the levels of structural relationship it reveals, and which of necessity have to be accounted for by the activity of conscious reflection, where reflection is initially defined to be the mode of inquiry (questioning) present in a field of conscious activity.

The formal structure evolved, representing these levels of interrelation brought into awareness through reflection, takes the form of an expanding *matrix* of terms in which the number of terms present increases according to a specific principle whenever a new level or perspective of reflection is taken. The generating principle, called the principle of Non-Identity, acts as a recursive formula producing a sequence of *self*-expanding terms. The sequence begins with a singular indeterminate primitive element e standing for any type of *e*ntity capable of being reflected upon (i.e. any object, structure, relation, or more generally, any event present to a field of consciousness). The process of reflection, R, is an operation transforming e into e′–i.e. $(R)e = e'$. Reflection of e into e′ will produce three terms for the first reflection or level. Repeating this operation *on e′*, i.e. $(R)e'$ or $(R)(R)e$ for a second reflection, will give three times three or a matrix of nine terms called e″. The nine term structure has *qualitatively* different modes of interrelation present than in the initial three term sequence.

In the limit, the R process produces an infinite sequence of terms–1, 3, 9, 27, 81 etc. according to the power expansion 3^n, where n stands for the successive reflections taken, representing a continual expansion of perspective moving from level to meta-level, and taking on the values of the positive integers varying from zero to infinity.[1] The fundamental recursive formula is, therefore, $(R)e^n = e^{n+1}$, defining, as yet without interpretation, the operation of *reflection.*

It is possible to give a non-contradictory account of the process of reflection. Being called the Principle of Non-Identity, it serves to determine and delineate the first universe of discourse *out of* the originally indeterminate posit called "e," and at the same time set up the conditions for the *negation* and transcendence of the very universe generated. In a sense, the process of reflection transforms a *pre*-formal indeterminate posit e into a *formal* determinate universe, such that a *meta*-formal perspective of the formal universe called e′ appears. Reflection is thus a shift from a pre-formal to post-formal situation, wherein a well-formed universe appears as an intermediate stage. The second reflection then regards this meta-formal e′ as a *new* pre-formal posit, ready for further determination, producing new relations within an expanded universe of discourse. Reflection is therefore a generating process in which an initially unformed element *becomes* formed, making reference to the element impossible without reference to the act of reflection. The activity of reflection becomes an integral aspect of the element reflected, and a process of continual reflection amounts to *self*-reflection—the initial element embodying reflection as its form.

2. *Logic: Reflection and the Principle of Non-Identity*

The initial step of reflection (R)e is called the *Assertion of* e, written (e) or +e, which *announces*

[1] In the limit, the number of terms are non-denumerable, i.e. as n approaches infinity step by step having the order of the natural numbers and hence being denumerable, the *content* of the orders of reflection approaches the indenumerable order of the continuum.

(affirms) something present in the field of consciousness, the parenthesis or plus sign indicating the *act* of reflection. However, the very fact that (e) or +e is different from e (as, e.g., the positive integer +4 is different from the natural number 4) implies that something *other* than +e must exist, *from which* +e is distinguished by being only the *positive* or *assertive* form of e, otherwise there would be no point in regarding +e and e distinctly. This "other-than-positive" is defined as its co-relative contrary −e (minus e), or, in opposition to (e), we can call this the logical *Negation of* e, written (-e) and called "not e," the parentheses about both e and -e indicating that a reflection has been taken, producing *two* terms as a result.[2] This means that unlike e, -e does not explicitly appear as an immediate pre-reflection given, but only makes its appearance *through* reflection, appearing *as* a reflected term (-e) *after* a reflection on e, producing (e), has implied that something *other than e* must exist *permitting* e to appear as a mediated term. Indeed, the notion of negation is regarded as the essence of reflection and mediation (and the act of questioning), since to mediate or reflect is to remove (negate) oneself from a situation of immediacy. The immediacy of -e is implicit, for by definition that which *is* immediate, and therefore *starting* our analysis, has been called e.

Thus the very act of *affirming* an immediacy, asserting or announcing a given, or recognizing what *is* present, is to set up the *condition* for its negation, since to affirm is to reflect, and allow for the *possibility of its negation.* Both +e and −e, or the assertion *of* and negation *of* e, are functions of e, which is to say that the *content* or reference-base e of assertion and negation is the same, expressed, however, in

[2] The short dash in -e means "not e," while the longer dash in −e means "minus e" such that +e = (e) and −e = (-e).

contrary forms. That which is initially given can be *referred to* positively as that which *is present* (called "positive presence") and negatively as that which is *lacking* (called "negative presence," since the given makes *itself* evident as a *lack*). The concept of negation viewed dialectically as a type of "negative presence" is therefore qualitatively different from the standard notion of logical negation. Given a term A, its negation not-A is usually interpreted to be a positive presence of something other than A, "-A," called, e.g., "B," such that A and B are not only distinct but *separable* "truth values." However the form "other than A" is actually a referral *to A* since no *content* different from A has been posited: to simply *deny* A is *not to assert* anything *else* in its place. Not A is *in*determinate as to *what* is asserted positively, referring only to the *denial of that which was intended.* A genuine negation is a negative presence which cannot without transformation be replaced by an affirming presence. If asked, "Where are you going?" and you respond: "I am *not* going to the theatre," this is a reference *to* the theatre in the mode of rejection.

Reflection on e polarizes e into two modes, distinct in form but inseparable and co-relative in content, since positive and negative as notions are not immediate givens, but mediated relations: each is itself only by virtue of excluding (and therefore having a reference to) its contrary notion: to assert e implies that e *could* have been negated, and vice versa. The *notions* of assertion and negation, mutually implying each other *as possibilities,* must *both* appear in a single act. Reflection is a questioning process producing determination by setting an element in opposition with *itself:* +A is seeing the element "from within" or "in-itself" as Hegel would put it, while −A is seeing the element "from without" or "for-itself." +A is a given *object* or system and −A is *its co*-determinate context or *space,* existing "*for*" the object, defining the object negatively.

Thus there is *one* content (the original e), *two* forms, and *three* phases present in the initial act of reflection (R)e: (e); (e) → (-e); (e) ↔ (-e), or *Assertion* of what is (Ae or +e), Assertion implying *Negation* (Ne or −e), and Negation in turn implying Assertion, making *both* co-relative, such that the negation of e is still a reference to *its* assertion, something which we shall call the *Self-Negation* of e (Se or + −e). Reflection, in attempting to determine or assert e, produces a self-negation of e, involving a coupling of contraries: the *original* pre-formal *non*-positive and *non*-negative e becomes transformed into a formed self-relation between *it*self (now appearing as +e) and *its* other −e, which as a whole is written + −e, i.e. something which is *neither* +e *nor* −e as such—neither "within" nor "without," but their mutual "boundary" state of mutual implication as possibilities. This now makes Se or + −e a *meta*-formed relation *about* the co-relativity *between* +e and −e, which cannot consistently be expressed by +e or −e themselves, regarding them as separable distinctions. Se or + −e thus expresses *explicitly* that which the original e was only *implicitly*, namely something *neither* positive nor negative, but rather *both* "in and for-itself" *as possibilities.* Reflection brings out (expresses) the original *ambiguity* of the pre-formal element, but can only remain true to this ambiguity by expressing the formed + and − aspects on a meta-formal, self-negative level, wherein the original immediacy or e now appears self-mediated through its co-relative mediation with its negation. (e) is the *assertion* of *immediacy,* which, however, because assertion is a reflection, gives us (e) → (-e), which *mediates* the immediacy, but, since mediation is doublefaced, (e) ↔ (-e) expresses the condition that while e is a function of (implies and therefore is mediated by) -e, -e is in turn a function of e, such that e becomes a function *of itself through* -e: e becomes *self-mediated* or self-negated. A cyclic triad of assertion, negation and self-negation, or immediacy, mediation and self-mediation, is produced through a *single* act of reflection: i.e. the so called thesis, antithesis and "synthesis" of Hegelian dialectic. The movement is directly from a pre-reflected, pre-formal thesis e, to a reflected, meta-formal synthesis +—e, producing a formed or reflected thesis +e and reflected antithesis —e along the way. The synthesis term then serves as a new pre-reflected thesis e′ for higher reflections.

The mutual implication which results, (e) ↔ (-e), is called the principle of Non-Identity, which is not necessarily contradictory since the form "p ↔ q" has *two* possible modes: either p and q are *both* (positively) *present* in one and the same notion, or p and q are *both lacking* (negatively present) in a single notion. If (e) and (-e) are both positively present, then this would violate the law of contradiction. However, if (e) and (-e) are mutually in a state of negative presence (regarding +—e as the boundary state between +e and —e which is *neither* as such)—i.e. if it is the case that "not(e) and not(-e)" or "-(e) and -(-e)" exists, then the law of contradiction is not violated, but the law of the excluded middle is. Put in this form, the principle of Non-Identity says that it is impossible to have both the law of contradiction *and* the law of the excluded middle, or it is impossible to be both consistent and complete at the same time since (as Quine points out) the notion of consistency demands that an element and its negation cannot *both* be present, while the notion of completeness demands that an element and its negation cannot *both* be absent. The law of Non-Identity hence states that it is not possible to regard (e) and (-e) as strict contradictories as initially intended, due to the coupling relation discovered *between* (e) and (-e) producing a term, which, while having a (negative) reference to (e) and (-e), is nevertheless different from either: they are either contraries or sub-contraries. The law of Non-Identity couples an element and its negation together in such a way that it is not possible for a completely determined system to appear—i.e. a system in which reference to *either* an element *or* its negation, but not both, can be made: ambiguity in some form must be present because no final distinction into *separable compartments* such as A and -A, "true" and "false," or present and absent, can be achieved.

The expression -(e) is not the same as (-e), nor is -(-e) the same as (e): if either or both were the case, a contradiction would result in the form "-(e) and -(-e)." Regarding (e) and (-e) as contraries we can then say that (e) → -(-e) or "the presence of (e) implies the lack or negative presence of (-e)" and (-e) → -(e) or "the presence of (-e) implies the lack or negative presence of (e)." It cannot then be the case that the converse is true, namely -(-e) → (e) and -(e) → (-e). Since -(e) is distinct from (-e), dialectic logic cannot dispense with parentheses in the formulation of negation operations.

In classical logic, parentheses can be dispensed with since an expression such as -(e) contracts into (-e) or -e, and -(-e) contracts into (e) or e. In intuitionalistic systems of logic we do not obtain a symmetric two value system of e and -e since -(e) contracts into -e, but -(-e) does not yield e: it is simply written as --e, and hence is asymmetric since both contracts do not occur. However, dialectic logic is doubly asymmetric since neither contraction is permissible and hence we are left with a new form of symmetry: a modified two-value logic which displays *levels* of negation. Initially on the first level there is (e) and (-e), but in addition this entire level is negated, giving -(e) and -(-e), which are distinct from the elements of the initial level, but negatively dependent upon them as (-e) was negatively dependent upon (e) *within* the original (first) level as the negation of e, the primitive "zero" level posit. The law of Non-Identity (e) ↔ (-e) can thus express both consistency (positively) and completeness (negatively) in that (e) and (-e), while positively absent, are still negatively present.

Analyzing the coupling relation +—e in this way indicates that we have already begun a reflection *on* our initial reflection (R)e. For regarding the meta-formal relation +—e as e′, a new pre-formal posit, (R)e′ produces two new expressions, (e′) and (-e′). But since e′ already represents the inseparable relation between (e) and (-e), the new reflection (R)e′ generates *four* terms: (e′) involves a relation between ((e)) and ((-e)) and (-e′) a relation between (-(e)) and (-(-e)). It should be noted that the first *parenthesis* about e was an indication that e *co-exists with its negation* -e, *each* term therefore appearing with a parenthesis, i.e. (e) and (-e), since each co-exists with the other. Similarly *two* parentheses about e, i.e. ((e)), indicates that not only do (e) and (-e) co-exist, but *their* negations -(e) and -(-e) exist, all *four* of which co-exist, producing the four terms ((e)), ((-e)), (-(e)) and (-(-e)). Thus a second reflection on e gives us the four expressions (e), (-e), -(e) and -(-e) originally implicit in the self-negation relation (e) ↔ (-e) except that now a second parenthesis appears indicating a *completed* second order reflection. A self-negation thus represents a *transition* state from one level of reflection to another. For example, the *formed* (e) and (-e) elements of the first reflection produced a universe of discourse which included a *non-determinate* relation (e) ↔ (-e) within it, which, however, could only *consistently* be expressed on a second level, where not only the (e) and (-e) terms appear (now as ((e)) and ((-e))) but also their *negations* (-(e)) and (-(-e)) *implicit* in (e) ↔ (-e).

On a second level, for example, ((-e)) can be called the second level assertion of an original first level negation, while (-(e)) in turn would be the second level negation of a first level assertion. The former, could, for example, be interpreted to mean that a certain X "is not moral" in the sense that X (is (not-moral)) while the latter might be interpreted to mean that the X which is not moral implies that X (is not (moral)). Hence the expression "X is not moral" can appear as an assertion or negation: i.e. we can say that "X *is* not-moral" (which could mean "X *is* immoral," equating immoral with not-moral) or "X *is not* moral," and it becomes meaningful to distinguish these otherwise obscure alternatives, for to state that X *is not* moral does not make a commitment: X could be *neither* moral *nor* not-moral (immoral)—being rather a-moral or in doubt as to the resolution of a certain issue.

A second level (n = 2) reflection, expressed in terms of plus and minus, becomes:

$$\underset{\substack{\text{1 term:}\\ n=0}}{e}: (R)e = \underset{\substack{\text{3 terms:}\\ n=1}}{(+e \rightarrow -e : +-e)} = e' : (R)e' =$$

$$\left\{\begin{array}{l} +(+e \rightarrow -e : +-e) \\ \downarrow \\ -(+e \rightarrow -e : +-e) \\ \because \\ +-(+e \rightarrow -e : +-e) \end{array}\right\} = \underset{\substack{\text{9 terms:}\\ n=3}}{e''}$$

It is obvious that a continued reflection process will generate a hierarchy of plus and minus terms, which together with their plus-minus coupling relations, represent levels of assertion, negation and self-negation, each new level marked off by a new parenthesis, and having a referral to the level it is a reflection of. Reflection, producing levels of relation n, thus yields a total of 3^n terms, including *both* the singular plus or minus terms, *and* their plus-minus co-relative terms. The single plus or minus terms, *generating* each level, however, form a sub-set of 2^n terms, indicating that a dialectic logic generalizes a two-value (+ and −) logic for n dimensions. From this point of view, dialectic logic has an indenumerably infinite number of "truth" values, as n approaches infinity.

Actually, however, dialectic logic is *fundamentally* a *uni*-valued logic (the original e), producing levels of self-opposition (+ and − e) and self-relation (+−e) resulting in an infinite number of levels of distinct yet inseparable forms. In this leveling process any particular *formed* (determined) level of relations is continually subject, by means of the coupling relation, to higher order indeterminacies, out of which higher order sets of determined relations are formed —as for example, the initial coupling of (e) ↔ (-e) gave rise, relative to the *first* level, to the indeterminate expression "-(e) and -(-e)," and then, on the next level, the determined forms (-(e)) and (-(-e)) in opposition to ((e)) and ((-e)). The appearance of an indeterminacy due to the coupling of contraries according to the law of Non-Identity indicates that a new level is in the process of formation—a level which becomes explicit in a higher order reflection, and which contains the previous level within it as a reference-base.

To illustrate that the above formulation generalizes the process of dialectic opposition, let us examine the second order reflection in a process of generating the third order reflection. (R)e′ = e″ and this gives us (e′) and (-e′) or a relation between the four terms: ((e)), ((-e)), (-(e)) and (-(-e)). However, the coupling term (e′) ↔ (-e′) = e″ has as its initial result either "(e') and $(-e')$" or "$-(e')$ and $-(-e')$." Thus a reflection on e'' ought to explicate the positive (e') and $(-e')$ terms and negative $-(e')$ and $-(-e')$ terms *implicit* in the meaning of e''. Now $(R)e'' = e'''$ implies that a third reflection has *eight* terms: the third level *assertion* of the four given terms inherent in e'' and the third level *negation* of the same four terms inherent in e'' such that $(R)e'' = e'''$ expresses a relation between (e'') and $(-e'')$. Assertion thus brings out the initial terms (e') and $(-e')$ of e'', and Negation $-e''$ brings out the implied negations $-(e')$ and $-(-e')$, giving us $(((e)))$, $(((-e)))$, $((-(e)))$ and $((-(-e)))$ for (e'') and $(-((e)))$, $(-((-e)))$, $(-(-(e)))$ and $(-(-(-e)))$ for $(-e'')$. Reasoning back to the original reflection $(R)e = e' = (e) \leftrightarrow (-e)$, this implies that e' brings out the *implied* opposition inherent in the initial e, namely e and $-e$, giving us (e) and $(-e)$ for its explication. The initial immediate e, as a *single* term, is in itself an implicit contradiction, which becomes negated into $-e$: e is originally potentially both itself and its other, a contradiction resolved by reflection into two *distinct* forms (e) and $(-e)$, giving us $e' = (e) \leftrightarrow (-e)$. Reflection therefore explicates the inherent opposition within any immediate, indeterminate element, such as e, producing in the process a determined (mutually distinguished) set of oppositions (e) and $(-e)$, which, however, due to the *coupling* of these determined forms demanded by the original e, collapses into a *new* mode of indeterminacy e', requiring an *additional* reflection into e'' to distinguish the *higher* modes of potential opposition, produced by the previous reflection, and *now* appearing as possibilities (i.e. (e') and $(-e')$).

Everything indeterminate and immediate (such as e, e', e'') is unstable, becoming negated and mediated by its own opposition, only to yield a higher mode of immediacy, having negatively present the previous modes of opposition it has negated. Only through a process of *continual* reflection are all oppositions and contradictions negatable, but this process cannot be completed at any *single* stage for new indeterminacies always appear. The e′ as (e) ↔ (-e) would be a *complete* resolution, but expressed as merely the positive terms "(e) and (-e)" e′ is a contradiction. To cancel the contradiction demands the negation of the co-relative terms, giving "-(e) and -(-e)," but now, while consistent, the expression e′ is incomplete. For now a new level has been started, namely (-e′) in opposition to (e′), requiring a new resolution e″ = (e′) ↔ (-e′) which repeats the above condition. The movement of reflection is therefore a continual movement of self-cancelling self-contradictions. Reflection is an infinite movement of self-realization that can never resolve itself in the form of a completed *product:* the whole *as a process* is incomplete; only the process *as a whole* or an infinite totality and *not* a product is complete. In this infinite process, no particular term remains as a non-negative term, each expression appearing only as a transitory step in a continual process of negation. Arresting the process at any point will result in a finite sub-set of opposites, the resultant term of which can only consistently express its component parts as negatively present due to the coupling of all contraries.

3. *Time: The Temporal Nature of Reflection*

What makes the above sequence of coupled contraries possible without explicit contradiction is the notion of negative-referral: i.e. realizing that an expression of the form "-(e)" is a referral to the *lack of (e)*. The notion of negative presence hence involves the presence of a memory process in which something is capable of being referred to in its negated state as a negative-presence. Indeed, the past is referred to through our memory process as that which once *was* and hence *is not,* but yet is capable of being referred to *qua past.* This must not be confused with the *act* of producing a memory, appearing in "the present": the content of the memory, or the memory itself is, however, a negative referral to a previously but now non-existing state. Hence dialectic logic is a type of "temporal" logic involving a memory system in which the negation of an element preserves the negated element as *that from which* the negation appeared. For this reason, not (notA) cannot be the same as A since not (notA) while negating the negation of A nevertheless has preserved within the parenthesis the fact that A *was negated* in the activity of a double negation. Thus negations are "non-conservative," since an attempted *re*turn or *re*petition from the initial A to notA and back to the initial A by means of a double negation retains within its representing structure the activity of movement that has *generated* the A which appears as a *result* of negation: one cannot return unmodified to the *original* state. In this way negated elements are preserved within the parentheses as *re*ference points for all future activity.

Unlike an "atemporal" logic, dialectic logic is asymmetric in that negation and reflection in general is a process of cancellation—a process of *aufheben* which retains any previous state as a perspective of orientation. An absolute or all-embracing negation would be equivalent to a total loss of memory, something which cannot be formulated within a memory system itself. It is hence impossible to "move backwards" through time in this analysis for this would involve an eradication of memory, an *event* not capable of *appearing within* the memory structure. (One can of course be aware of the loss of *something* which at one time served a certain function, but then we are not aware *of* that something itself, but only its contextual relatedness.) The significance of the quotation from the Rubaiyat appearing at the beginning lies in its poetic expression of this relentless irreversibility of time.

It is important to recognize that the indeterminate nature of negation (i.e. notA is a referral to the *absence of* A and is indeterminate as to what *is* present) has as its intuitional foundation the notion of time. Since we are considering the process of reflection to be an asymmetric process appearing through time (and indeed, as we shall see, defining the very nature of time) this implies that the various elements to be generated cannot at any stage all be present. Hence we are not dealing with an already form*ed* and determin*ed* universe of discourse, but with one that is in the process of *being formed,* and therefore the system is intrinsically incomplete and must exhibit this incompleteness through the indeterminacy of its variables. Only within a completed system (and hence one that is essentially finite *in description)* is it possible to state that the negation of a given element x is all that which is "left over," namely an un-ambiguous "not-x" such that *not*-notx is in turn x! Since we are dealing with a continually expanding universe of discourse, not-x is an *inde*terminate reference to what *is present,* having only a *de*terminate reference to that which has been *excluded.* Once a negation has been determined and de-limited within a given frame of reference (as for example -e appearing as (-e), and thus *binding* or coupling -e in relation to what is excluded, namely e, giving (e) $\leftrightarrow$ (-e), this then implies that the *entire universe of discourse* (now called e′) can be negated, producing higher order negations that initially are likewise indeterminate (i.e. giving us -e′ or -(e) and -(-e). It is thus important to distinguish between the genuine indeterminate negation, *opening* a system up to elements *beyond* those already formed, and a determined negation expressing a *previous act* of negation, and which co-exists *with* and is thus bound *to* its co-relative assertion *within* an already formulated universe. Thus -(A) is open, and (-A) is closed: the former states that an x does *not have* a property A, while the latter states that an x *has* a property notA. In sequence, the negation of an element A as *not*A gives the indeterminate form -A, but *re*cognizing that reflection yields notA determines the negation as (-A), permitting *not* (-A) or -(-A) to appear *and its* determination not(-A) or (-(-A)) etc. The genuine indeterminate negation produces *levels* of negations (and *co-relative levels* of assertions such as (A), ((A)), ((-A)) etc.), and ignoring this distinguishing nature of dialectic negation reduces negative presence to positive presence, and "spatializes" time: non-dialectic logic is a-temporal, corresponding to a view of the universe as essentially determined and *given* "in space," and merely in need of *description.*

Dialectic logic is asymmetric as the time process is, and ". . . the systematic development of truth in scientific form . . . lies in the form and shape in which the process of time presents the existence of its moments."[3] Also, Hegel informs us in the introduction to his *Logic,* that

> The one and only [*sic*] thing for securing scientific progress is the knowledge of the logical percept that Negation is just as much Affirmation as Negation, or that which is self-contradictory resolves itself not into nullity, into abstract Nothingness, but essentially only into the negation of its *particular* content, that such negation is not an all-embracing negation, but is *the negation of a definite something,* which abolishes itself, and thus is a definite negation; and that thus the result contains in essence that from which it results —which is indeed a tautology, for otherwise it would

[3] Hegel, *Phenomenology of Spirit,* trans. J. Baillie (2d ed.; New York: Macmillan, 1931), pp. 70–71.

> be something immediate and not a result. Since what results, the negation, is a definite negation, it has a content. It is a new concept, but a higher richer concept than that which preceded: for it has been enriched by the negation or opposite of that preceding concept, and thus contains it, but contains more than it, and is the unity of it and its opposite. On these lines the system of Concepts [i.e. Hegel's system] has broadly to be constructed, and to go on to completion in a resistless course, free from all foreign elements, admitting nothing from outside.[4]

Thus there is only *one* starting point: the indeterminate e, such that all reflections are indeed *self*-reflections *on* and *about* e (and thereby "free from all foreign elements"). Thus -e is not a mere negation of e, but has a reference *to* e (as "the negation of a definite something"), such that when the non-identity relation uniting e and -e into (e) $\leftrightarrow$ (-e) appears to express the condition that the "richer concept" which results "is the unity of it [the original concept] and its opposite," the possible self-contradiction of positing *both* (e) and (-e) "resolves itself not into nullity," but only into the "negation of its *particular* content," i.e. into "-(e) and -(-e)." The "synthesis" of e and -e is hence a *negative unity of opposites* bringing e and -e together into a relation which is "*neither* (e) *nor* (-e)," i.e. into a relation which is defined in terms of that which it is not. Thus the "synthesis" concept of Becoming for Hegel is that "which is not either Being [affirmation] or Nothing [negation],"[5] but rather the indeterminate *state* of transition between that which is and is not: becoming is defined in terms of that which it is not.

Hegel's synthesis of becoming as the coupling of

[4] *Science of Logic,* trans. Johnston and Struthers (New York: Macmillan, 1929), I, 64–65.

[5] *Science of Logic,* I, 95.

being and nothing—as well as the relation "-(e) and -(-e)" in general—can be regarded as a single "boundary zone," representable as a "line" distinguishing yet connecting two mutually opposed "regions" called (e) and (-e). This boundary line can be regarded as a mathematical *limit* relation between two *distinct although inseparable* spaces, and hence, being a limit relation, it expresses that which the two spaces approach, without having the two spaces *positively* present in the boundary zone. Rather the very notion of a mathematical limit entails the *negative* presence of *that* which is limited: "-(e) and -(-e)" is a boundary *of* (e) and (-e), and being a reference *to* (e) and (-e), it is therefore defined in terms of what it is not. Similarly $+-$e can be regarded as the "zero" point *limit* of +e and $-$e.

Unity is therefore the *transcendence* of that which is unified, and transcendence as a *movement* from an initial state (e) to its negation (-e) is a *unity* of both: a negative unity (e) $\leftrightarrow$ (-e). In this unity, each opposite is *aufgehoben,* i.e. (a) it is cancelled, yet (b) preserved *as* a negative presence and (c) raised to a higher or "richer" level in that *as* a negative presence each element (e) can be conjoined with its opposite (-e) expressing a state of transition "-(e) and -(-e)" without contradiction.

The synthesis or self-negation of a term, resolving itself into a negative unity of opposites, thus illustrates that the definition of dialectic opposites are "positive contraries which become negative subcontraries upon their mutual implication in a non-identity relation." Thus (e) and (-e) are positive contraries meaning that they cannot both appear together in any one relation. However the very act of writing the denial of inconsistency or contrariness "-(e) and -(-e)" allows us to consider the negative presence of (e) and (-e), wherein they now appear as negative sub-contraries. This means that as *negative* relations, they cannot both be absent in any one relation. Thus, the first term

(e) implies -(-e) or the negative referral to its opposite (-e), and the second term (-e) implies -(e) or a negative referral to its contrary (e), while the synthesis term (e) ↔ (-e) is a negative referral to *both,* i.e. it is "-(e) and -(-e)." Being negative sub-contraries is the other side of the coin of being positive contraries, and in this way we guarantee a condition of negative completeness: there will always be a negative reference to either (e), (-e) or both. Hence the dialectic of a synthesis term lies in the fact that it is *both* terms (negatively) yet *neither* (positively) at the same time, spelling out the essence of dialectic opposites: to be inseparable yet distinct.[6] We can now construct a table of opposition, showing how dialectic opposites complete an otherwise incomplete structure. It also illustrates that dialectic opposites, *like contradictories,* are a combination of contraries and sub-contraries but in a different way. Let X stand for impossible, and / for possible:

Type of opposition	Reference to *Both* (e) and (-e)	Reference to *Neither* (e) nor (-e)
Contraries	X	/
Sub-Contraries	/	X
Contradictories	X	X
Dialectic opposites	/	/

4. Logic and Time: The Problem of Identity in General

Regarding the dialetic process intuitively, reflection takes an immediately given entity called e, and "places" this entity e in context with its other called

[6] Speaking about the unity of Being and Nothing, of which Hegel says "all that follows . . . all philosophical concepts, are examples of this unity," the essential point is "that they are absolutely distinct, and yet unseparated and inseparable . . . their truth is . . . this movement of one into the other." *Science of Logic,* I, 97; 95.

not e or o, implicitly present within itself as the entity's potentiality for being questioned or reflected (i.e. negated as an immediacy), such that the result is now neither e nor o as such but the transcending and unifying *movement* or *relation* eo. *In* this relationship of context, e itself becomes transformed and determined as (e) and not e or o likewise becomes determined as (o), while the *relationship* eo is the co-relativity and hence transcendence of these individual determinations. The basic structure of reflection can now be intuited as a *movement* from a *singular indeterminate term* e, to a *singular meta-determined relationship* eo, the process $(R)e = (e \rightarrow o{:}\ eo)$ being called e′, indicating that reflection has been a self-determining process *of e.* The negating o term represents the *expansion* brought about by the *explicating* reflection process, and is not something alien to e. To reflect on something is to view that element and not some other element from a plane of perspective and hence a *reflection is a double negation whereby the original immediate posit disappears and reappears in context with the implicit negation inherent in the process of reflection,* i.e. with the questioning of the given. If we did not have a temporal logic, a reflection on e would simply be e itself. But a temporal logic regards reflection as an *activity* in which the very questioning of an initial posit changes the nature of the posit present. Thus we have a conceptual counterpart to the indeterminacy principle in physics, which states that the very activity of a subject measuring an object modifies the object (and also subject) involved. For example, reflection on or thinking about a conceptual object changes the *way* in which the object appears to the field of consciousness, and reflection or thought about an emotional state itself transforms that state from one of bare immediacy to reflective mediation, bringing to bear implicit associated feelings. Reflection on a perceptual object will alter the frame of reference with which the object is viewed and hence will alter the relevant information that the subject takes as essential for the perceived object, since perception involves not only seeing, but also the operation of *looking-for,* i.e. discovering "in" that object an example of some conceptualized relation forming part of the evaluative perspective negatively present in the field of viewing consciousness. Experiments indicate that an altered perceptual mode even transforms what is seen.

The principle of Non-Identity holds that entities appear as *events* within a field of consciousness and are basically neither determined nor not-determined, but rather in a process of *being*-determined: e.g. e is being determined to be e′. This implies that the problem of Identity or defining "what is" must include the negation of reflection as an *integral* aspect: *what* is defined cannot be severed from the *act* of definition. In a non-temporal structure, the principle of Identity would hold: once something is given, e.g. an object A, *re*ference can be made to the *same* A despite modifications of context. Thus it would be possible to write "A is A" or "A $\leftrightarrow$ A." However, to *say* that "A is A" is to give an answer to an implied question, namely "A is ?" since the statement "A *is* A" is a *re*flection on the *immediately* given A and in effect becomes "A is (A)." Reflection, *reveals* A co-existing with -A, such that (A) $\rightarrow$ -(-A): "A is A" means that A is A and *not* something else. *Re*cognition of immediacy or a *re*ference to it, *transforms* it into mediation. Within a temporal context, the very fact that A *re*appears (i.e. appears *twice* in "A is A") means that the *unquestioned* immediacy of an original A has been modified by the questioning process: it appears as something mediated (i.e. it appears a *second* time, now *in relation to* -A) and not immediate (appearing only a *first* time). The dialectic of something appearing a second time is therefore based upon the dialectic of the notion "to reappear." For something to re*appear* means on one level that it indeed does *appear* again, but in that it *re*appears, means that the *mode* of appearance *transforms* the object present and appearing into something mediated and not immediate: *all repetition is therefore transformation* since a repeated state has negatively present in its memory structure the fact that it has already happened in the past. The law of Identity is not false: it is simply empty since "A *is* A" is not definable within a temporal context.

We could of course say that "A *was* A" meaning that the present state of *what is* is being bracketed, and the temporal aspect introduced by taking into consideration the effects of an observ*ing* and persist*ing* field of consciousness is ignored. In that case, with the suspension of the on-going temporal process, we have a hypothesized past which *qua-being-past* remains unchanged. Thus the law of Identity operates for a system whose members are taken to be *already fixed by definition:* it operates within a system in which the ambiguity of definition is eliminated by fiat. Thus, every element is well-form*ed in-itself,* and is not influenced by *contextual* relatedness: the A within a formula "x + A = y" is the "same" A as within a formula "z + A = w," since "A ↔ A" rejects any coupling A may have with a contextual "-A." Thus the law of Identity can be regarded as a type of sub-set within a law of Non-Identity, referring to the *past* aspect of the time process. This can be formally stated in the form of a meta-principle of Non-Identity called -I′: calling the principle of Identity I (e ↔ e or (e) ↔ (e)) and the principle of Non-Identity -I (-(e ↔ e)) or (e ↔ -e) or ((e) ↔ (-e)), a meta-principle of Non-Identity would read -I′ = (I) ↔ (-I). Therefore Identity can be expressed as a function of some higher order Non-Identity; being appears as a function of time and becoming, and the past appears as a function of an enlarged temporal structure which includes the negating present. Indeed, the very attempt to show that a law of Non-Identity negates *itself* by a self-reflection reestablishes a higher form of Non-Identity. Calling the law of Non-Identity N, a coupling of N with its negation -N gives us $N' = (N) \leftrightarrow (-N)$. Unlike a law of Identity, the law of Non-Identity expresses itself through its opposite, and ceases to express itself if it is not related to its opposite.

Regarding logical structures explicitly in terms of temporal development permits a reformulation of certain basic concepts, which would otherwise seem foreign to the region of logic. First of all, the problem of Identity is no longer merely "formal," in that the *process* of formation, itself non-formal, is seen underlying the *act* for formation. Therefore, there is a dialectic between formal and non-formal: i.e. "content" reappears in the guise of the activity of formation—a content which is dynamic and reflective in nature. Thus, as we have seen, the *element* formed and the *process* of formation called reflection are inseparable, which means that dialectic logic expresses a philosophy of *phenomenology*. The element present is any object or *event,* and the *field* it is present to is the field of *consciousness,* which reflects on the event. We are thus conceiving consciousness as *a persisting field of presence to events* (either conceptual or perceptual) and hence since it persists, an accumulating memory field develops, reflective of its continuity of presence. Therefore, consciousness is defined phenomenologically as a subject (field of presence)—object (event) interrelation in which neither field nor event, subject nor object have meaning independent of their state of interaction. Consciousness is thus a co-relativity between the contraries S and O (subject and object) giving rise to the form $(S) \leftrightarrow (O)$ and, as we shall see later, capable of expressing *levels* of subject-object relation, S', O', S'', O'' etc. Dialectics, phenomenlogically based, avoids being either a subject-centered idealism or an object-centered materialism. The subject-object relation of phenomenology is the *content* of the dialectic process, which as a structure in turn is the very *form* of the subject-object phenomenology of consciousness: *Dialectic Phenomenology* is what results.

However, besides being descriptive of consciousness, Hegelian dialectic explicates the very structure of time itself. The triadic movement (e → o: eo) is no other than a triadic movement between past, present and future. The initial indeterminate element e is, as such, pre-temporal, before reflection. Without an act of reflection upon the intuitively given there would be no recognizable differentiation between the intuitively present events and the field of conscious presence, reflectively distinct from the occurring events. There would merely be the continual presence of "events-within-a-field," the continual presence of whatever (state, process, relation) is given, and no notion of differentiation or temporality could be *explicated:* the pre-reflective present is a type of "eternal" or "continual" *indeterminate* presence of what-is. Recognition of differentiation implies the existence of *negating* events (events that take on a *determining,* negating characteristic) within a field of presence such that a meaningful *contrast* appears between something given and something *not*-given; between a sustaining and *persisting* field of conscious presence preserving what has already been given within its memory field (reflective of its *continuity* of presence), and a non-persisting and hence "fleeting" or negating set of events as something not-given but "happening" and therefore in contrast to the persistency of the field. This can then be shown to yield the triadic relation: (the *negated* yet preserved given) → (the *negating* not-given) : (the process of the given *being negated* by the not-given) as (e → o: eo).

The *act* of reflection will now be defined *phenomenologically* to *be* the negating event (the not-given) within the interacting subject-object (field-event) system which "fixes" or "focuses" upon something intuitively given, transforming the given into the *past* as something determin*ed*, and hence *removed* from the indeterminate flux of sheer presence, becoming part of the persisting memory field, such that the reflective act itself at the same time becomes the *present-act* of negation and determination, and such that past and present as contrary differentiations mutually imply each other as opposites. Being phenomenologically defined, the act of reflection must not be thought of as a merely "mental" state; it is rather a function of the combined field-event or subject-object process of interaction: reflection depends upon the object as well as the subject.

The act of reflection negates the immediacy of the initial e, giving us (e) as that which *has been determined* as given, and equally *determines* the present as a *specific* not-given or (-e). The net result is an asymmetric temporal process of the *past* being established through a negating *present,* defining in this transition, and co-relatively between past and present, or (e) and (-e), the notion of the *future* as that which is *neither* the given and past, *nor* the specific negating not-given or present, but the past-to-present act of transition: the future is the transcending *movement* of negative unity—the *act* of becoming, transcendence or determination itself; it is the process of something *being-given* and is bound neither by the given nor by the not-given. The future "exists" not as something already predetermined, yet not manifest; the future is a "transcending presence" between two temporal states, expressing the given past in a process of continually becoming *transformed* by a negating present. The future is the mode of self-transformation—the mode of the given seen as a *process* of being-given which is neither positive nor negative, but self-negative. Seen as self-transformation, the future of a given is a "*pro*ject" or *goal of becoming,* and must not be seen as a *separate* presence, disjointed from the past as another separate presence neither of which are thereby capable of appearing in an immediate present. Actually all three modes of past, present and future appear in a *single* act of reflection in which an *indeterminate* presence (the original e) becomes transformed into a *transcending* presence (the reflected e called e′), coupling the *positive* presence of the past, as the already establish*ed* and determined, and the *negative* presence of the present as the negation of the given. The past is the negat*ed,* the present is the negat*ing,* and the future is the process or *state* of nega*tion* of something be*ing* negat*ed,* i.e. a state of self-negation and transcendence which as a state is *completely open:* it is *neither* positive *nor* negative but explicates the original *in*determinate presence it is a reflection of; the essence of the future is freedom.

Logic, time, phenomenology and ontology are therefore all interwoven in one overall concept of dialectic and the principle of Non-Identity: indeed, with logic we have assertion +e, negation −e and self-negation +−e; with time we have past, present and future; with phenomenology we have subject (the persisting field of presence), object (the negating events) and the subject-object relation; and with ontology we have being, nothing and becoming.

Dialectic logic can therefore be regarded as a systematization of the mode in which elements, appearing within a consciousness that persists through time, *become* determined, and indeed it can be said that the structural nature of an element generated becomes a reflection of its history: space (structure) and time (history) become inseparable. However, this does not prevent a formalization of dialectic, given as a mapping of the ongoing temporal process within a persisting structure that is being generated, and which, once generated, *remains* present. It becomes important, however, not to confuse that which is *being* determined with the *elements* determined, which *once* set down qua-determined (including the determination that a certain element is indeterminate) are regarded *independently* of the generating process that produced them and transforms them by continually *re*producing them within newer contexts. From the intuitive perspective, the various stages e, e′, e″ are all part of a *continual* expansion of the *one* original indeterminate e, whereas from the formal perspective, *each singled out* stage such as e′ appears as an *independent* member having qualitatively different relations from the other stages since they obey the sub-ordinate law of identity—something which of course can and must be expressed since identity and the persisting past is a part of the temporal process.

Therefore, the development of the dialectic matrix, representing the form in which *levels* of reflection appear, will be presented as a *formal* structure of A (Assertion), N (Negation) and S (Self-Negation) operators, a *logical* interpretation as assertion, (e) or +e, negation, (-e) or −e, and self-negation, (e) ↔ (-e) or +−e, and an *intuitive* process using the e, o and eo symbols. As intuitive symbols, e and o are to be regarded as elements-in-continual-transformation, capable of having a reference to formal counterparts, but essentially symbolizing that which is in a state of continual temporal self-transformation.

5. *The Relationship between Ordinary Logic and Dialectic Logic*

From the perspective of a principle of Non-Identity, dialectic logic can be taken as a way of generalizing Goedel's theorem, and instead of regarding it merely as a *limitation* to the expression of consistent systems in ordinary logical structures, it now becomes the *starting point* for a dialectic logic, which regards these limitations as the essence of its structure. According to Goedel's theorem, our present mathematical-logic system is so constituted that consistency and completeness appear as contraries: given one, the other cannot necessarily be shown. But as we have seen, the principle of Non-Identity equally presents us with that contrariness. Indeed, it is significant that the formula giving rise to Goedel's result is similar in form to the principle of Non-Identity: i.e. it is possible to construct a true formula G such that its demonstration is implied by and implies the demonstration of its negation. This is symbolized by Dem (G) $\leftrightarrow$ Dem (-G), which results in the conclusion that while true the formula G cannot consistently be expressed *within the given* formal system without expansion, which would then only produce higher order incompleteness, namely another formula G′ having a fate similar to G.[7]

The above situation appears as a limitation of expression only if we view formal structures merely from the perspective of the law of Identity, wherein we regard the essence of a given term as already fixed and formed, independent of the activity of reflection. Reflection, however, opens up any given X to an indeterminate -X, placing the given thus in a new context, *within* which both the given X and the -X become transformed due to the mutually limiting nature of the coupling relation expressing the *co*-existence of X and -X. Hence X appears determined as (X) in relation to an equally mediated (-X), produc-

[7] It is interesting to note that G represents the statement "G is not demonstrable," i.e. G says *of itself* that it is not derivable from the axioms. Goedel's theorem hence formalizes a self-negative and self-reflective condition, which, while true, cannot be *derived* without contradiction.

tive however, of a *transformed* X called X′ representing the coupling (X) ↔ (-X). The coupling relation thus acts to *delimit* and form both *X and -X* by a relation of mediation (i.e. X mediated by -X gives (X) and -X mediated by X gives (-X)), yet is *itself* a transcendence of that *which* it forms, standing as it does for the *act* of formation. Thus, of necessity, reflection will always produce potential contradictions, for a contradiction is always a contradiction *in terms,* and the terms formed by the coupling relation, while delimited by a mutual limiting relation and thus *excluding* ambiguity *in themselves,* have nevertheless only *achieved* this determination by a coupling relation which as a meta-determination to the determined forms *itself* exhibits the ambiguity it has eliminated from the formed terms. Thus the only way out of the contradiction of terms resulting from *delimited* terms *exhibiting* the ambiguity of the act that produced them, namely the co-relativity relation (X) ↔ (-X), is a *redefinition* of terms, allowing for an *expansion* of the universe of discourse: instead of merely (X) and (-X), we have ((X)), ((-X)), (-(X)) and (-(-X)).

Numbers were originally regarded merely as rationals, i.e. in the form p/q. The operation of squaring a rational would always give another rational. Now the *inverse* operation of square-rooting, while a meaningful *property* of a number, *could* produce a non-rational, and hence *not* a number as initially conceived. However, an expansion of the number concept to real numbers, including both rationals and irrationals, resulted in a widening of context, within which the older notion of number, otherwise subject to contradiction, appeared in modified form. But irrationals turned out not to be identical with nonrationals, since further expansion into imaginary, complex and hyper-complex numbers could also be achieved. In mathematics, the transition from natural numbers to integers, rationals, real, complex, hypercomplex etc. represents a continual process of redefinition of number, to allow for expansion of context needed to overcome potential contradictions resulting from generalizations of already formed concepts. Contradictions are therefore *not* to be regarded as a catastrophy, but rather as a sign that the delimited universe of discourse *needs* a redefinition of identity to allow for the appearance of the ambiguity and indeterminacy *previously eliminated* by fiat. Any *formed* expression is *by* definition (!) incomplete in that it is thereby taken out of the *process* of formation—a process which is itself not formed.

Thus if we regard the *process* of formation—the dialectic of reflection—as the foundation of formal structures, then it is possible to reintroduce the notion of *completeness* with the notion of consistency, in that the act of redefinition is now regarded not as an *ad hoc* intervention from without merely to preserve consistency or distinctness, but rather redefinition is regarded as expressing the nature of the ever-present formation process and as an *expansion* of the *given* terms, having the original given terms *negatively present* as part of an accumulating memory structure which preserves and hence is complete with respect to *all* that it transforms and negates as *part* of a growing structure. We thus evolve a stratified theory of types or levels X, X′, X″ etc., which, unlike the Russell theory of types, does not appear as an *extra*-logical device introduced to preserve consistency, but is rather an integral aspect of the *logic* itself.

From the law of Identity perspective, Goedel's theorem would regard an expression such as Dem(G) ↔ Dem(-G) or (X) ↔ (-X) as giving rise to only *two* alternatives: (a) either we get "(X) and (-X)", expressing a contradiction in that while inseparable, (X) and (-X) are also indistinct, or (b) "-(X) and

-(-X)" expressing incompleteness in that, while distinct, (X) and (-X) are also separable, productive of a formed relation that is *neither* (X) nor (-X), but a *third* alternative. This alternative goes *beyond* (X) and (-X) and has *no* reference to them, since they have been rejected. This type of reasoning leads to a meta-level analysis in which there is no *continuity* of content from level to level: each new level becomes a completely distinct *and* separable formed expression which does not retain a reference base to that which has been transcended.

However, with the notion of negative-referral, the expression (X) $\leftrightarrow$ (-X) in the form "-(X) and -(-X)" expresses a coupling relation which says that the opposites are both distinct *and* inseparable, i.e. while positively absent, they are negatively present, and positive contraries are transformed into negative subcontraries. This means that there will *always* be reference to (X) and (-X) negatively: the condition for positive consistency is equivalent to a condition of negative completeness. (Also, while we do not have positive completeness, neither do we have negative consistency, meaning that *both* (X) and (-X) can be conjoined as negative referrals in a boundary condition expressing a state of transition and transcendence.) Thus, when a new level is revealed, enlarging the universe of discourse by redefinition, from single to multiple parentheses structures, the enlarged structure is a development of the previous level and does not appear as an *ad hoc* enlargement. Dialectic logic, therefore, does not concentrate on the problem of consistency *versus* completeness as such. Rather it considers the basic problem to be that of *Identity* and indeed considers the notions of consistency and completeness (as well as the parallel notions of the law of contradiction and the law of the excluded middle) to be imbedded *within* the formulation of the concept of identity. Calling A by the symbol p, and notA by q, we can construct, according to the standard meaning of operations in classical logic, the following relations:

$$[-(p \,\&\, q) \text{ and } (p \text{ or } q)] \leftrightarrow (p \leftrightarrow -q) \leftrightarrow (p \leftrightarrow --p) \rightarrow (p \leftrightarrow p)$$

Law of Contradiction	+	Law of Excluded Middle	=	Law of Double Negation	→	Law of Identity, I
Consistency	+	Completeness	=	Well-determined System	→	Identity
p and q are contraries	+	p and q are sub-contraries	=	p and q are Contradictories	→	p is self-identical: no relation to q

However, if we deny the law of Identity, holding that p is not self-identical (because reflection relates p to q), or deny the condition of *strict* Contradiction we get $-I \rightarrow -(p \leftrightarrow --p) \leftrightarrow [-(-(p \,\&\, q)) \text{ or } -(p \text{ or } q)]$. In other words, the possibilities open are either inconsistency or incompleteness: the law of Identity is not only a necessary condition for a well determined system, but its negation leaves us right in the beginning with the notions of consistency and completeness set against one another.

Dialectic logic, *starting* with a law of Non-Identity, hence regards as its basic essence the opposition between consistency and completeness, but because it formulates Non-Identity in terms of a temporal logic involving negative-referral, the opposition is transcended by becoming an expression of the fact that entities reflected upon are in a continual state of *becoming* and self-transformation, and are therefore *being*-determined, and thus neither determin*ed* nor not-determin*ed* as such. Underlying the essence of Goedel's theorem is the need to reformulate *Identity*, permitting it to express Non-Identity and self-generation.

Thus the essence of dialectic analysis lies in the fact that it forces reformulations and transformations of presently accepted and artificially fixed conceptualizations. It is opposed to any type of fixed-substance notion, whether the concepts apply to the self, world or self-world interaction. Identity is not something *given* or defined: it is something that has to be continually achieved and reaffirmed, involving the anxiety of non-identity and self-negation. The *act* of *de*finition itself, i.e. that X *is* A, which underlies the basic structure of formal systems, is what must be transformed: upon *reflection* X is also A′ or $(A) \leftrightarrow (\text{-}A)$. When a predicate X such as "is in motion" is analyzed from a formal perspective, it is important to introduce levels (meta-levels) wherein it is necessary to distinguish motion taken in different senses, i.e. motion_1, motion_2, motion_3, etc. in order to avoid contradiction. However, this is but another form of the consistency-completeness conflict, since one is forced either to (a) consider *one* expression such as motion_1 as complete and including all its variations within its scope with the result that *inconsistencies* occur, or (b) consider any one expression such as motion_1 as well defined and *incomplete* regarding other senses of the term in order to maintain consistency. However, all the various senses of motion are nevertheless still references to an overall *idea* of motion (otherwise we would not refer to them as *motion* with *sub*scripts), which as an idea undergoes self-transformation in its identity as further reflections are made.[8]

In dialectic logic, the various terms e, e′, e″ are so regarded as referring to only *one* content, namely e, seen in a mode of continual redefinition—a redefinition

[8] Such self-transformations of concepts reflect the dialectic nature of consciousness or the Self, i.e. an activity that manifests itself by becoming transformed through self-consciousness: i.e. $(R)S = S'$ or a reflection on Self produces a higher order notion of self that includes itself in relation to the not-self or the objects of consciousness. Hence S′ is the dialectic unity $S \leftrightarrow O$, where S is Self, subject or field, and O is World, object or events.

that is part of the implicit definition of the original e. Dialectic logic, dealing directly with the problem of identity within difference, regards notions as vehicles of *conscious expression* that have continually to expand their delimited boundaries in order to be true to the indeterminate temporal nature of consciousness. For this reason dialectic logic would be a fruitful ingredient in the area of conceptual model-building since it addresses itself not to the primary data of a particular science as such, but to the developed or quasi-developed theoretical structures *of* the sciences. Dialectic ought therefore to be an integral part of *meta-science,* i.e. that discipline which has as its task the problem of ascertaining criteria for choosing *which* plausible hypotheses or conceptions—out of a whole set of possibilities *each* one of which could equally well apply to the requirements of primary data—would be in better form for *expressing insight and predicability* that leads beyond the *given* data: the subject matter of meta-science is the *history* of theoretical structures and thus involves the *temporal* development of scientific *consciousness.* Meta-science analysis is thus open to empirical validation since the effectiveness of theory can be judged in time. In this way dialectic is intended as a bridge between science and phenomenology, making the subject-object structure of consciousness, viewed as a field-event complex productive of dialectic opposition, the *criterion* of meta-science analysis. Conceptions must be *both* objective and subjective, displaying oppositions as distinct *and* inseparable, and any theoretical structure showing a tendency to express its elements in a one-sided (abstract) way would require reformulations transcending these reductionisms to reified self-identical absolutes: *ultimate* particles, *absolute* velocities, *complete* unity or duality, *rigid* bodies, *total* vacuums, *complete* indeterminacies, etc. would have to be transcended. The aim of dialectic analysis would be one of investigating primary formulations, reformulating conceptions which lead either to incompleteness or inconsistencies due to claims of rigid *identity.*

Recognizing, therefore, that the law of Identity is a subset to a larger and more encompassing law of Non-Identity is tantamount to recognizing that negation and contradiction, far from opposing affirmation and identity, are rather an integral aspect of identity seen now as the identity *of* non-identity, or the being *of* becoming, i.e. seeing that to be is to become and face the anxiety of non-being.

> But the life of spirit is not one that shuns death, and keeps clear of destruction; it endures death and in death maintains its being. It only wins to its truth when it finds itself utterly torn asunder. It is this mighty power, not by being a positive which turns away from the negative . . . on the contrary, spirit is this power only by looking the negative in the face and dwelling with it. This dwelling beside it is the magic power which converts the negative into being. That power is just what we spoke of above as subject [consciousness], which by giving determinateness [negation] a place in its substance, cancels abstract immediacy [i.e. that which is void of being concrete and related to its opposite] i.e. immediacy which merely *is,* and by so doing becomes the true substance, becomes being or immediacy that does not have mediation [negativity-determination] outside it, but is this mediation itself.[9]

6. *Expansion of Dialectic Logic into Higher Order Reflections*

We will now briefly indicate, given the principle of Non-Identity, how higher order levels of reflection manifest themselves as dialectic matrices displaying

[9] *Phenomenology of Spirit,* p. 93–94.

triadic movement in several dimensions simultaneously. Calling the self-negation term $(e) \leftrightarrow (-e)$ by the symbol $(--e)$, thus reflecting the double-implication and double-negation structure of the self-negation operation (negating *both* e and -e), the *initial* triad obtained through (R)e involves the terms (e); (-e) and (--e). The expression (--e) also indicates that the synthesis term $+-e$ is a negation of the negation of the original e, in that it is a *return* to the non-positive and non-negative nature of the original e, seen however on a more developed plane.[10] We can now write: $(R)e = (A \rightarrow N\text{: } S)e = (Ae \rightarrow Ne\text{: } Se) = ((e) \rightarrow (-e)\text{: } (--e)) = e'$, where A, N and S stand for the assertion, negation and self-negation operators.

The problem remains as to what the second order reflection $e'' = (R)e' = (R)(R)\,e = (A \rightarrow N\text{: } S)(A \rightarrow N\text{: } S)e$ entails. Let us write $(R)e' = (Ae' \rightarrow Ne'\text{: } Se')$, and since $e' = (A \rightarrow N\text{: } S)e$, we get the following: $e'' = (R)e' = (A(A \rightarrow N\text{: } S)e \rightarrow N(A \rightarrow N\text{: } S)e\text{: } S(A \rightarrow N\text{: } S)e)$. This can be better seen as a two-dimensional structure or matrix:

$$\begin{Bmatrix} Ae' \\ \downarrow \\ Ne' \\ \because \\ Se' \end{Bmatrix} = \begin{Bmatrix} A(A\rightarrow N{:}S)e \\ \downarrow \\ N(A\rightarrow N{:}S)e \\ \because \\ S(A\rightarrow N{:}S)e \end{Bmatrix} = \begin{Bmatrix} AAe\rightarrow ANe{:}ASe \\ \downarrow \quad \downarrow \quad \downarrow \\ NAe\rightarrow NNe{:}NSe \\ \because \quad \because \quad \because \\ SAe\rightarrow SNe{:}SSe \end{Bmatrix}$$

(formal matrix)

$$= \begin{Bmatrix} ((e))\rightarrow & ((-e)){:} & ((--e)) \\ \downarrow & \downarrow & \downarrow \\ (-(e))\rightarrow & (-(-e)){:} & (-(--e)) \\ \because & \because & \because \\ (--(e))\rightarrow & (--(-e)){:} & (--(--e)) \end{Bmatrix} = \begin{Bmatrix} (e') \\ \downarrow \\ (-e') \\ \because \\ (--e') \end{Bmatrix}$$

(logical interpretation)

[10] The *immediate* form of self-negation, seen as a direct union of e and -e, would be --e, which, like -e, can only be *implicit:* -e and --e *appear* only through reflection, and thus in the *form* (-e) and (--e).

Thus levels of assertion, negation and self-negation correspond to writing levels of e, -e and --e within ordered parentheses. The immediate observation is that nine terms appear, involving four non-synthesis terms (AA, AN, NA, NN), four partial syntheses (AS, SA, NS, SN) and one complete synthesis SS. The diagonal of the matrix AA, NN, SS represents the complete second level Thesis, Antithesis and Synthesis.

In order to obtain an *intuitive* grasp of the above two level triad of nine terms, it must be remembered that *dia*lectic logic is essentially a two-valued (two-formed) logic, involving a continual cyclic feedback relation between the e and o or assertion and negation inherent in the original eo or (e) $\leftrightarrow$ (-e) term. This means that upon reflection, the presence *of e* is a reference to the absence *of o,* and the presence *of o* is a reference to the absence *of e.* Now the function of the Assertion operator has been to *leave-present* that which *is* present. Hence Ae is a reference to the presence of e, and Ao is a reference to the presence of o. On the other hand, Negation has been conceived of as a reference to that which is not-present or *absent.* Now with e present, o is absent, while with o present, e is absent. Thus it follows that Ne must be a reference to the presence of o, and No must be a reference to the presence of e. But if we set Ne equal to o, then No or NNe must be a reference to the presence of e: a negation of the *negation of e* must reflect the presence of that which the *negation of* e says is absent, namely e. From this point of view, a continual negation process on e, such as NNNN. . . . . e gives rise to a *cyclic* series: e, o, e, o etc., reflecting the co-relativity of mutual implication between e and o—between e *itself,* or "in-itself," and e as *its other* or "for-itself." However, at the same time, each operation must preserve as a negative presence the previous stages it has negated. Hence a sequence such as e o e coming from NNe should be written as e, o(e), e(o(e)) indicating that the second e of the sequence appears from a previous o, which in turn appeared from a previous e. Thus the act of cyclic repetition is actually an asymmetric process of transformation, since no complete *return* to the initial condition of *pre*-reflective immediacy is possible: it is ever present as a negative context.

Thus a double negation of e NNe or (- (- e)) is not purely *cyclic* (i.e. where NNe is the *same* e), nor is it purely *linear* (i.e. where NNe is not e, but a third element *different* from e or o), which standard classical and intuitionalistic logics are respectively. A dialectic double negation is a combination of both, i.e. it is *spiralic,* meaning that it returns to the same element on a new level, a higher level in that (- (- e)) must have a reference to the original e that has been *negated* and which must of necessity be negatively present.

Starting with e as an unreflected term, the sequence Ae, Ne, Se of the *first* reflection can intuitively be written as e(e), o(e), eo(e) respectively, indicating that the *triple* sequence (e → o: eo) *originated* from an *unreflected e* (now appearing within parentheses) by a *single* act of reflection, giving us (R)e = (e(e) → o(e): eo(e)).[11] Thus, remembering that the A operator leaves present any symbol combination, the N operator replaces any e symbol by an o, and any o by an e, and finally that the S operator *combines* the

[11] Thus Ae or the *Assertion of* e means to reflect *on* e, *leaving it* present, yet the very reflection called "leaving e present" implies a change of state: the e *left* present is now a *mediated* e–i.e. an e that exists in juxtaposition with its opposite possibility "*not* to leave present." Hence writing Ae = e(e) indicates that the immediate non-oppositional e is transcended yet preserved *within* a parenthesis, replaced by itself as a mediated e existing *outside* the parenthesis. Ne is naturally o(e)–e being replaced by o–and Se is eo(e)–e being replaced and seen *as* the transcending movement or relation eo.

result of A and N together in the *order* A + N (i.e. Se is the relation eo and *not* oe, indicating that (R)e = (e → o: eo) is a transition *from* e, the initially present, to eo), we are now prepared to interpret the *second* order matrix in terms of the *intuitive* symbols e and o. In order to simplify symbolic appearance, we shall drop the common reference, from the *first* reflection, which *all* terms have to their origin term e:[12]

$$\begin{Bmatrix} AAe \rightarrow ANe : ASe \\ \downarrow \quad \downarrow \quad \downarrow \\ NAe \rightarrow NNe : NSe \\ \cdot\cdot \quad \cdot\cdot \quad \cdot\cdot \\ SAe \rightarrow SNe : SSe \end{Bmatrix} = \begin{Bmatrix} Ae \rightarrow Ao : Aeo \\ \downarrow \quad \downarrow \quad \downarrow \\ Ne \rightarrow No : Neo \\ \cdot\cdot \quad \cdot\cdot \quad \cdot\cdot \\ Se \rightarrow So : Seo \end{Bmatrix}$$

$$= \begin{Bmatrix} e(e) \rightarrow o(o) : eo(eo) \\ \downarrow \quad \downarrow \quad \downarrow \\ o(e) \rightarrow e(o) : oe(eo) \\ \cdot\cdot \quad \cdot\cdot \quad \cdot\cdot \\ eo(e) \rightarrow oe(o) : eooe(eo) \end{Bmatrix} = \begin{Bmatrix} e'(e') \\ \downarrow \\ o'(e') \\ \cdot\cdot \\ e'\ o'(e') \end{Bmatrix} (R)e'$$

(Intuitive matrix)

It is clear that the dialectic e o eo process is happening in two dimensions simultaneously. In the original first level triad, eo is the negative unity of e and o, all three of which now become the *given* elements of a second reflection (the given element for a first reflection being the original e). The entire triad is called e′, and a second reflection (R)e′ producing e′ (e′) → o′ (e′): e′ o′ (e′) means that the *result* of the first reflection e′ appears negatively present within parentheses at each stage. This means that each stage of the second triad will itself have reference to the ne-

[12] The NNe term *would* be e(o(e)) if *both* second *and* first order reflections retained reference to previous terms: for the first reflection NNe would be No(e), and the second No(e) would be e(o(e)). However, we are writing NNe = No = e(o) with the understanding that *all* terms *derive* from e.

gated first level *triad* e′, giving us a triad of triads or nine terms. The first triad e′ (e′) is none other than e, o, eo itself, now seen as a double structure, both itself as the *past* origin (within parentheses) and itself as *still present* (un-negated). The second triad o′ (e′) then *inverts* the e o eo or e′ relation, giving us o e oe or o′, i.e. a *counter*-triad, and the final second level triad e′ o′ (e′) *combines* the initial and inverse triads e′ o′, giving us an e and o relative to e (called eo(e)), an inverse e and o relative to o (called oe(o)) and the combined movement eooe relative to eo (called eooe(eo)).

Intuitively, this second order reflection, and all others, can be represented as a tree of continual expansion by mutual interpenetration:

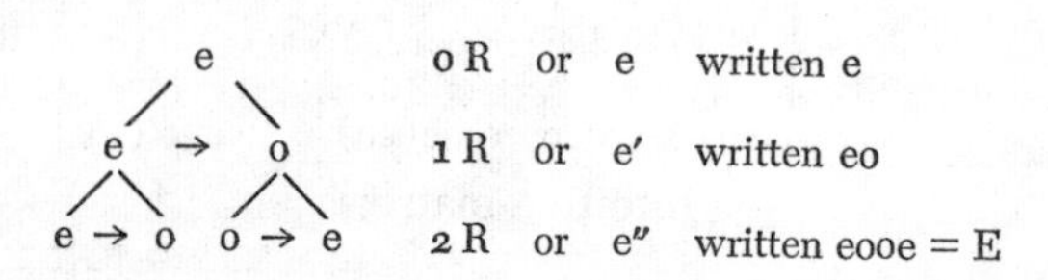

Reflection is an outward movement from the initial e to its contrary o such that every element generated *likewise* mirrors a movement from itself to its contrary. The eo synthesis of the first reflection, being a *negative* unity, means that while e and o are co-relative, they are not identical. Since e and o are *distinct* while united, this can only mean that the unity eo *between* e and o must appear reflected *within* e and o themselves, as indeed any boundary between e and o (i.e. eo is a boundary) must also be a boundary *of* e and a boundary *of* o: a boundary does not "exist" by itself. Hence what appears as an "external" synthesis between e and o on the first reflection now becomes internalized within e and o on a second reflection: e becomes a movement from e to o (i.e. e within-itself reflects as part of *its* meaning the boundary condition eo by reflecting a reference to o) and likewise o becomes a movement from o to e, such that a second reflection is an explicit *self-reflection:* an overall movement from e (within e) *to an externalized e* (within o). The term eooe means that e has been *self-determined through its other,* and this is written E: instead of merely being *other*-bounded as in e → o, we have a condition of *self*-boundedness, *eo* → *oe.* The diagonal of the intuitive matrix e(e), e(o), eooe(eo) spells out the net movement of the second matrix. Clearly the first three terms within the "e column" (e(e), o(e), eo(e)) of the intuitive matrix represent the e, o synthesis relative to e, the "o column" represents the e, o synthesis relative to o, and the "eo column" represents the e, o synthesis relative to itself: eo is now both e to o *and* o to e.

A third order reflection would make every e and o another double term, giving us a movement from e o o e to eo oe oe eo, or a movement from E to O, where O is the self-determination of o: oeeo. Just as the second reflection eooe or E is a negation of the negation of the zero order e, the third reflection EO is a negation of the negation of the first order eo: even number reflections are e-directed and odd numbered ones are o-directed. In the limit, there would not be any level of relation *between* two terms on level n that is not a reflection *within* the terms on level n + 1. The Absolute would represent a state of complete interpenetrability—something not expressible within a finite number of levels. For in any *finite* order, the last sequence of e and o terms would appear *either* inconsistent *or* incomplete. Either the e and o terms on the *last* level appear distinct and separable, preserving their individuality but not expressing their various forms of negative unity within-themselves as further sub-components, or the last level regards each of the e and o terms as expressing their unities within themselves on the *same* level, meaning that, while complete, the system is inconsistent, for now every e is both e and o identically: e and o become inseparable but indistinct. Only with an infinite progress can we express both completeness (inseparability) and consistency (distinctness), for the unity produced by a coupling relation always demands a further and deeper level of possible sub-relations *ad infinitum* such that there is *neither* an ultimate (indistinct) unity producing inconsistencies *nor* an ultimate (separable) duality producing incompleteness. It is as if we had two types of paint, one black, e, and the other white, o, which because they are co-relative, are infinitely mixed such that in *essence* black is distinct from white, but in *existence*, they are inseparable, no *particular* region of white existing without black in it and vice versa. Unity and duality have been transcended by an infinite system of levels: the Absolute is the very process of this continual transformation and redefinition, and does not appear at any *particular* stage as such, expressing rather the *principle* of Non-Identity that to be is to become, and becoming is the foundation of being.

With such a matrix structure, it is possible to give an unambiguous interpretation to the philosophical *structure* of Hegel's system, showing how the *Phenomenology* and the *Encyclopedia* form a single whole. According to a detailed analysis given in my thesis, "The Dialectic of Consciousness in Hegel's *Phenomenology of the Spirit,*" the original element e, starting the dialectic, is the *un*reflected subject S, representing the initial state of a given persisting *presence* which is in-itself the potential contradiction of being both itself and its negating objects or events. The nature of the pure (unreflected) subject lies in its being potential Spirit: a reflection on S gives us the first triad ($S \rightarrow O$: SO) or (reflected) subject, object and subject-object experience. This is S′ or what Hegel calls the state of *pure* sensation. Out of sensation or S', develop S', O' and $S'O'$, called sensation, perception and conception (understanding). Hence sensation or $S' = SO$ is a movement from subject to object (i.e. the subject revealing its dependency upon a sensed object), perception or $O' = OS$ is a counter-movement from object back to subject (i.e. the object in turn revealing its dependency upon a perceiving, looking and interpreting subject), and conception is the combined movement from subject to object and object to the now externalized (i.e. non-original) subject–a subject externalized by means of the objects it is dependent upon: conception is SOOS or S''. Instead of $S \rightarrow O$: SO, we have now $S' \rightarrow O'$: $S'O' = S''$. In conception we have a self-negation or self-mediation of pure sensation: the subject senses or sees its *own* essence within the external world of objects, formulating objects according to trans-objective laws and rules of behavior. However, it was shown that higher order relations would reveal a continual interpenetration of subject and object, revealing not only modes of external consciousness, but self-consciousness, and *their* combinations, until the Absolute at the end expresses the *state* of infinite subject-object interpenetrability that *has been* for a fact always been express*ing* itself.

However, once the Absolute is *revealed*, a new level of infinite-valued relations appear. For a reflection on the Absolute itself reveals three component Absolutes within the Absolute, i.e. *each* of the three generating components S, O and SO is *itself* infinite, reflecting the *entire* S, O dialectic *within* itself from its *own* perspective. The nth level of reflection ($S, S', S'' \ldots S^n$), $S^n \rightarrow O^n$: S^nO^n, will give $S^\infty \rightarrow O^\infty$: $S^\infty O^\infty$, as n goes to infinity (∞). Now the nth level of reflection generates the $n + 1$ level (e.g. $e' \rightarrow o'$: $e'o'$ is called e''). A reflection (meta-reflection) on S^∞ would thus give $S^{\infty+1}$, which is however still S^∞

since infinity plus one is still infinity. Indeed, the $S^{\infty+1}$ term is formed by combining the three S^{∞}, O^{∞}, $S^{\infty} O^{\infty}$, terms together (as e.g. the *nine* terms of e″ is the combination of the three *three-termed* e′ o′ and e′o′ elements), but three infinities still give infinity: $3\infty = \infty$. Thus each sub-part is in a one to one correspondence with the whole, which is the defining characteristic of an infinite totality. According to a tentative analysis, it appears that the three sub-infinities correspond to the triadic division of Hegel's *Encyclopedia:* Logic (S^{∞}), Nature (O^{∞}), and Spirit ($S^{\infty}O^{\infty}$). This means that the infinite subject S^{∞} is regarded as the Logic or Essence of the *Phenomenology* taken as a whole, wherein all reference to an *external* object has already been mediated in principle *within* an all-pervading and persisting subjective or inner presence. Similarly, the infinite object O^{∞} is regarded as the external or object counter-part to Logic, namely Nature or the Existence of this Logical essence, wherein all reference to a subject appears mediated within the external, negating object. Within Logic, the subject matter becomes the *conceptions* of ontology, namely Being, Becoming etc., and within Nature the subject matter becomes the objectified counter-parts to Being, namely a space-time, matter in motion analysis. Thus the *Phenomenology* of Subject-Object analysis represents *Being,* being defined, since Hegel clearly indicates in his *Logic* (p. 84) that ". . . pure Being is the unity into which pure knowledge returns," which is to say that the Absolute of pure knowledge obtained from the *Phenomenology* appears as an overall totality called pure Being—the starting point for Hegel's Metaphysics (*Encyclopedia*). Hence Metaphysics for Hegel is a type of Trans-Phenomenology, and Being is defined solely in terms of the Absolute nature of consciousness: the phenomenological condition of subject-object interaction.

There is no Being except that which in its *immediacy* is in essence completely self-mediated. "It is in this respect that Pure Being, the absolutely immediate, is also absolutely mediated."[13]

Finally, the synthesis of Logic and Nature is the infinite Subject-Object experience called Spirit itself, $S^{\infty} O^{\infty}$, which represents the Spirit or Reality of the *Phenomenology,* i.e. the combined "inner-outer" subject-object mode of presence in which *no* reference is made to subjects or objects *in-themselves.* Here Hegel deals with such notions that are explicitly objective *and* subjective, namely notions of the animate soul as a mind-body complex serving as the basis for self-world and self-self interaction. The point which is essential to realize, however, is that the regions of Logic, Nature and Spirit entirely overlap: there is no separate logical, natural and spiritual world. Essence, Existence and Reality, Subject, Object and Experience, Logic, Nature and Spirit, being infinite subtotalities of an infinite total, are merely three different *modes* of viewing one and the *same* universe. Each is a *concrete universal* in itself, including all other three within itself: each is both *particular* yet *universal,* i.e. the *universal relation* between the three "parts" S, O, SO called $S \rightarrow O$: SO is reflected within *each part* on every level. Hence there is no "mysterious jump" from Logic to Nature: they are *co-relative as infinite* totalities. Neither is there a radical jump from the *Phenomenology* to the *Encyclopedia.* Rather the transition is a transition from *finite* subject-object analysis, to *infinite*-leveled subject-object analysis, wherein one takes the perspective of an infinite process *as already completed in essence.* The *Phenomenology* studies the whole *as a process,* and the *Encyclopedia* studies the process *as a whole,* in terms of variables each of which is regarded as essentially infinitely mediated within

[13] *Science of Logic,* I, 84.

itself. This gives the *Phenomenology* a temporal character, and the *Encyclopedia* its a-temporal flavor, but they are really two sides of the same coin—of whole-process or whole-part dialectic. The Absolute does not exist "in time," but is rather the process of temporality itself—the eternal presence of continual transcendence, whose parts existing "in-time" each reflect the a-temporal whole of transcendence.

"Triad building" is therefore not a *linear* process, in which one mechanically goes from thesis to synthesis and again from thesis to synthesis. As with all things of subtlety in the modern world, it is non-linear and multi-dimensional, giving rise to triadic movements existing simultaneously on several levels. As an example of what a nine-term matrix would look like, let us look at Hegel's analysis of Becoming. The initial triad of Being (B), Nothing (N) and Becoming (BN), has already been described. The state of becoming or B′ = BN upon reflection becomes internalized within being and nothing, respectively, producing notions called dynamic being BN(B) and dynamic nothing NB(N). Using a simplified "e o eo" type matrix we get:

B *Being* →	N Nothing :	*BN* *Becoming*	= B′
↓	↓	↓	
N(B) Passing →	B(N) : Arising :	NB(BN) Equilibrium	= N′
··	··	··	
BN(B) Dynamic → Being	NB(N) Dynamic: Nothing	*BNNB*(BN) Dynamic Equilibrium: *the Being of Becoming*	B′N′ = B″

Starting with the zero state of pure Being, the first reflection reveals that Being manifests itself in two forms: Being "in itself" or B and Being "outside of itself" or Nothingness N. Becoming as the synthesis expresses the condition that any immediate notion of presence or Being B will reveal itself as a state of Becoming BN, in which any mode of B is placed in relation to its contrary N. The triad as a whole is called B′, which upon a second reflection in turn will reveal the negation of Becoming, N′ and the self-negation of Becoming, B′N′. The negation of becoming is a type of "anti-becoming" in that every movement from B to N makes possible a counter movement from N to B: i.e. any negated state of Being will have to reveal Being once again. This inverse state we shall call Equilibrium N′ or NB(BN) indicating that the negated BN becomes balanced by an inverse NB. However, the synthesis of B′ and N′ gives us something which is neither becoming nor in equilibrium as such, but rather a state of dynamic equilibrium in which becoming *self*-negates itself. This means that we have a system in which becoming gives rise to an equilibrium B′ → N′ which still has reference to the *originating* state of becoming N′ → B′ not as something *negated,* as in Equilibrium, but as something co-existing with it. This means that we must have a double movement from B to N and N to B giving BN NB, or a state in which whatever is becomes negated *in order to* reveal itself once again *out* of the state of negation. Being *maintains* itself through a process of becoming, i.e. Being returns to itself not within itself, but by having itself manifested through and from its opposite, Nothingness. As a *whole,* we have a state of Being or equilibrium since B moves into itself in BNNB, but only by virtue of a self-negating activity in which every component *part* is in a state of becoming or anti-becoming. As with the notion of the conservation of momentum, the system as a *whole* is in equilibrium, but each of the *component* elements are subject to change and becoming, such that every positive change is off-set by a negative change. This describes the Being *of* Becoming. Reflection from B to B′ to B″ is a movement from *Being* to *Becoming* to the *Being of Becoming.*

Relative to the variables B and N, a second reflection on Becoming amounts to a crossing of terms, such that each becomes an explicit function of the other, *within* itself. Thus N(B) means Nothingness coming or having come from Being or what Hegel calls "Passing Away," and B(N) means Being having come from Nothingness or "Arising." The synthesis of Passing and Arising is that which is neither as such, i.e. the state of Equilibrium. Thus Being and Nothing combine to give the boundary state of Becoming, which breaks up into two sub-boundaries called Passing and Arising, which in turn combine and transcend themselves into Equilibrium. However, the complete picture demands that both B and N reveal the entire *triadic* movement of B and N co-relatively *within* themselves—giving us B (or B(B)), N(B) and BN (B) and N, B(N), and NB(N). Here Being is viewed as that which *within* itself has the property of passing into or displaying negation (BN(B)), i.e. Being as dynamic is potential Nothingness, while Nothingness is the potential of arising Being. In modern physics, the essence of a particle is not its mass but its energy from which the particle is seen as that which can be annihilated as a localizable particle. Similarly, the modern vacuum is seen as potential being, displaying field-energy properties which have the ability to *create* particles.

Thus a second order reflection reveals that the opposites are now not simple Being and Nothing, giving simple Becoming, but rather the opposites appear self-mediated into Dynamic Being and Dynamic Nothingness such that a unity *of Being* and *Nothing* already exists *within each* term as a potential unity, meaning that the unity of Being and Nothing BN is really a *double* unity or a unity of unities. When B and N appear as BN, we really express a unity of BN(*B*) and

NB(*N*) giving BNNB(*BN*). The Becoming which results is thus a two-level state of becoming expressing the becoming (self-negation) of becoming or the Being of Becoming. The diagonal of the matrix presents the net result: Being moving *into itself* as an externalized Being through the vehicle of its own negation (and thereby *internalizing* N between itself as B moves into B), written $B \rightarrow B(\mathrm{N})$: *B*NN*B*(BN), or more fully as $B(\mathrm{B}) \rightarrow B(\mathrm{N})$: *B*NN*B*(BN).

Having outlined the essential structure of dialectic logic, three main tasks remain. First would be a detailed analysis of Hegel's philosophy, seeing how well the actual structure (of the *Phenomenology* and *Encyclopedia*) and the proposed matrix interrelate. A superficial analysis of the table of contents of Hegel's *Logic,* for example, seems to indicate that it might be possible, with minor changes, to regard the transitions outlined in his triadic structure as equivalent to triadic changes in e, e′, e″ etc. Being, Nothing, Becoming would be e o eo, which as a whole is labelled Being (Total Being) or e′. The second triad of (Total) Being, Determinate Being and Being-for-self would be e′, o′, e′o′ which is called Quality or e″. This would make Total Being a type of Becoming, Determinate Being a type of Equilibrium, and Being-for-Self a type of Being-of-Becoming according to our previous analysis of B′ N′ B′N′. The third triad is Quality, Quantity and Measure or e″, o″, e″o″ which is called Being (in General) or e‴. Quality would have the structure E = eooe and Quantity O = oeeo, indicating that quantity represents *externality* "o" or Negation "N" in a state of self-determination in which N returns to itself *through an externalized B:* Quality is the *internalization* of Non-Being and Quantity is the *externalization* of Being. Finally the fourth triad is Being EO, Essence OE and Concept EOOE or e‴, o‴ e‴o‴, giving e⁗, which is the Logic itself explicated in four steps. It is interesting to note that, from this perspective, EO or Being (in General) is regarded in the mode of becoming, i.e. *Quality* E revealing Quantity O, while Essence, starting from externality regards *Quantity* O in the mode of re-revealing Quality E as its *inner* nature, making the Concept or Logic EOOE the *self*-determination *of Quality.* Thus for EO or Being, the terms Quality and Quantity, E and O or "inner Being" and "outer Being" are simply opposed as *immediates* E vs. O or *EO;* for Essence E and O *mediate* each other giving O(E) and E(O) as the components of Essence or *OE*(EO), and for Concept E and O *self-mediate* themselves, *each* being a function of *both* or EO(E) and OE(O): in Concept, EOOE, inner being reveals *itself* from any externalized being. We have a self-determination of a *whole* in EOOE in which *each element* (i.e. E and O) is *itself* self-determined. The generating principle 3^n, where n = 4, thus gives 3^4 or 81 *basic* categories obtained by only *four* reflections! It would be possible, however, to extend the analysis indefinitely, each time increasing the subtlety and complexity present by a more *detailed* explication in depth of the ever-present Absolute of infinite interpenetrability. Thus Hegel's system would have to be regarded as essentially *open*, subject to continually higher modes of reflection.

A second task remaining is that of subjecting the entire formal and logical treatment of the matrix to a rigorous logical-mathematical analysis especially in relation to Goedel's theorem. Finally, matrix analysis, within the manifested spheres of Nature and Spirit, has the task of interpreting the concrete natural and social sciences from a *meta-science* point of view, hopefully giving structural insight into complex notions such as space, time, matter, motion, organic systems, feedback mechanisms, ego and ego-ego systems, as they appear both objectively and subjectively. Perhaps in this way, the Hegelian structure, viewed now as a modern temporal logic of Non-Identity and levels of negation, can help synthesize and orient modern theories of science by means of a language and form more suitable to the style in which problems are now formulated. In this way, dialectic would become an essential structure of philosophic speculation, grounded upon a firm basis capable of formalization and projecting conceptions open to empirical validation within an historically developing consciousness, dealing with notions that underly the foundations of human and natural existence.

X. HEGEL ON FREEDOM

Richard L. Schacht

No concept is more central to Hegel's philosophy than his concept of freedom. He refers to "freedom realized" as "the absolute end and aim of the world" (PR, §129).[1] His *Philosophy of Right* is really a discussion of freedom, for he holds that "freedom is both the substance of right and its goal, while the system of right is the realm of freedom made actual" (PR, §4). Freedom is also the central concept in his philosophy of history: "World history," he says, "is the progress of the consciousness of freedom" (RH, p. 24). Hegel further terms freedom the very essence of spirit or mind (*Geist*): ". . . the essence of spirit—its substance—is freedom" (RH, p. 22). And since on his view spirit is not merely man's basic nature but also the fundamental principle of reality, freedom is suggested to be the nature of that most basic of metaphysical categories, the Notion or Concept (*Begriff*): "The Notion is the principle of freedom, the power of substance self-realized" (LH, §287).

This essay was written especially for this volume.

[1] In identifying citations from Hegel, I shall employ the following abbreviations:

LH—*The Logic of Hegel* (Wallace's translation of the *Lesser Logic*).

PS— *Phenomenology of Spirit* (translated by Baillie as *Phenomenology of Mind*).

PM—*Philosophy of Mind* (Wallace's translation of the third part of Hegel's *Encyclopedia*).

PR— *Philosophy of Right*.

RH—*Reason in History* (R. S. Hartman's translation of the Introduction of Hegel's *Philosophy of History*).

As in the cases of so many of his other concepts, however, Hegel's concept of freedom is rarely clearly understood. He is frequently accused on the one hand of presenting a concept of freedom too abstract to have any bearing on real life, and on the other, of merely giving lip service to the concept of freedom while in reality taking a kind of quasi-totalitarian position diametrically opposed to the exercise of real freedom.[2] It is true that his understanding of freedom is not identical with that of many philosophers—not to mention men in the street. But such accusations only show that those who make them have not read Hegel very carefully. If it is true, as he remarks in the Preface to his *Phenomenology of Spirit,* that "the familiar is not understood simply because it is familiar," it is all the more true that the *un*familiar will never be understood. One may in the end decide to reject Hegel's idea of what true freedom involves. But if one rejects it, one ought at least to do so for reasons relating to what he actually holds.

In what follows, I shall attempt to clarify his view of freedom and then briefly consider what is to be made of it. While I shall have something to say about freedom in the context of his philosophy generally, I shall concentrate upon his discussion of it in connection with the concepts of the will, personality, subjectivity, and "ethical life"—in short, his discussion of freedom in his *Philosophy of Right.*[3] His logic, philosophy of nature, and philosophy of history may contain little that would profit philosophers today; but quite the opposite is true of his *Philosophy of Right.*

[2] See, e.g., pp. 291f. below.

[3] Hegel covers the same ground in the third part of his *Encyclopedia,* §§469–552. But the *Philosophy of Right* is more accessible, more readable, and more detailed; and, most importantly, it represents Hegel's final statement of his views on freedom and subjects relating to it.

Before turning to Hegel himself, it is helpful to take notice of certain concepts and views of several of his predecessors that bear importantly upon his discussion of freedom. His insistence upon the continuity of his philosophical views with those of his predecessors is well known, and the present case is one in which this continuity is significant and illuminating.

I

In his *Essay Concerning Human Understanding*, Locke gives the following definition of liberty: "*Liberty* . . . is the power a man has to do or forbear doing any particular action according as its doing or forbearance has the actual preference in the mind; which is the same as to say, according as he himself *wills* it" (II.21.15). Hume gives a virtually identical explication of liberty in his *Enquiry Concerning Human Understanding:* "By liberty . . . , we can only mean *a power of acting or not acting, according to the determinations of the will;* that is, if we choose to remain at rest, we may; if we choose to move, we also may" (Section VIII, Pt. I; p. 103). Concerning these characterizations of liberty, which may be taken to represent a fairly commonsensical understanding of freedom, several points should be noted: First, what is at stake is the source of determination of some particular course of action. Second, the decisive consideration is taken to be that of whether the individual's course of action is one that he himself has decided upon; when his will is done, his action is considered free. In other words, liberty or freedom is here conceived in terms of self-determination in the realm of action. And third, both Locke and Hume consider liberty or freedom so conceived to be quite compatible with determinism; both deny that human actions that satisfy their definitions have the status of uncaused events, and hold that such actions are subsumable under general laws no less than are natural events.

Next, several Aristotelian ideas should be noted that have a greater relevance to Hegel's understanding of freedom than may be immediately apparent. One is the idea that things—or at least substances—have essences. "The essence of each thing is what it is said to be *propter se*. . . . What, then, you are by your very nature is your essence" (*Meta.* VII: 4; 1029b). Not that which is peculiar to the individual, but rather the trait or traits in virtue of which his species is set off from others, constitute his essence. So, for example, Aristotle conceives man's essence in terms of rationality, on the ground that "what is peculiar to man" is the "life of the rational element" (*Nich. Eth.* I: 7; 1098a).

Another relevant Aristotelian notion is that of the distinction between potentiality and actuality. Aristotle employs the distinction in connection with "coming-to-be" generally: ". . . for coming-to-be necessarily implies the pre-existence of something which *potentially* 'is,' but *actually* 'is not'; and this something is spoken of both as 'being' and as 'not-being'" (*Gen. et Cor.* I: 3; 317b). Applied to a discussion of essence, this suggests the possibility of something that exists and is potentially a thing of a certain sort but has not yet come to be actually what it is potentially. A child, for example, as a human being, is according to its essence a rational being, but it may be rational only potentially, and not yet actually.

Finally, notice should be taken of Aristotle's conception of two sorts of "originative source of change." He distinguishes between "originative source of change in another thing or in the thing itself *qua* other" (*Meta.* IX: 1; 1046a). Both sorts may be seen to be operative in the case of an organism such as an animal. The movements of animals, which appear to be their own doing, are "not strictly originated by them," according to Aristotle; rather, the "originative source of change" here is to be found in the animals' environment (*Phys.* VIII: 6; 259b). When we consider not their movements but their growth to maturity, on the other hand, we are confronted with a "change" that has its "originative source" in the animal itself. The law of its development is contained in it itself. Of course, its growth and development require the proper environmental conditions. But when these are present, it is "through its own motive principle" that the changes in the organism constituting its growth toward maturity occur. This process might be characterized as the organism's self-realization, the actualization of its essence not through an external agency but through its own.

Spinoza's God embodies the principle of self-determination much more completely than do Aristotle's organisms; and in Spinoza this principle is explicitly associated with the idea of freedom. Spinoza gives the following definition of a free being: "That thing is called free which exists from the necessity of its own nature alone, and is determined to action by itself alone" (*Ethic,* Pt. One, Df. VII). Something is free, for Spinoza, only if it contains within itself not only the "originative source" of all that it does once it is in existence, but also the source of its own being—in short, only if it is *sui causa.* That which "by another is determined to existence and action" is not free, but rather "compelled" (*ibid.*). Freedom so conceived cannot be a property of any particular existent, but rather only of God; thus Spinoza says, "God alone is a free cause" (*Ethic,* Pt. One, Prop. XVII, Corol. 2).

Since what is essential to freedom on Spinoza's view is complete and absolute self-determination, freedom is by no means incompatible with necessity. On the contrary, he often speaks of "the necessity of the divine nature" and holds that every actual attribute of God is a necessary one. Similarly, he sees no incompatibility between the notions of freedom and of law. God acts according to laws and yet is free, because "God acts from the laws of His own nature only, and is compelled by no one" (*Ethic,* Pt. One, Prop. XVII). It is in the absence of dependence upon and determination by an external agency, rather than the absence of necessity and subjection to law, that freedom as Spinoza conceives it consists. Freedom does not even imply that one is subject only to laws of one's own *making;* God did not choose what "the laws of His own nature" would be. It is necessary that these laws should be what they are. What makes God free is the fact that they are not imposed upon him from without. They are not laws of his own making, laws he has given to himself, but rather "laws of His own *nature*" —of his very essence. Of course, if his nature had some external source he would not be free. But it is not determined by anything external to himself; he is *sui causa.*

Among finite things, according to Spinoza, matters are otherwise. No finite thing is *sui causa* with regard to either its nature or its existence. The human will is no exception: "The will cannot be called a free cause, but can only be called necessary." For "it requires a cause by which it may be determined to existence and action" (*Ethic,* Pt. One, Prop. XXXII). Human action thus constitutes no exception to the determinism that prevails throughout nature, on Spinoza's view. The actions of God alone are truly self-determined and therefore free.

Finally, reference must be made to several ideas of Kant's.[4] Spinoza calls the free being he discusses "God"; he conceives this "God" not in terms of self-

[4] Citations are from his *Critique of Pure Reason,* tr. Norman Kemp Smith; henceforth "KRV."

consciousness or will, however, but rather as "substance." Thus he speaks of "God, or substance consisting of infinite attributes, each one of which expresses eternal and infinite essence . . ." (*Ethic*, Pt. One, Prop. XI). This substance consisting of infinite attributes is eternal, determined by nothing external to itself, and the cause of all finite things, but it is not a self-conscious subject. It is precisely of such a subject, on the other hand, that Kant predicates freedom: "There is in man a power of self-determination, independently of any coercion through sensuous impulses" (KRV, A534/B562). Indeed, Kant goes so far as to hold that being free involves acting under the idea of freedom; or at least, that it is the consciousness of freedom we have in the consciousness of obligation that shows freedom to be more than a theoretical possibility.

In attributing freedom to a being that is not a self-caused, eternal substance consisting of infinite attributes, but rather a finite subject having the character of reason, self-consciousness, and will, Kant thus differs radically from Spinoza. He agrees with Spinoza, however, in conceiving of freedom in terms of self-determination, as the above passage indicates; though he does not conceive of it as extending to one's very existence, as Spinoza does. One can be said to be free only if one's will is not determined by any external agency but, rather, autonomously. Kant further agrees with Spinoza that nothing that is merely a part of nature is self-determined in this way; but unlike Spinoza, he does not feel that the human will falls entirely into this category. He argues that it is not self-contradictory to suggest that there is in man a faculty capable of initiating a new causal series in the world—a *causa noumenon;* or, as he says, "that causality through freedom is at least *not incompatible with* nature" (KRV, A558/B586). Kant is quite certain that reason as such is free, or self-determined:

"We can *know*," he says, "that it is free, that is, that it is determined independently of sensibility" (KRV, A557/B585; emphasis added). The only question, on his view, is whether or not it can be said "to have causality with respect to appearances." That this is "at least possible" is a fact that he contends can be established on purely theoretical grounds (KRV, A548/B576). And he finds a practical confirmation of this idea in the experience of moral obligation, which he takes to be incompatible with the view that the will is not autonomous. "That our reason has causality, or at least that we represent it to ourselves as having causality, is evident from the *imperatives* which in all matters of conduct we impose as rules upon our active powers" (KRV, A547/B575).

For Kant as for Aristotle, man's reason sets him apart from all merely sensuous existence. Indeed, he regards it as definitive of man's essential (noumenal) nature. If the determining ground of the will is reason, therefore, the will is self-determined in a way in which it is not when its motive principle is some mere natural impulse. For the determining principle of one's volition then lies in one's own rational nature, rather than in some agency external to it. If one were not essentially a rational being, action from a law prescribed by reason would not be free, for it would not in any sense be self-determined. Kant is able to term such action free, however, precisely because of his conception of man's essential nature in terms of reason. Action determined by a law prescribed by reason is free because it is self-determined—determined, that is, by a principle that is constitutive of one's own essential nature. It should be observed, however, that for Kant only the form of the law actually derives from reason; the content, on the other hand—as in the case of perception—derives from nature.

One further point remains to be noted: Kant's distinction between "negative freedom" and "positive freedom." He says of the freedom associated with reason: "This freedom ought not . . . to be conceived only negatively as independence of empirical conditions. The faculty of reason, so regarded, would cease to be a cause of appearances. It must also be described in positive terms, as the power of originating a series of events" (KRV, A553–54/B581–82). Our freedom thus has both a negative aspect and a positive aspect. To say that an action is free in the negative sense is simply to assert that it is not determined by any agency external to the will of the acting agent. It does not follow, however, that a free action is an undetermined one. Rather, it is one that has its "determining ground" in something other than "empirical conditions," namely, reason. To say that an action is free in the positive, fuller sense is to make this explicit. It is only when reason prescribes laws, and action is based upon them, that action is free in the positive sense. And action is not even free in the negative sense, short of this. Freedom is actual, or action is actually free, only when reason has prescribed a law and when the will is determined in accordance with it.

II

With these views of Hegel's predecessors in mind, a preliminary account of his own understanding of freedom in relation to theirs may now be given. As a first approximation, he would accept Locke's and Hume's explications of freedom in terms of the self-determination of one's actions. He would agree with Kant, however, that if what prompts one to act in a certain way is some mere impulse or inclination, one's action is not really free at all. For then the decision or choice upon which the action is based does not have its "originative source" or "determining ground" in the mind of the agent at all; rather, it is just as completely determined by the operation of laws of sensuous nature as is any other natural event. Hegel readily allows that many human actions have precisely this character: they are free in the Lockean and Humean sense that they are what the agent has decided or chosen to do, but they are not free in the sense that what the agent decides or chooses to do is determined by natural laws.

He differs from Locke, Hume, and Spinoza, however, and agrees with Kant in holding that a more significant sort of self-determination—freedom that is not the mere illusion of freedom—is possible: namely, self-determination at the level of the decision on which the action is based, or, in Hume's phrase, in "the determination of the will" itself. Like Aristotle and Kant, Hegel holds that man has an essential nature, and conceives of that essential nature in terms of thought or reason. "Thinking," he says, in a manner reminiscent of Aristotle, "is the characteristic property by which man is distinguished from the beasts, [while] he has feeling in common with them" (PM, §400). And like Kant, he further holds that reason is capable of providing men with laws on which practical decisions can be based; so that, when their determinant is a law of reason, they are determined by a principle constitutive of the individual's essential nature. As such, they are self-determined, and are therefore free. A person is free, for Hegel as for Kant, if and only if the "determining ground" of his practical decisions is nothing external to reason, but rather is reason itself. Human freedom, therefore, is to be conceived not simply in terms of the self-determination of one's actions in accordance with one's will, but rather in terms of their *rational* self-determination, or determination in accordance with a will the principle of which is a law of thought rather than a law of mere nature.

It would not be entirely accurate to say simply that

Hegel rejects the idea of freedom as caprice or the ability to do whatever one wants, in favor of the idea of freedom as action in accordance with a law of thought or reason. He does reject the former view of freedom, but only because he quite agrees with the determinists that actions answering to these descriptions, far from being truly self-determined, remain in the toils of nature. He adopts the latter view of freedom because he sees in action determined in accordance with laws of reason the only alternative to action governed by natural laws. In the Aristotelian notion of development in accordance with a law of one's own essential nature, and in the Spinozistic notion of freedom as action in accordance with the same, Hegel saw the idea of a kind of action that did not require the assumption of the existence of uncaused events, but that at the same time answered to the description of independence of external agency. Such action alone, he felt, could truly be said to be self-determined, and therefore free. As for Kant, therefore, freedom for Hegel cannot be conceived merely negatively, as "independence of empirical conditions." It must also be conceived positively, in terms of conformity to a law of reason. For action is independent of empirical conditions only where it has its "originative source" in the only other place it could have it: namely, in reason.

More remains to be said, however; Hegel holds that action is truly free only if it involves self-determination that is not only rational but also *self-conscious.* If one's self-determination in accordance with one's rational nature does not take place consciously, as in the case of Spinoza's God (whose nature was that of a substance rather than a self-conscious subject), it has the character of a blind and mindless necessity. Kant had maintained that freedom can be predicated only of a self-conscious subject, and that action is free only when it is determined not only in accordance with a rational principle but also under the idea of freedom; and it was this in which Hegel felt the superiority of his understanding of freedom over Spinoza's consisted. To be sure, an action is not free on Hegel's view merely if it is self-consciously self-determined; it must further be determined in accordance with a law of reason. Yet it also is not truly free—though it may be said to be *implicitly* free—if its determining ground is a law of reason but is not self-consciously so determined. Freedom, for Hegel, is thus to be conceived in terms of self-conscious rational self-determination rather than in terms of self-determination *simpliciter,* though in spelling it out in this way Hegel took himself simply to be making explicit what the idea of self-determination essentially involves when applied to a thinking being.

III

At this point it might seem that Hegel's understanding of freedom does not differ significantly from Kant's. In point of fact, however, Hegel breaks decisively with Kant on a number of counts—even while granting that Kant does have an essentially correct and adequate grasp of the concept of human freedom. Perhaps most fundamentally, Hegel rejects the Kantian notion of the thing-in-itself and with it the idea that the will has a noumenal as well as a phenomenal existence, upon which Kant bases his entire discussion of freedom. It may be, as Kant argues, that it is *not self-contradictory* to suppose that there is in man a *causa noumenon*, or faculty of initiating a new causal series in the world; but, for Hegel, such a supposition has no cogency whatsoever. The only thing-in-itself of which it makes any sense to speak, on his view, is the system of reason that constitutes the essential structure of all appearance. This system of reason, however, does not constitute a noumenal world over against the phenomenal. It does not exist at all except in so far as it is embodied in phenomena. And there are no noumenal entities of any sort—material, psychic, or divine. The experience of freedom of which Kant makes so much is taken by Hegel not to indicate that the will has a noumenal as well as a phenomenal existence, but rather to reflect the fact that what are commonly referred to as the laws of nature do not govern the whole of phenomenal reality. And Kant's real service in stressing it, on Hegel's view, was not that he showed it to provide a practical proof of the non-phenomenality of the will, but rather that he supplied an important corrective to Spinoza's characterization of freedom by bringing out that freedom involves acting under the idea of self-determination.

Hegel further differs from Kant on the matter of the law or laws of reason, in relation to which self-determination may become rational. For Kant, action is free only if the law on which it is based derives from reason. Actually, however, for Kant it is only the *form* of the law (universality) that derives from reason; its content derives from nature, i.e. from our natural inclinations. On Hegel's view, action based on a law of this sort is still action in the toils of nature. It is only if the whole of the law—its content as well as its form—derives from reason, that it truly deserves to be called a law of reason; and it is only if action is based on a law of this sort that it deserves to be called self-determined in accordance with reason, and therefore free. Hegel contends that virtually any maxim having as its origin some natural inclination can pass the test of universalizability. The requirement of reason that the maxim of one's action be universalizable, therefore, does not of itself eliminate the natural basis of the determination of action and replace it with reason. In short, if reason could do no more than impose this requirement upon us, it would follow, on Hegel's view, that rational self-determination would be but an empty phrase and freedom would still be but an illusion.

This, however, is not Hegel's conclusion, for he holds that reason is by no means so limited in what it can do. Rather, he contends that it can and does give rise to laws the content as well as the form of which derive from it itself. And to the extent that these laws are made the basis of one's actions, rational self-determination ceases to be an empty phrase and becomes a genuine reality. For action then ceases to have its originative source in natural inclination, and instead is rationally determined through and through. Kant failed to discover the existence of such laws, because he did not look for them in the right place; or perhaps because he failed to grasp what Hegel takes to be the true significance of the phenomena that constitute these laws: namely, the laws and institutions of the social order.

Hegel holds that these laws and institutions, which constitute what he terms the "substance" of a "state," are by no means a mere conglomeration of practices bearing no relation to rational principles. On the contrary, he contends that they are to be viewed as an inherently rational system, manifesting the Idea or system of reason itself in concrete form. They "are not accidental, but are rationality itself," and the state they collectively constitute is "the divine Idea as it exists on earth" (RH, pp. 49, 53). The establishment of this thesis is one of Hegel's central aims in the *Philosophy of Right*. He holds that it is in these laws and institutions, and in them alone, that the individual can find a basis for the determination of his actions that is rational and, so, in conformity with his essential nature, and that guarantees their independence of mere impulse and inclination. To the extent that the individual determines his actions in accordance with them, therefore, and only to this extent, he is rationally self-determined and thus free. "For law is the objectivity of spirit; it is will in its true form. Only the will that obeys the law is free, for it obeys itself and, being in itself, is free" (RH, p. 53).

Though once again it must be added that he is truly free, according to Hegel, only if he apprehends that in determining his actions in accordance with these laws and institutions he is determining them in accordance with the very reason that constitutes his essential nature, rather than something alien and external to him. His awareness of them has the character of a "knowing presence to him of his own essence of rationality" (RH, p. 52). His actions are rationally determined, and he is conscious of the fact that, in so acting, the only necessity he is obeying is one that derives from his own essential nature. His freedom is not the freedom of caprice; but such freedom is no true freedom at all—rather, it is merely a disguised form of subjection to natural laws. He cannot be said to have given the law of his actions to himself, since the law of his actions is determined by the nature of reason itself. But, like Spinoza's God, he is at least subject to no laws other than those of his own essential nature, and therefore is self-determined. And this is the only form of freedom, on Hegel's view, that it is possible for man to enjoy. "The rational, like the substantial, is necessary. We are free when we recognize it as law and follow it as the substance of our own being" (RH, p. 53).

IV

Having given this preliminary characterization of Hegel's conception of freedom, and before considering his development of it in his *Philosophy of Right* in more detail, I should like to comment briefly on two of his more general and speculative contentions involving references to freedom: namely, that freedom realized is "the absolute end and aim of the world," and that the Hegelian Absolute—the *Begriff* (Notion or Concept)—"is the principle of freedom."[5] The former contention already becomes more comprehensible when taken in conjunction with the latter; for if there is an Absolute, and if the ultimate end and aim of the world is conceived in terms of it (as would only be reasonable), and if, further, this Absolute is to be conceived in terms of freedom, then it quite logically follows that the end and aim of the world is to be conceived in these terms as well.

It remains, then, to determine what could have led Hegel to characterize the Absolute in terms of freedom. And this is not difficult if one bears in mind that he understands freedom in terms of self-conscious rational self-determination. For the Absolute is conceived by Hegel precisely in terms of self-determination, rationality, and self-consciousness. As Absolute, it quite obviously must be self-determined; for if either its existence or its nature were dependent upon anything external to it, it would not be absolute. Further, as Hegel states in the Preface to the *Phenomenology of Spirit,* it has a twofold nature: it is both substance and subject.[6] Considered as substance, it has the character of a system of reason; hence the appropriateness of the terms Idea and Notion or Concept. Its specific determinations therefore are preeminently rational. At this point it is well to recall Spinoza's Absolute—God or substance, conceived as a self-determined, rational system—and his characterization of it as free.

Spinoza's basic error, on Hegel's view, lay in his failure to realize that the Absolute is not only substance so conceived, but also subject. Self-

[5] See p. 289 above.
[6] Kaufmann tr., p. 388.

consciousness is just as essential to it as is its substantial nature. The term *Begriff*, as a more concrete specification of the nature of the Absolute, has a double appropriateness: it conveys the idea of a conceiving or conscious apprehending as well as the idea of a concept or system of reason. It is only when the system of reason is grasped in consciousness—only when it achieves the form of self-consciousness—that it is something actual. Simply in itself, it lacks the form of existence—contrary to Spinoza, for whom the existence of the substance is inseparable from its pure essence. For Hegel, the nature of the Absolute does require that it exist; but that is because it is to be conceived not only as substance or pure essence, but also as subject or self-consciousness. Just as, on Hegel's view, Spinoza's understanding of freedom must be modified to the effect that freedom is to be conceived in terms of *self-conscious* rational self-determination; so also he contends that Spinoza's conception of the Absolute must be modified in such a way that reference is made not only to its self-determined, rational structure, but also to the form it takes in its actual existence—namely, self-consciousness. The Absolute or the *Begriff* is thus conceived by Hegel in terms of self-determination, rationality, and self-consciousness. And since self-conscious rational self-determination is freedom, as Hegel understands it, he employs this term to convey the general nature of the *Begriff* in a nutshell, saying, "The *Begriff* is the principle of freedom."

Hegel's use of the term "freedom" in his metaphysics may thus be seen to be both comprehensible—once it is seen how he is using this and certain other terms—and consistent with his use of the term in his less metaphysical writings, such as the *Philosophy of Right.* It is upon these writings, however, that current interest does and perhaps should largely center. For this reason, I shall devote the remainder of my discussion to his conception of freedom as it is developed in them.

V

It is perhaps best to begin, as Hegel does in the *Philosophy of Right*, with a consideration of the question of the freedom of the will, before turning to the question of the relation of freedom to social institutions.[7] He elsewhere observes that "the term 'freedom,' without further qualification, is indefinite and infinitely ambiguous. Being the highest concept, it is liable to an infinity of misunderstandings, confusions, and errors and may give rise to all possible kinds of extravagances" (RH, p. 25). At the very outset of his discussion, therefore, he undertakes to remove the misunderstandings and confusions so commonly associated with the use of the term, by considering precisely how the notion of the freedom of the will is to be understood.

The first point to be made is that the will is not to be conceived as a mental faculty distinct from thought or reason. It is essentially nothing other than "thinking reason resolving itself to finitude" (PR, §13R)—that is,

[7] The *Philosophy of Right*, in its present form, consists of numbered paragraphs to which Hegel himself frequently appended Remarks, and to many of which Additions have been added, derived from notes taken at Hegel's lectures. I shall identify quotes by giving Hegel's paragraph numbers, adding an "R" when the material cited appears in a Remark, and an "A" when it occurs in an Addition. The Additions obviously do not have the authority of what Hegel himself submitted to print. They are often illuminating, however; and because they are generally considered to be reasonably faithful to what Hegel actually said, I shall on occasion draw upon them. I have followed Knox's translation, except where a rendering different from his has seemed to me to be desirable. (See, e.g., p. 309, Note, below.)

thought in its practical employment, engaged in determining a course of action in the world, choosing and deciding what to do. In saying that the will is "the point of origin" of freedom (PR, §4), Hegel is not associating the idea of freedom with some extrarational principle, but rather is simply suggesting that it is thought, in so far as it is concerned with action, with which one is dealing in speaking of freedom. "As will, the mind steps into actuality; whereas as cognition it is on the soil of conceptual generality" (PM, §469). He continues to speak of "the will," but this doubtless is merely because it is more convenient to do so than to use such cumbersome formulations as "thinking reason resolving itself to finitude." It is important to keep in mind that this is a terminological convenience rather than a label for some mysterious faculty. Men are thinking beings who engage in action; and Hegel's talk of "the will" merely specifies that what he is considering is thought applied to action.

It is, then, necessary to distinguish the question of whether willing is something *determinate* from the question of whether it is something *determined.* The will, on Hegel's view, is both indeterminate and determinate. It is indeterminate in the sense that I have the "ability to free myself from everything, abandon every aim, abstract from everything" (PR, §5A). That is, willing is not to be associated with any specific course of action; no particular decision is implied by the general ability to decide. The act of deliberation involves a consideration of alternatives, and therefore a disassociation, at least in principle, of the deliberating consciousness from the particular alternatives before it. In this sense, the will contains an "element of pure indeterminateness" (PR, §5).

On the other hand, actual willing or deciding always involves resolving upon *some* particular course of action. In this sense, an act of willing is always determinate. I cannot will without willing this rather than that; I cannot act without acting in some specific or determinate way. The will, therefore, whenever it is concretely active, is determinate. And it is something actual only when it is active. If freedom is conceived merely in terms of its "pure indeterminateness"—that is, merely negatively—then it is conceived in such a way that freedom and action exclude each other. Such freedom amounts to nothing in the world of action. It constitutes an essential moment of true freedom, in that "freedom itself is to be found only in the reflection of spirit into itself" (PR, §194R). That is, freedom involves a consciousness of oneself as independent of everything determinate; and such a consciousness emerges with the awareness of the "pure indeterminateness" of the will. By itself, however, such freedom is abstract and insubstantial. In this "unrestricted possibility of abstraction from every determinate state of mind which I may find in myself or which I may have set up in myself . . . we have negative freedom, or freedom as the Understanding conceives of it. This is the freedom of the void" (PR, §5R). If the concretely active will is to be considered free, its freedom must be recognized to contain both an element of indeterminateness and an element of determinateness. So Hegel says:

> Freedom lies neither in indeterminateness nor in determinateness; it is both of these at once. . . . Freedom is to will something determinate, yet in this determinateness to be by oneself and to revert once more to the universal (PR, §7A).

So far, nothing has been said that affects the issue of whether or not the will, in settling upon some determinate course of action, is *determined* or *undetermined.* For the indeterminateness associated with the ability to disassociate oneself from everything determinate does not imply that one's decision to pursue this or that particular course of action is not determined. On the contrary, it is quite compatible with the deterministic thesis that every particular decision made and every particular action undertaken is determined by the laws of nature. It is for this reason that the question of the will's determinateness and indeterminateness must be distinguished from the question of whether particular volitions and actions are determined or undetermined.[8]

Hegel is in complete agreement with the determinists in so far as they are concerned to deny that decisions are or can be undetermined by general laws and that even the most spontaneous and arbitrary decisions have the status of uncaused events. He grants that people often make decisions that may be described as arbitrary, and that they are often accompanied by a feeling of spontaneity. He contends, with the determinists, however, that this does not establish that they originate solely in "the will of a single person in his own private self-will" (PR, §29R) and are independent of everything external to "his own private self-will." On the contrary, he holds that they are determined by inclinations and impulses that are subject to general laws of sensuous existence. As such, they are not in fact self-determined at all; and the feeling of spontaneity is but the illusion of freedom.

[8] In his translation of the *Philosophy of Right,* Knox confuses the issue by employing the terms "determinacy" and "indeterminacy" both when Hegel is discussing the issue of the will's determinateness and indeterminateness and when he is discussing the issues of whether or not determinate volitions are determined and in what ways they may be determined. He has as an excuse the fact that Hegel uses the same German terms in both cases. But he would have done better to avail himself of the alternate English renderings of these terms, to bring out the difference between the two issues with which Hegel is dealing.

> Determinism has rightly pointed to the content which, as something met with, . . . comes from outside. . . . Since, then, arbitrariness has immanent in it only the formal element in willing . . . while the other element [i.e., the content of the volition] is something given to it, we may readily allow that, if it is arbitrariness which is supposed to be freedom, it may indeed be called an illusion (PR, §15R).

It should be observed that this is Hegel's conclusion wherever the content of a decision derives from a natural impulse or inclination, whatever its form may be. It thus applies even when the form is that of self-consistent universality. Kant, in other words, still leaves us with but the illusion of freedom.

Yet this is not the end of the matter; for, though determinate decisions are always determined in accordance with general laws, it does not follow that the only laws in accordance with which they may be determined are those governing mere sensuous existence. Decisions could still be free if the laws in accordance with which they were determined were laws deriving from the individual's own essential nature; for then they would in a significant sense be self-determined, even if not by "the will of a single person in his own private self-will." This in fact is possible, according to Hegel. The will can be free—but only in the sense that "its self-determination consists in a correspondence between what it is in its existence . . . and its concept," i.e., its essential nature (PR, §23). The will is thought in its practical employment; and thought, Hegel holds, is essentially rational. To the extent, therefore, that particular decisions are based upon laws deriving from reason, they are self-determined in the above-mentioned sense. This may not be the way in which freedom is ordinarily understood; but Hegel is saying that self-conscious rational self-determination is the only alternative to remaining subject to the laws governing all natural existence —the only sort of freedom man can have that is more than the mere illusion of freedom.

Such freedom, it perhaps goes without saying, is not a birthright, except as a potentiality. For example, "Children," Hegel says, "are potentially free and their life directly embodies nothing save potential freedom." Yet theirs is "a freedom still in the toils of nature" (PR, §174). And adults no less than children remain merely potentially free, and in the toils of nature, unless and until they realize their potential freedom by basing their decisions upon laws deriving from reason and apprehending themselves as obeying the law of their own essential nature in doing so. For since freedom is conceived not in terms of the ability to choose, but rather in terms of self-conscious rational self-determination of one's actions, it is not a reality in the life of an individual unless his actions are in fact so determined. Then and only then is his will free not merely potentially, and free not merely in the abstract and negative sense of pure indeterminateness, but free actually and in a concrete and positive sense.

It should be observed that though this conception of freedom does differ from the ordinary understanding of freedom, it is not so far removed from the ordinary understanding of what freedom involves as to no longer deserve to be called freedom at all. For freedom is ordinarily conceived in terms of self-determination; and Hegel, starting from this idea and preserving it throughout, simply attempts to show what is involved in the only sort of true self-determination of which we are capable. It so happens that much of what we ordinarily take to be self-determined is not, and that true self-determination involves acting along lines of which we are not used to thinking in these terms. But the concept of freedom itself that emerges from Hegel's discussion preserves at least the basic outlines of our ordinary concept of freedom; and therefore his retention of the term is not unreasonable.

VI

So far, we have been dealing only with Hegel's development of the *concept* of freedom—a development that is presented only as the Introduction to his *Philosophy of Right.* The body of the work is devoted to a consideration of what is involved in the emergence of freedom as a reality in the world, or freedom as Idea. It consists of a presentation of the developmental sequence that, if completed, results in actual self-conscious and rational self-determination in the actual practical life of the individual. Hegel distinguishes three basic stages in this developmental sequence. In brief: In the first, self-determination becomes a reality, in the sense that a sphere is marked out in which the actions of the individual are not subject to the direction of anyone else, but rather are determined by his own decisions and choices. In the second stage, a self-consciousness emerges in which the individual comes to understand his essential nature properly; i.e., not in terms of his particular characteristics and idiosyncracies, but rather in terms of rationality and universality. And in the third stage, his concrete decisions and choices—and therefore his actions—are brought into line with his essential nature, acquiring the character of rationality and universality, through their determination in accordance with a set of objective laws and institutions that are rational and universal in nature. With the conclusion of this development, the practical life of the individual has the character of self-conscious rational self-determination, and thus freedom is an existing reality.

Hegel begins by observing that freedom is nothing in the absence of the opportunity to act without let or hindrance by others; and that it is the existence of things, together with the establishment of property rights in relation to them, that first of all affords us and secures for us this opportunity. He says:

> If the free will is not to remain abstract, it must in the first place give itself an embodiment, and the material primarily available to sensation for such an embodiment is things, i.e., objects outside us. This primary mode of freedom is the one which we are to become acquainted with as property, the sphere of formal and abstract right. . . . The freedom which we have here is [that of] what is called a person (PR, §33A).

The sort of freedom I have when an external sphere is secured in which I can do as I please, however, is only freedom in an "abstract" sense, according to Hegel. For it is only in an abstract sense that I can be said to be self-determined in so acting. My actions are self-determined in that they are not determined by the will of anyone else. To conceive of self-determination simply in these terms, however, is to conceive it in a merely negative and superficial way. A more adequate understanding of it cannot be achieved until attention is diverted from the action in so far as it is unhindered and uncoerced by others, to the action in so far as it is determined by oneself. This involves a shift of attention from the objective (the action) to the subjective—the choice or decision determining the action, and more basically the self making the choice or decision. The sort of freedom now before us is termed "subjective," in that it involves a consciousness of oneself as the determining source of one's decisions and choices. What has been added to freedom of the former sort is this element of explicit self-consciousness. And this is an important addition:

> In this way a higher ground has been assigned to freedom; the Idea's existential aspect, or its moment of reality, is now the subjectivity of the will. Only in the will as subjective can freedom or the implicit principle of the will be actual (PR, §106).

Hegel's point is relatively simple. One cannot really be said to be free so long as he is not explicitly aware of himself as being free. The consciousness of oneself as free is not itself a guarantee of true freedom: it may be only the illusion of freedom, and is compatible with determinism. But it is a necessary condition of true freedom in that if one does not grasp one's actions as deriving from decisions and choices of one's own making, they cannot truly be said to be one's own. To act unhindered by others, and yet to do so unself-consciously and without explicitly viewing one's act as one's own, is to be free at most only in principle, or in Hegel's terms, implicitly. Self-determination that is not self-conscious is a poor sort of freedom.

Thus Hegel distinguishes subjective freedom, or the freedom of the subject, from abstract freedom, or the freedom of the person, in terms of the explicit self-consciousness that distinguishes the *subject* from the *person,* who lacks it: "This reflection of the will into itself and its explicit awareness of its identity makes the person into the subject" (PR, §105). The individual's attention ceases to be absorbed in the things on which he acts and goes further than his freedom from coercion by others: "Its personality—and in abstract right the will is personality and no more [i.e., is not self-conscious]—it now has for its object" (PR, §104). Freedom is now associated not merely with the right of the individual to do as he wants with what is his, but rather with the more fundamental "right of the subject to find satisfaction in the action" (PR, §123)—

> . . . to recognize as its action, and to accept responsibility for, only those presuppositions of the deed of

> which it was conscious in its aim and those aspects of the deed which were contained in its purpose (PR, §117).

But now the question arises of the content of the aim and purpose on the basis of which the subject self-consciously determines his actions, and of the origin of this content. For he can be said to be truly self-determined only if he himself is the origin of this content—only if this content on the basis of which he decides and chooses is itself self-determined. Initially, however, the subject differs from the person only in that the "person" has the character of unself-conscious personality, while the "subject" has the character of self-conscious personality. The content of the aims and purposes of the subject, therefore, still reflects the nature of personality. Personality, according to Hegel, is to be conceived in terms of "a differentiation and singling out of the modes which nature gives; we find it as the special temperament, talent, character, physiognomy, or other disposition and idiosyncracy, of families or single individuals" (PM, §395). The content of the aims and purposes determining its action, therefore

> . . . the still-abstract and formal freedom of subjectivity possesses only in its natural subjective embodiment, i.e., in needs, inclinations, passions, opinions, fancies, etc. The satisfaction of these is welfare or happiness (PR, §123).

The *welfare or happiness* of the particular self-conscious person—the subject—is the result of his self-conscious determination of his actions in accordance with such things as these. But is he thereby also free in so far as he is able to achieve such satisfaction? Hegel's answer is that, once again, we are dealing with something that can be called freedom only in an "abstract and formal" sense. Although self-consciousness has now been added to the absence of coercion, the individual whose aims and purposes are determined by factors of the sort mentioned above is still not truly self-determined. For if they are determined by the particular configuration of "the modes which nature gives" that constitutes his personality, they are not truly self-determined; rather, they are ultimately determined by the natural laws that govern the occurrence and interaction of these modes. One's self-consciousness of self-determination notwithstanding, therefore, the individual enjoys but the illusion of true freedom or self-determination so long as the content of his aims and purposes is a function of the needs, inclinations, passions, etc., associated with his particular personality. Hegel finds a basis for the determination of action other than a configuration of "the modes which nature gives," yet one that accords with the individual's own essential self, in the objective and determinate system of "ethical life" (*Sittlichkeit*)—and only in it.

> Ethical life is the Idea of freedom in that on the one hand it is the good become alive, . . . while on the other hand self-consciousness has in the ethical realm its absolute foundation and the end which actualizes its effort. Thus ethical life is the concept of freedom developed into the existing world and the nature of self-consciousness (PR, §142).

The term "ethical" here has a sense rather different from that which it ordinarily has in English usage. The German term *Sitte* means "custom"; and while Hegel does not simply have customs in mind in speaking of *Sittlichkeit,* he does have in mind something similar: namely, the laws and institutions of a social, cultural, and legal nature that inform the life of a people. It is Hegel's contention, in the above passage, that true freedom is to be found only in self-conscious self-determination, in accordance with such laws and institutions. They constitute "a stable content independently necessary and subsistent in exaltation above subjective opinion and caprice" (PR, §144). In so far as they determine one's aims and purposes, therefore, these aims and purposes have a content quite different from that which they have when they derive from the particular personality of the individual—a content, moreover, that is inherently rational:

> It is the fact that the ethical order is the system of these specific determinations of the Idea which constitutes its rationality. Hence the ethical order is freedom or the absolute will as what is objective, a circle of necessity whose movements are the ethical powers which regulate the life of individuals (PR, §146).

This may seem to be rather paradoxical: the ethical order is said both to make freedom possible and to constitute a "circle of necessity" regulating the lives of individuals. For Hegel, however, there is no contradiction here; for he holds that an individual whose existence corresponds to his essential rational nature will be at one with the ethical order and its laws and institutions:

> They are not something alien to the subject. On the contrary his spirit bears witness to them as to its own essence, the essence in which he has a feeling of his selfhood, and in which he lives as in his own element which is not distinguished from himself (PR, §147).

In ethical life all opposition between the individual and the ethical order vanishes; for the individual perceives his essential nature to be rational, and further perceives the ethical order to constitute a rational system. He thus sees that in determining his actions in accordance with the laws and institutions of the ethical order, he determines them not in accordance with an alien law, but rather in accordance with the law of his own essential nature. So Hegel says, "Duty is the attainment of our essence, the winning of positive freedom" (PR, §149A). Duty is not incompatible with self-determination if it is the law of one's own nature that determines one's duty. On the contrary, if this is the case, duty and self-determination coincide:

> The bond of duty can appear as a restriction only on indeterminate subjectivity or abstract freedom, and on the impulses either of the natural will or of the moral will which determines its indeterminate good arbitrarily. The truth is, however, that in duty the individual finds his liberation . . . from dependence on mere natural impulse. . . . In duty the individual acquires his substantive freedom (PR, §149).

It should be emphasized that in speaking of duty, Hegel has in mind neither the deliverances of the individual's own conscience, nor the categorical imperative, but rather the objective duties determined by the laws and institutions of the ethical order. They include, and indeed culminate in, the duties one has as citizen or member of the state. Hegel considers the state to be "the actuality of the ethical Idea" (PR, §257) because he holds that it is only with the emergence of the state that the laws and institutions informing the life of a people acquire the character of an integrated and complete rational system. This is the basis of his contention that "The state is the actuality of concrete freedom" (PR, §260). It should be observed, however, that Hegel's state is not one in which the interests of the individual—even *qua* particular person—are sacrificed to interests of the state that are inimical to those of the individual. On the contrary, it is Hegel's view that "my interest, *both substantive and particular*, is contained and preserved in another's, i.e., in the state's . . ." (PR, §268; emphasis added). The state as Hegel conceives of it is so constituted that as a member of it, I both attain that rationality in my actions which renders them self-determined and therefore renders me free *and* find my personal well-being secured and enhanced far beyond what would be possible in the absence of the state. This, at any rate, is the situation in the "genuinely organized" state; and it is only in so far as a state is "genuinely organized" that Hegel considers it to be "absolute rationality" (PR, §258) and "the actuality of the ethical Idea" (PR, §257).

> The essence of the modern state is that the universal is bound up with the complete freedom of its particular members and with private well-being. . . . The universal must be furthered, but subjectivity on the other hand must attain its full and living development. It is only when both of these moments subsist in their strength that the state can be regarded as articulated and genuinely organized (PR, §260A).

The force of these remarks is simply that the state of which Hegel speaks is not totalitarian: life in it is not so regimented that personality disappears. But this involves no retreat from the position that one is truly self-determined, and enjoys more than the mere illusion of freedom, only in so far as what one does is determined in accordance with an objectively existing law or institution. The fact that Hegel would allow much of what the individual does to be determined by his personal desires and inclinations, does not mean that he regards the status of such actions any differently than has been suggested above. Actions determined in this way are actions determined in accordance with "the modes which nature gives," and thus are determined in accordance with the general laws that govern these modes, rather than being truly self-determined. That there is occasion for actions of this sort is owing to the fact that reason is incapable of engendering a system of laws and institutions that would govern the whole of life. Laws regulating matters that Hegel leaves to personal discretion may in fact exist. A state in which there are such laws, however, is not a "genuinely organized" state on Hegel's view, since its laws are not strictly conformable to reason. In a "genuinely organized" state, certain matters are governed by laws and institutions, and others are not. In the case of the latter, the individual enjoys that sort of freedom discussed by Hegel in connection with personality and subjectivity. Such freedom, however, is not true freedom. The individual is truly free only where his actions are rationally as well as self-consciously self-determined—only, that is, where they are determined in accordance with objective rational laws and institutions.

VII

Knox, in his article "Hegel and Prussianism," suggests that Hegel's problem in the *Philosophy of Right* is this: "How is it possible to combine the individual Greek's complete devotion to his city with the modern emphasis on the paramount importance of individual freedom?"[9] No one would deny that his suggested solution captures well the first element mentioned. Many commentators question, however, whether the freedom he finds compatible with it deserves to be called freedom at all. E. F. Carrit, in his reply to Knox, gives expression to a common sentiment about the matter:

> No doubt Hegel professed (as who does not?) and even persuaded himself (as who cannot?) that he

[9] T. M. Knox, "Hegel and Prussianism," *Philosophy*, Vol. XV, No. 57, p. 53.

> was an admirer of freedom. And he managed to do this by giving the word a peculiar meaning of his own. Freedom is not the power of doing what you like (*P.d.R.* §15) nor what you think right (§140). He holds that those and only those are free who desire above all things to serve the success and glory of their State.[10]

Carrit, it would appear, holds that to be free is to be able to do what you like and/or what your conscience tells you to do. To be sure, one will not find Hegel's understanding of what true freedom involves appealing if one is committed to some such view of freedom. Aside from the fact that Carrit quite ignores Hegel's analysis of the concept of freedom, he fails to take account of the fact that Hegel thinks he has shown that what Carrit understands to be freedom is no true freedom at all. One may *prefer* to do what one likes, or what one's conscience dictates—this Hegel does not deny. He agrees with the determinists, however, that to do so is not at all to be self-determined, the feeling of spontaneity notwithstanding. To the protest "But this is what we *mean* by freedom!" he replies that, rather than rest content with an understanding of freedom that amounts to but the illusion of true self-determination, he prefers to associate the term with a type of action that does in fact answer to this description. This is hardly "giving the word a peculiar meaning of his own." Rather, it involves maintaining that the meaning of the word requires a different application of it from that which is customary if it is to have any true applicability at all.

This move is by no means as arbitrary and unreasonable as Carrit implies. It remains to be determined, however, whether or not Carrit is correct in asserting

[10] E. F. Carrit, "Discussion: Hegel and Prussianism," *Philosophy*, Vol. XV, No. 58, p. 194.

that in practice Hegel's reapplication of the term comes down to the following: ". . . those and only those are free who desire above all things to serve the success and glory of their State." This, it seems to me, is a ludicrous caricature of Hegel's actual position. To state Hegel's position as baldly as possible, those and only those are truly free who live in a rationally organized state, who desire above all things to do what their state requires of them, and who determine their actions in accordance with its laws and institutions. Even this is misleading, if it is not added that according to Hegel the rationally organized state will require of them only that which is in the "substantive and particular" interest of all concerned. He would reject the suggestion that such a state would pursue its "success and glory" at the expense of this twofold interest of its citizens. A state might do this; but to the extent that it did, it would not be the sort of state Hegel endorses. Even when he says that the individual must be prepared to sacrifice all when the state is threatened (PR, §324), he is not suggesting that the interests of the individual are to be subordinated to its "success and glory." Rather, his point is that the state is what makes possible both the maximum satisfaction of the individual's particular wants and needs and the realization of his essential nature and true freedom, and that he therefore must be prepared to make sacrifices to preserve the state, upon which his own interests depend.

One may conclude that objections of the sort made by Carrit are not legitimate ones, however, and still consider Hegel's account to fall short of being satisfactory. For example, it may be that in a "genuinely organized" state the laws and institutions would be such that the individual could embrace them without reservation. But, surely, few if any existing states are organized so adequately that their laws and institutions conform completely to "the ethical Idea" and have the character of "absolute rationality." Under these circumstances, one cannot be entirely happy with Hegel's disparagement of those who live in an ethical order and yet raise questions about what one really ought to do: were they serious, he says, "they would have clung to what is substantively right, namely to the commands of the ethical order and the state, and would have regulated their lives in accordance with these" (PR, Preface, pp. 3–4).

The basis of the individual's identification with the ethical order is supposed to be his recognition that it embodies the same rationality in terms of which his own essential nature is to be conceived. If, upon turning from Hegel's discussion of the genuinely organized state in the *Philosophy of Right* to his own state, the individual discovers significant discrepancies, and further finds the fault to lie in the organization of the latter, he will have a problem. He may agree that true self-determination consists in action in accordance with a rational system of objective laws and institutions, and therefore is impossible outside of the state. But if the laws and institutions of his own state are not rational, the determination of his actions in accordance with them can hardly have the character of self-determination for him. Hegel's suggestion, therefore, that true self-determination is in fact possible in this way is conditionally true at best; and the most obvious condition on which its truth depends is by no means as adequately satisfied as the position he adopts would seem to require.

Ultimately, of course, the plausibility of Hegel's understanding of what true freedom involves depends upon the plausibility of his conceptions of man's nature and of the nature of the ethical order. These are matters that lead straight to the heart of Hegel's metaphysics, and cannot possibly be gone into here. It should be clear, however, that it is Hegel's understanding of the natures of man and the world—rather than the Prussianism or the totalitarian inclination so often attributed to him—that leads him to take the position he does on the nature of human freedom and the relation between freedom and the state. One who would maintain that his position is untenable cannot merely point to the prevalence of a different understanding of what freedom involves, but rather must show the untenability of one or more of the views on which his position depends.

Hegel's line of reasoning may be briefly summarized as follows: To be free is to be self-determined. Indeed, it is to be self-consciously self-determined; for it would be inappropriate to term a being "free" unless it were aware of its determinations as its own. Further, to be free is to be self-determined not only in one's actions, but also in one's choosing and deciding to act in various ways. Self-determination implies not only the absence of coercion by other men, but also the independence of one's choices and decisions of any factors alien to one's self. In speaking of man's self, what is intended is not his merely physical or sensuous nature, but rather his true or essential self, which is to be conceived as mind or spirit. Mind or spirit, in turn, is to be conceived not in terms of the feelings, impulses, inclinations, and desires associated with mere physical or sensuous existence, but rather in terms of rational thought. Both sorts of phenomena are governed by laws; and all phenomena of human life are governed by laws of one sort or the other. The laws of reason, however, are not subordinate to or determined by the laws governing sensuous existence. They constitute a system determined by the nature of reason itself. One who determines his choices and decisions—and so also his actions—in accordance with laws of reason, therefore, is self-determined in a way in which one who determines them in accordance with his impulses and inclinations is not. He alone is truly free, for he alone is truly self-determined. A being who is essentially rational is self-determined only if he governs himself in accordance with the laws of his essential rational nature, and is thereby liberated from subjection to laws that are not laws of his own essential nature.

Man's essential rationality, however, does not of itself guarantee that the individual by himself is capable of governing himself in accordance with the laws of his essential rational nature, even if he should desire to do so. He has the capacity to come to think and act in accordance with reason; but he exists at least initially as a merely particular person, moved by natural needs and inclinations and having a determinate nature or personality the character of which is a function of the operation of the laws of sensuous nature. So long as the aims and purposes of his actions are determined subjectively, on his own, they can have no source other than his particular personality—which, as the determinists correctly observe, is by no means self-determined. This is so even when these aims and purposes appear as the dictates of conscience or are given the semblance of rationality through being universalized. The individual can escape the condition of non-self-determined particularity only if he can find an objective basis for the determination of his actions that is not subject to the influence of his particular impulses and inclinations. Such an objective basis obviously cannot be determined subjectively, on one's own; for nothing determined in this way can have the requisite objectivity or independence of subjective influences. There is only one thing that does have this character: the ethical order, with its objectively existing laws and institutions.

Of course, action determined in accordance with them could not be considered free at all if, in spite of their objectivity, they were something utterly alien to the individual's own nature. In the properly organized state, however, they are nothing other than laws of reason itself, concretely embodied; and as such they are not something alien to the individual's own nature at all. On the contrary, they embody objectively the very rational structure in terms of which the individual's essential rational nature is to be conceived. In determining his actions in accordance with them, therefore, the individual at once escapes the toils of nature and brings his actions into conformity with the law of his own essential nature. He thereby achieves rational self-determination in the only way in which it is possible for him to do so. To be free is to be self-determined. Here, and here alone, is one truly self-determined. Here, and here alone, therefore, is one truly free. It follows, of course, that true freedom becomes possible only with the emergence of the properly organized state as an existing reality. But this is a proposition that Hegel explicitly affirms. And it is only in this light that one can see why he attaches so much importance to the state.

A number of the contentions upon which Hegel's understanding of freedom depends seem questionable, to say the least—in particular, his characterization of man and of the state as essentially rational, and moreover as corresponding in their essential rational natures. Yet I wonder. Many irrationalist accounts of man's nature have appeared since Hegel wrote, and all discussions of man's nature have fallen into disrepute in recent years. Still, I would venture to suggest that there is something too obviously true to be denied in the observation that man has the ability to think rationally, and that there is something quite plausible about the contention that rational thought is central to all human activity in connection with which it is tenable to speak of genuine self-determination. Further, it may be that the metaphysical underpinnings of Hegel's theory of the state are implausible and that he exaggerated the rationality of the modern state. Still, I would venture to suggest that the laws and institutions of which he speaks do—or at least in principle can—provide a basis for the determination of action that raises it above the level of natural impulse and inclination and renders it more rational than it could be in the absence of such laws and institutions. Whether the elements of truth in what Hegel says about these matters—if they are such—are sufficient to establish the validity of his understanding of what freedom involves, either as it stands or in some modified form, is certainly open to question. It does seem to me, however, that a negative answer is by no means obviously indicated.

Works Cited

Aristotle, *The Basic Works of Aristotle,* ed. McKeon (New York: Random House, 1941).

Carrit, E. F., "Discussion: Hegel and Prussianism," *Philosophy,* Vol. XV, No. 58 (April 1940), pp. 190–97.

Hegel, G. W. F., *The Logic of Hegel,* tr. W. Wallace (Oxford: Oxford University Press, 1892).

———, *Phenomenology of Spirit,* Preface, tr. W. Kaufmann. Included in Kaufmann's *Hegel: Reinterpretation, Texts, and Commentary* (New York: Doubleday & Co., 1965). The entire work is translated by J. B. Baillie under the title *Phenomenology of Mind* (London: Macmillan & Co., 1949).

———, *Philosophy of Mind,* tr. W. Wallace (Oxford: Clarendon Press, 1894).

———, *Philosophy of Right,* tr. T. M. Knox (Oxford: Clarendon Press, 1942).

———, *Reason in History,* tr. R. S. Hartman (New York: Liberal Arts Press, 1953).

Hume, David, *An Enquiry Concerning Human Understanding* (La Salle, Ill.: Open Court, 1952).

Kant, Immanuel, *Critique of Pure Reason,* tr. Norman Kemp Smith (London: Macmillan & Co., 1963).

Knox, T. M., "Hegel and Prussianism," *Philosophy,* Vol. XV, No. 57 (Jan. 1940), pp. 51–64.

Locke, John, *An Essay Concerning Human Understanding* (London: Cummings & Hilliard and J. T. Buckingham, 1813).

Spinoza, Benedict (or Baruch), *Ethic,* tr. W. H. White. Included in *Spinoza Selections,* ed. John Wild (New York: Charles Scribner's Sons, 1930).

XI. HEGEL REVISITED

Shlomo Avineri

The varying and changing interpretations to which Hegel's political and historical theories have been subjected in his native Germany during the last 150 years run parallel to some of the basic trends in German intellectual history since the Napoleonic period. When the first Hegel Congress met in 1930 at the Hague, Hegel was virtually forgotten in Germany: in his inaugural address, Richard Kroner, one of the foremost Hegelian scholars in Germany, lamented the fact that while Hegel was widely influential abroad, his impact in Germany was hardly visible.[1] Today, a look at the present philosophical and political literature in Germany would give a very different impression. The bulk of the present literature on Hegel has not, however, achieved a consensus of opinion about either the meaning or the evaluation of the Hegelian legacy itself.

For ever since Hegel's own days, few philosophies have been subjected to so much uncritical praise and equally unjustifiable abuse as the Hegelian system. Not only philosophers, but also theologians, historians, sociologists, social scientists and social critics, historians of ideas—in short, almost everyone writing on modern intellectual life has his own image of Hegel and has to profess an attitude. While one can be luke-

Reprinted from the *Journal of Contemporary History*, Vol. 3, No. 2, 1968, by permission of the author and the editor of the *Journal of Contemporary History*.

[1] *Verhandlungen des ersten Hegelkongresses vom 22. bis 25. April 1930 in Haag*, ed. B. Wigersma (Tübingen-Haarlem, 1931), 19.

warm about Locke and objectively detached even about Kant or Rousseau, Hegel brings out the partisan in everyone: one is either for or against, and in a rather extremist fashion. As an enthusiastic but not always very perceptive 'left' Hegelian once put it, 'There has never been, ever since man began to think, a system of philosophy as comprehensive as that of Hegel. Logic, metaphysics, natural philosophy, mental philosophy, the philosophy of law, of religion, of history, all are united in one system, reduced to one fundamental principle.'[2]

The literature is really immense, and it is still growing: the 1965 volume of *Hegel-Studien* lists 116 items for 1962–63 alone. The rediscovery of the strongly Hegelian manuscripts of the young Marx added further dimensions to the study of Hegel both in the West as well as in some of the communist countries.

One of the main issues which continues to agitate those who comment on Hegel is his political philosophy and his philosophy of history which is closely related to it: even people who would not feel like discussing Hegel's philosophical system *per se* are ready to take issue with his political theory. Could it be plausibly argued that the great ideological schism of the first half of the twentieth century is nothing else than a secularized version of the rift between 'right' and 'left' Hegelians?[3] Was Hegel the originator of the modern racist-totalitarian state?[4] Or was he rather a

[2] F. Engels, 'The Progress of Social Reform on the Continent: Germany and Switzerland', *New Moral World,* 18 November 1843. Engels significantly adds: 'The Hegelian system seemed quite unassailable from without, and so it was; it has been overthrown from *within* only, by people who were Hegelians themselves.' Cf. my article 'The Hegelian Origins of Marx's Political Thought', *The Review of Metaphysics,* September 1967.

[3] Cf. G. Lichtheim's Introduction to the Torchbook edition of Hegel's *The Phenomenology of Mind* (New York, 1967), xxxi.

[4] K.R. Popper, *The Open Society and Its Enemies* (Princeton, 1950), 255–73.

shrewd observer of social and political change, cautiously suggesting to temper reform with tradition and reason with history?[5]

An overall re-assessment of Hegel's political philosophy is badly needed, though it cannot be undertaken here: the last comprehensive study of Hegel's political views within the context of his general philosophical system was undertaken almost fifty years ago by Franz Rosenzweig in his monumental *Hegel und der Staat* (1920). Yet the ambiguity about the meaning of the Hegelian heritage is not of recent vintage: it dates back to the immediate impact Hegel's philosophy had on his contemporaries. The political circumstances of nineteenth-century German history added further twists and new aspects to the dilemma. Looking at some of the reactions Hegel's thought evoked among his contemporaries and immediate successors may help us to understand some of the more recent attitudes toward his philosophy. Most of the current views about the Hegelian system and its political implications seem to be prefigured in these early reactions, which may also shed some further light on those undercurrents of German intellectual history which became so violently dominant in the twentieth century.

The tone struck by Hegel's disciples and successors at Berlin University on his death in 1831 was panegyric to the extreme. They promptly announced plans for the publication of a complete edition of his works, and the flowery language in which they extolled their master seems excessive even by the baroque standards of the period. Philip Conrad Marheineke, who was one of the speakers at the official funeral ceremony at the University, likened Hegel's death to Christ's leaving the terrestrial realm in order to return to the ethereal

[5] Z.A. Pelczynski, Introductory Essay to *Hegel's Political Writings* (Oxford, 1964). Cf. W. Kaufmann, *Hegel* (Garden City, 1965), 249–90.

heights of the spiritual kingdom.[6] In a turn of phrase whose ambiguity must have escaped him, the other speaker at that ceremony, Friedrich Förster, compared Hegel's system to the Tree of Knowledge. Hegel, Förster claimed, was a deeply devout Christian thinker who taught his students how really to understand Christ. Like Leibnitz and Kant, Hegel was a testimony to the greatness of Prussia and the German spirit. Hegelian philosophy was about to sweep the world like Alexander's Macedonian troops. The Kingdom of the Spirit had been definitely established by Hegel's teachings.[7] And the Prefaces to the various volumes of Hegel's works reflected a similar adoration on the part of his editors, including, besides the two speakers already mentioned, Eduard Gans, Heinrich Gustav Hotho, Leopold von Henning, Karl Ludwig Michelet, Karl Rosenkranz, as well as Hegel's son Karl, a scholar in his own right.

Yet this praise by the Hegelian establishment was quickly offset over the next few years by an undercurrent of philosophical and political polemic which undercut much of Hegel's influence and presented his philosophy to the general public in a light that was to bedevil it for generations. This was made easier by the untenable position his followers manoeuvred themselves into. While editing their master's works, the 'official', 'right' Hegelians in their own writings made the Hegelian system even more incomprehensible, less exciting and more conservative than it originally was. Having accepted Hegel's claim that his system was the close of philosophy, his disciples consciously resigned themselves to the role of *epigoni*, thus endorsing one of the more questionable and least

[6] *Zwei Reden bei der feierlichen Bestattung des königl. Professors Dr Georg Wilh. Fr. Hegel, am 16ten November, gesprochen* (Berlin, 1831), 6.

[7] Ibid. 12–14.

dialectical positions of their master. In politics their philosophy came to represent an enlightened rationalization of the Prussian state; and while this was ultimately also Hegel's position, to praise Prussia in the context of 1840 was a totally different thing from seeing it in 1819 as the best chance for rational, controlled progress. Gone also was the ambivalence which always permeated Hegel's attitude towards Prussia, and what in Hegel sometimes represented lip-service became the ultimate rationalization of a political system which by then looked very different from the one Hegel found to conform more than others to his idea of a state based on the universality of legal norms.[8]

The mantle of dialectical critique and philosophical innovation thus fell on the unorthodox 'left' Hegelians who brought out the revolutionary potential inherent in their teacher's dictum that 'what is rational is actual'. But the radical implications of such a reading of Hegel shocked many observers into conceiving Hegelian philosophy itself as basically subversive.[9] This of course seems to be quite a correct understanding of the potentialities of Hegelianism, but the consequence was that both right and left Hegelians put themselves, for different reasons, into ultimately isolated positions. Thus besides the esoteric debates of the different Hegelian schools, there emerged a *public* debate about Hegel which was often conducted not by Hegelians but by outsiders. The effect of this climate of opinion could be gauged later by the impact of Haym's book *Hegel und seine Zeit* when it was published in 1857.

Ironically enough, one of the first discussions of

[8] H. Lübbe (ed.), *Die Hegelsche Rechte* (Stuttgart, 1962), 7–17.

[9] K. Löwith (ed.), *Die Hegelsche Linke* (Stuttgart, 1962), 7–38; H. Stuke, *Philosophie der Tat* (Stuttgart, 1963); J. Gebhardt, *Politik und Eschatologie* (Munich, 1963).

Hegel to appear in print shortly after his death was a pseudonymous play published in 1832. Under the improbable pen-name of Absolutulus von Hegelingen, its author, the writer O.H. Gruppe, attacked Hegel and Hegelianism in a most unbridled way. Nothing could be more in contrast with the pontificating tones of the Hegelian establishment than the play's title: *The Winds, or, A Wholly Absolute Construction of World History by Oberon's Horn.*[10] This grotesque caricature, modelled on a combination of Aristophanes' *The Birds, A Midsummer Night's Dream,* and *Faust,* is without any literary value, yet its general argument (so far as it has an argument) prefigures many of the later standard charges against Hegel.

The plot is relatively simple: living in the charmed environment of Fairyland is the main character, Hegel, disguised as *Absolutus, Philosoph zu Utopien.* His mumbo-jumbo is law in that distant cloud-cuckoo land of Utopia: he is surrounded by councillors, secretaries, secret secretaries, and other bureaucratic dignitaries of this Prussianized Utopia. He is the hero of a bunch of noisy, pushy, garlic-smelling disciples, and the play tells of the tribulations of three of them—Arroganz, Absalom, and Israel, all sons of one Aaron Ganz, 'a Jewish innkeeper and distiller of concrete spirit'. Old Aaron Ganz distils pure 'being', and sells it as a drug to demagogues and other subversive elements; his three sons are determined to find their way to the philosopher and become his direct disciples in Utopia. But the journey to Utopia is difficult. Israel dies, Absalom goes mad, and Arroganz goes back to his father's tavern and becomes what he should always have been—an innkeeper. But before relegating the

[10] Absolutulus von Hegelingen, *Die Winde, oder ganz absolute Konstruktion der Weltgeschichte durch Oberons Horn* (Leipzig, n.d. [1832]).

Jews to their proper place in society ('Leave therefore books and pens / The shop counter is your lectern'), the author depicts Hegelian philosophy as a meaningless swindle aimed at subverting existing society. Most interestingly, Hegel's philosophy is accused of hidden materialism and hence of denying Christianity; that his philosophy so strongly attracted so many of the young emancipated Jewish intelligentsia is another proof of that.[11] On the one hand Hegel is accused of having private and illicit connections with the powers that be; yet the French Revolution, Napoleon, modernism and atheism—all are conceived as consequences of the secret formula concocted by Absolutus. At the end of the play the formula is stolen and Utopia then vanishes into what it has always been—thin air. Absolutus's philosophy proves to be nothing more than pure air spinning around itself.

This worthless, though in its way delightful, little farce, combining rabid anti-Hegelianism with antisemitism, would not have warranted any mention had it not been the case that many of the same accusations were to be repeated by later and perfectly respectable authors. In 1835 a Jena professor, Carl Friedrich Bachman, published a tract called *Anti-Hegel* in which he professed his own belief in a personal God, contending that the Hegelian system denies this and should therefore be suppressed. He goes on to compare Hegel—and German idealism in general—to Jacobin terrorism and to the idea underlying Robespierre's radicalism.[12]

[11] Ibid. 10. The deep fascination exercised by Hegel on the first generation of emancipated and secularly educated Jews has recently been discussed by H.G. Reissner, *Eduard Gans: Ein Leben im Vormärz* (Tübingen, 1965). For Hegel's own view on the Jewish question, see my article 'A Note on Hegel's Views on Jewish Emancipation', *Journal of Jewish Studies*, April 1963.

[12] C.F. Bachman, *Anti-Hegel* (Jena, 1835), iv–v, 2–3.

That Hegel was thus opposed both as an arch-conservative and as a radical revolutionary does, of course, poetic justice to the dialectical nature of his theory of identity and his philosophy of history. In the Preface to his *Philosophy of Right* Hegel did after all proclaim that 'What is rational is actual and what is actual is rational.'[13] He thus opened his philosophy to both a radical and a conservative interpretation: if the rational actualizes itself as history, rational reform will ultimately triumph; on the other hand, the argument from history seems to endow existing institutions with a rational legitimacy.[14] It is true that in section 6 of his *Enzyklopädie der philosophischen Wissenschaften* Hegel tried to explain that his statement in the *Philosophy of Right* should not be construed in a quietistic way, namely that *all* reality is rational: here he explicitly introduces the distinction between 'actuality' (*Wirklichkeit*) and mere 'existence' (*Dasein*), and it is only the former that is rational. Yet this gloss only deepened the ambiguity: in 1837 a *Privatdozent* in Halle wrote that Hegel should not be made responsible for everyone who happens to lift an idea from the Hegelian system: almost every shade of opinion can be defended by a reference to one or another aspect of the Hegelian corpus.[15] Similarly, another writer cried out in agony that recent critics had made Hegel the universal whipping horse, accusing 'Hegelian philosophy of being a poisonous amalgam

[13] G.W.F. Hegel, *Philosophy of Right,* Eng. trans. (Oxford, 1942), 10. For the way in which Engels misquoted and emasculated this sentence, see Marx-Engels *Selected Works* (New York, n.d.), I, 420. Engels made Hegel say that 'All that is actual is rational and all that is rational is actual.'

[14] On this ambivalent legacy, see N. Rotenstreich, *Basic Problems of Marx's Philosophy* (Indianapolis, 1965), 6 ff.

[15] J. Schaller, *Die Philosophie unserer Zeit* (Leipzig, 1837), iv.

of irreligiosity and mysticism, of revolution and despotism'.[16]

But the strongest attack on Hegel in pre-1848 days was yet to come. It came in 1839 from K.E. Schubart in his book *On the Irreconcilability of the Hegelian Theory of State with the Highest Living and Developing Principle of the Prussian State.* Schubart explains that he concentrates his polemic on Hegel's political and historical views since they are unacceptable to him as 'a Prussian and a Protestant'. He brings Hegel's latent Spinozism strongly into focus by his contention that Hegel's God who unfolds himself in history is not a true personal God, since 'he cannot create anything that he does not have to transcend *(aufheben)* later . . . God must be a creative, not self-unfolding being'. Schubart's objections to Hegel's political ideas are even stronger. He takes issue with Hegel's view of Prussia as a constitutional monarchy: to Schubart, this is too much a rational justification of the Hohenzollern state. Prussia is a dynastic state, Schubart argues, its essence is epitomized in the subjective element of the dynastic principle. If Prussia is seen as a constitutional monarchy, then the essence of the state is transferred from the person of the monarch to the dynasty's relationship to objective institutions. To Schubart, a constitutional monarchy is a republic in monarchical garb, and therefore a subversive idea, irreconcilable with the principle of the Prussian state. Prussia is a 'pure', absolute monarchy, and hence Hegel's remark (in §280 of the *Philosophy of Right)* that the monarch only puts the dot on the 'i' means that to Hegel the monarchy is incidental and not essential to the state. Whereas for a dynastic state like Prussia, 'it is always the monarch through whom all others act and can act'. While Hegel insists that the state is based on

[16] Karl W.E. Mager, *Brief an eine Dame über die Hegelsche Philosophie* (Berlin, 1837), iii.

the objectivity and universality of its legal norms, Schubart detects in such an attitude a reversal from Christian subjectivity to Old Testament narrow legalism; Hegel is 'Judaizing' the Prussian state: 'We have here the hard, avaricious Jewish formalistic state.'[17]

Such a line of argument became even more popular when Young Hegelian theological criticism focused more attention on the ambivalence of Hegel's religious views. Heinrich Leo, writing in 1839, reviewed and attacked Bruno Bauer, Ludwig Feuerbach, David Friedrich Strauss and others for their criticism of biblical and especially evangelical traditions. The Hegelians, he wrote, 'deny the existence of a personal God. . . . From the standpoint of all hitherto existing Christian churches . . . this implies that this party preaches atheism in the open. . . . This party denies the human incarnation of God in Christ. . . . It denies the immortality of the soul.'[18]

As in the work of many other writers who criticized the implications of Hegel's religious views, there is a strong anti-Jewish undercurrent in Leo's book. Though almost all the Young Hegelians whose writings he criticizes are of good Gentile stock, Leo refers to the Hegelians as 'Messrs Jenkel, Schmuel and Levi' (p. 46), and the hidden 'Judaism' and Spinozism of Hegel's system are attacked several times. The irony of the matter is that Leo was himself considered by many of his contemporaries to be either a converted Jew or coming from a converted Jewish family, and

[17] K.E. Schubart, *Über die Unvereinbarkeit der Hegelschen Staatslehre mit dem obersten Lebens- und Entwicklungsprinzip des preussischen Staates* (Breslau, 1839), iv, v, 7–9, 16, 13.

[18] Heinrich Leo, *Die Hegelingen* (Halle, 1839), 1–4. Though Leo's book is aimed primarily at the 'young' Hegelians, he also attacks some of the orthodox Hegelians, especially K.L. Michelet's *Geschichte der letzten Systeme der Philosophie in Deutschland*.

in his book he went to quite humiliating lengths to disavow this rumour.[19]

The vehemence of attacks from religious quarters on Hegel can perhaps be compared to the reaction in England to Darwin: few people have been so violently criticized for subverting religion and public order. J.A. Wendel criticized Hegel for a-historical abstractness: the monarchy in Germany should not be defended on general theoretical grounds, as in Hegel, but because it was a peculiar *Germanic* institution, determined by centuries of ethnic *völkisch* existence: echoes here of Hegel's disagreement with Savigny's historical school of jurisprudence.[20] Hegel's logical absolutism and Spinozistic panlogism were attacked by Ferdinand von Sommer.[21] A Swiss author, de

[19] *Die Hegelingen*, 85–7: 'My occidental ancestry cannot be doubted. . . . I view with deep agony those half-bred creatures, who though of Jewish ancestry and thus possessing a physical and psychological physiognomy distinct from the Germanic, proclaim themselves as representatives or correctors of our German, native interests and circumstances. A politically-reasoning Jew or half-Jew is one of the ugliest sights provided by life. Both my parents, my four grandparents, my eight great-grandparents, and my sixteen great-great-grandparents were all of documentarily proved occidental race. Nowhere has there ever been a hint of Jewish relations. . . . The family name is Italian. . . . My family has therefore nothing to do with Palestine. . . . You may call me a 'half-wog' *(Halbwalch)* in old German parlance —I have nothing against that. But I do not have the honour to be numbered among the princely Sons of Israel or to be half-Jewish.' This incredible piece was written in 1839, not 1939.

[20] J.A. Wendel, *Beurteilung der Hegelschen Philosophie* (Coburg, 1839), 40.

[21] F. von Sommer, *Hegels Philosophie widerlegt aus dem Standpunkt des System selbst, dem der anderen Philosophen und dem der gesunden Vernunft* (Berlin, 1843), v, 65, 98–9. As late as 1852 an accusation of Hegelian Spinozism was used to suspend one Dr Hansch from his chair at Charles University in Prague. An anonymous tract defending the suspension was

Valenti, saw Hegel's system as anti-Christian, God-less, blasphemous, lying, unashamed, unphilosophical, and unscientific.[22] While acknowledging Hegel's greatness as a philosopher, another devout Protestant author, Trahndorf, saw the main danger in Hegel's introduction of rational criteria for the evaluation and scrutiny of religious and theological traditions; through Bauer and Strauss, Hegel had undermined the belief in Christian tradition and miracles. After Hegel, one was left wondering whether 'religion is of divine origin or a mere human artefact.'[23] The accusation of subverting religion was levelled not only at the Young Hegelians, but was also provoked sometimes by statements by the more orthodox, professorial old Hegelians like Marheineke: the kernel of dialectical criticism was strong even there.[24] A more sophisticated approach was used by Franz Anton Staudenmaier, who pointed out that Hegel himself conceded that his system was Christian in content, though not in form: this admission allowed the use of Christian criteria for a critique of Hegel and such a critique would not be external to the system. Staudenmaier saw the Hegelian *List der Vernunft* as basically un-Christian and was repelled by the dialectical necessity of evil in Hegel: it was almost

---

published under the title *Der verderbliche Einfluss der Hegelschen Philosophie* (Leipzig, 1852). Here the accusations against Hegel include revolutionary radicalism (12–17) and a similarity to the teachings of Spinoza and Philo Judaeus (6). Hegelianism, the author contended, should be eliminated root and branch, since 'it attacks like a miasma the health of spiritual life in Germany' (4).

22 de Valenti, *Hegel-Strauss und der Christenglaube* (Basel, 1843), 13, 19, 20–1, 24.

23 K.F.E. Trahndorf, *Wie kann der Spiritualismus sein Recht gegen Hegels Philosophie behaupten* (Berlin, 1840), 4.

24 Cf. J.J. Rohovsky, *Unvereinbarkeit der Hegelschen Wissenschaft mit dem Christentume und der christlichen Theologie* (Breslau, 1842).

Manichaean.[25] A spirited attempt to distinguish 'true' Hegelianism from 'false' Hegelian interpretation, and thus save 'true' Hegelianism from the suspicion of radicalism, did not prove very successful or convincing.[26]

Several attempts were made to counter the impression created by all this violently anti-Hegelian literature. One of the first to take issue with Schubart was Immanuel Ogienski in a pamphlet written in 1840. Ogienski's main contention was that Schubart misunderstood both Hegel and the nature of the Hegelian state. Though initially the dynasty was the only link welding together the various territories of the Hohenzollerns, Prussian history provided ample proof for a continuous trend towards the emergence of objective institutions, basing political allegiance on legal norms and not on a personal nexus. Prussia, Ogienski argued, was well on its way to becoming a constitutional monarchy, and it was this tendency which Hegel emphasized in his *Philosophy of Right*.[27] A similar argument was advanced by Förster in an article in the *Hallische Fahrbücher* of 1839: Schubart's identification of the Prussian state with the Hohenzollerns may have been true in the past, but it no longer corresponded to contemporary reality. By themselves the Hohenzollerns were of no import—only insofar as their efforts were aimed at something that could be described as a common weal had they acquired historical significance. The controversy between Hegel and Schubart was one between rationalism and romanti-

[25] F.A. Staudenmaier, *Darstellung und Kritik des Hegelschen Systems aus dem Standpunkte der christlichen Philosophie* (Mainz, 1844), 560.

[26] G.A. Gabler, *Die Hegelsche Philosophie* (Berlin, 1843).

[27] I. Ogienski, *Hegel, Schubart und die Idee der Persönlichkeit in ihrem Verhältnis zur preussischen Monarchie* (Trzemessno, 1840), 6.

cism, and the Prussian state, whatever its dynastic subjectivist origins, was becoming an institutionalized modern state. Paradoxically, Förster argued, if one wanted to disagree with Hegel's view that the monarch put the dot on the 'i', one should do so because there was an authoritarian undercurrent in such a statement, not because it had republican overtones.[28]

The most influential *apologia* for Hegel was, of course, Karl Rosenkranz's monumental *Hegels Leben* (Berlin, 1843). This was the first full-scale intellectual biography of Hegel and it brought to light for the first time many of Hegel's unknown manuscripts and letters. Its main thrust was to portray Hegel as a German classic in the tradition of Goethe, combining *Deutschtum* and *Menschtum* in the best traditions of the Enlightenment. In this study, Hegel's philosophy of history, as well as his political theory, were deemphasized, and the treatment of these themes is the least satisfactory aspect of Rosenkranz's book. By attempting to neutralize the political and theological arguments and counter-arguments about the Hegelian system, Rosenkranz hoped to integrate Hegel into the mainstream of German *Kulturleben.*[29]

But the weaknesses of such a treatment were obvious, both because the impact of the Hegelian schools of political and religious thought was tremendous, and because political life in Germany was moving quickly in a direction where the issues raised by Hegel's political philosophy could not be sidetracked.

Thus Rosenkranz's biography only invited that kind of reassessment of Hegel that would strike at the ambiguities laid bare by attempting to neutralize the

[28] F. Förster, 'Noch ein Dennunciant der Hegelschen Philosophie', *Hallische Fahrbücher für deutsche Wissenschaft und Kunst,* No. 46, 26 February 1839.

[29] The parallel with Goethe was especially successful; cf. E. Rehm, *Goethe und Hegel: Eine historische Parallele* (Oels, 1849).

impact Hegel had on the German political mind. The soul-searching of the German liberals in the post-1848 era provided a favourable intellectual climate for such a debate. Rudolf Haym's *Hegel und seine Zeit*, published in 1857, capitalized on both the frustration of 1848 and the ambivalences in Hegel's thought in general and his attitude to Prussia in particular. To an 1848-vintage liberal-nationalist like Haym, Prussia symbolized the *ancien régime* that frustrated the hopes for German unification: he credited Hegel both with reactionary politics and with subservience to Prussia. While he thus correctly brought out the conservative ingredient always present in Hegel's political theory, he made it into the only component of his system. And with an astonishing disregard for the historical dimension, he equated the reformist Prussia of vom Stein and Hardenberg with the romantic, reactionary Prussia of the 1840s and 1850s. Hegel thus emerged as the protagonist of reaction and obscurantism; by implication, the romantic nationalists of 1813 became the prophets of freedom and progress. This was not surprising in a generation that naively equated national independence with political liberalism, but it set the liberal *imprimatur* on some of the most obnoxious, chauvinistic, xenophobic, and racist attitudes that were to bedevil German politics for generations. Rosenkranz tried to counter this emasculation of Hegel and his *Zeitgeist* by a pamphlet of his own, but his attempt was feeble and utterly unconvincing: bowing to the prevalent German national-liberal spirit, he tried to rescue Hegel by recourse to a me-tooism that was doomed to fail.[30] Making Hegel into a nationalist, as he tried to do in another book in 1870, was even more damaging to the Hegelian image than Haym's initial attack. Hegel became both a Prussian and a national-

[30] K. Rosenkranz, *Apologie Hegels gegen Dr. R. Haym* (Berlin, 1858).

ist: the picture of Hegel as the precursor of Bismarck was thus created by foe and friend alike.

In his 1870 book, Rosenkranz went out of his way to pay homage to the insurrection of 1813, totally overlooking the fact that Hegel was utterly opposed to this nationalist outburst. The last phase of Hegel's philosophy of history, 'the Germanic world', which in Hegel is coeval with Western Christendom, was turned by Rosenkranz into a racial philosophy in which the Germans represent the cream of the 'Caucasian race'[31]—utter nonsense in Hegelian terms, since race never figures in Hegel, nor do 'Caucasians'. While extolling the virtues of Prussia, Rosenkranz viciously attacked Austria, which 'out of all German tribes' never gave the nation even one philosopher and was thus also incapable of becoming a focal point of German unity (p. 5). In Rosenkranz's mind, Sadowa seems to have been related to philosophic excellence rather than to strategy.

Rosenkranz's *volte face* was aided by the publication in 1870 of fragments of a manuscript written by Hegel in 1801–2 in which he advocated a modernization of the political institutions of Germany, doing away with the decrepit and obsolete institutions of the Holy Roman Empire of the German Nation. Portions of this manuscript were published earlier by Rosenkranz and over the years the nameless manuscript received the misleading title *Die Verfassung Deutschlands,* which helped to present it as if it were a nationalist tract.[32] And though Hegel rejoiced in the Prussian defeat at Jena in 1806, bitterly opposed the anti-French campaign of 1813 and the plans for

[31] K. Rosenkranz, *Hegel als deutscher Nationalphilosoph* (Leipzig, 1870), 149–50, 173. For Hegel's attitude during 1813, see my 'Hegel and Nationalism', *The Review of Politics,* October 1962.

[32] Cf. *Hegel's Political Writings,* 143–242.

German unification in 1815, a selective publication of portions of the so-called 'Constitution essay' helped to create the image of Hegel as a forerunner of German nationalism.[33] When the essay was published in full for the first time in 1893 (by Georg Mollat), its image as a nationalist tract, based on previous slanted selections and a tendentious title, had already been firmly established. Few took the trouble to have a close look at it, which would have revealed that when it came to questions pertaining to the idea of nationalism, Hegel had very little sympathy with it, as is clearly shown from the following passage:

> In our day the tie between the members of a state in respect of manners, education, language, may be rather loose or even non-existent. Identity in these matters, once the foundation of a people's union, is now to be reckoned among the accidents whose character does not hinder a mass from constituting a public authority. . . . Thus dissimilarity in culture and manners is a necessary product as well as a necessary condition of the stability of the modern state.[34]

Another conclusion one may be tempted to draw from this passage is how little Hegel really grasped the modern *Zeitgeist*.

It was this projection of 1871 on to 1917 which led to several of the later views about Hegel's political

[33] K. Köstlin, *Hegel in philosophischer, politischer und nationaler Beziehung* (Tübingen, 1870).

[34] *Hegel's Political Writings*, 158. In 1935 Mollat published a new edition of the *Constitution*, this time entitled *Die Verfassung des Deutschen Reiches* (Stuttgart, 1935), thus upgrading Hegel from a proponent of mere 'Germany' to a prophet of the 'German Empire'. In his new Introduction he warmly recommended Hegel as relevant to 'the new age of German history'.

theory and his philosophy of history. It was this selective, historically anachronistic view of Hegel that has been expressed in such erudite–yet basically defective–studies as Herman Heller's *Hegel und der nationale Machtstaatsgedanke in Deutschland* (1921). The romantic Prussia of Friedrich Wilhelm IV, Bismarck, and Treitschke were all read into Hegel, despite the fact that insofar as one could argue on the basis of the Hegelian texts themselves, Hegel always opposed those attitudes which prefigured such later manifestations.

Ironically, it was the nazis who knew better. For them Hegel was absolute anathema: like some of the Jew-baiting early anti-Hegelians, Rosenberg and other nazis quickly realized that the rationalist and critical elements in Hegel have little in common with the Myth of the Twentieth Century or the Thousand Year Reich.[35] Even so, some attempts were made to prove Hegel's compatibility with the Third Reich. A legal theoretician tried to stretch Hegel's concept of emergency powers to legitimize encroachment upon civil society,[36] while another author attacked the rationalist, liberal interpretation of Hegel as an emasculation of his system. Such an interpretation, this author conteded, was the outcome of nineteenth-century 'liberalism, individualism, and abstract thinking'; it should be replaced by a new, authoritarian under-

[35] For an excellent résumé of this see the chapter on 'National Socialism versus Hegel' in H. Marcuse's *Reason and Revolution* (New York, 1941). Some proto-nazis, like Carl Schmitt, also understood that historical subjectivist romanticism has very little to do with Hegel. Cf. his *Politische Romantik*, 2nd ed. (Munich, 1925), 46 ff.

[36] P. Bockelmann, 'Hegels Notstandslehre', *Abhandlungen des kriminalistichen Instituts der Universität Berlin*, IV. Folge, 3. Bd., 4. Heft (Berlin, 1935).

standing of Hegel.[37] A nazi jurist wrote that in looking for a new, national-socialist idea of justice, they should go back to the primeval idea of Teutonic popular justice, to which Hegel could be a very valuable guide.[38] What the textual evidence for this was remains a mystery, since Hegel's utterances about original Germanic law and custom are far from flattering. With these few exceptions, the general tone of the nazi attitude towards Hegel was extremely negative, epitomized in Alfred Rosenberg's statement that nazism stood opposed to the French Revolution, Hegel, and Marx as doctrines 'alien to our blood'.[39]

In other countries, the interpretation of Hegel's political thought followed a different course, but in Germany the dividing line seems clear. The political debate about Hegel thus appears as just another phase in the battle between the rationalists and the romantics—with the national-liberals neatly split right down the middle. For the romantics, Hegel stood for 1789 and universalism, against historicist nationalism and the *völkisch* virtues. Hegel's *Volkgeist* is one constituent in a universalist and rationalist *Weltgeist*, not the sovereign expression of a particular and subjectivist ethnic culture. Though it may be true that Hegel was politically timid, his political philosophy could never serve the same aims as that of Burke or Gentz. The irony of the matter has, of course, been the fact that Hegel was so utterly wrong in his understanding of his own *Zeitgeist*. His philosophy of history

[37] G. Dulckheit, *Rechtsbegriff und Rechtsgestalt: Untersuchungen zu Hegels Philosophie des Rechts und ihrer Gegenwartsdeutung* (Berlin, 1936), 13.

[38] E. Mewes, *Hegel und der deutsche Richterideal* (Urach, 1937), 2.

[39] A. Rosenberg, *Der Mythus des 20. Fahrhunderts* (Munich, 1933), 525.

postulated a conscious trend towards the unification of European culture;[40] he considered the subjectivist romanticism of his age a dangerous yet basically marginal phenomenon, a voice from the past. When it became the wave of the future, it submerged Hegel's political philosophy along with the option for an alternative course of German history.

One should not, however, be misled in the other, equally extreme direction: if Hegel germanized the French Revolution, he still should not be made into an individualist liberal: his quest for a meaningful community, epitomized in the state, was always too strong for that. But then individualist liberalism has never been a real force in Germany, possibly because the existence of a historically coherent body politic is a prerequisite for such liberal-individualist postulates, and such a premise was lacking in Germany. Hence the utter impotence—and ultimate capitulation—of German liberalism. When it met its fate, first at the *Paulskirche* and then at Sadowa, the German academic establishment, nourished on the illusion that liberalism and German nationalism go hand in hand, was irrevocably compromised. 1933 had already been prefigured in 1871, and it may be idle to wonder whether, had political Hegelianism been stronger in both cases, the outcome might have been different. Be that as it may, with a short exception in the early 1830s, Hegel's political ideas were always 'out' in Germany. Hegel never really had a chance.

I would like to thank the Penrose Fund of the American Philosophical Society for a grant that greatly facilitated the reseach on which this paper is based.

[40] G.W.F. Hegel, *Vorlesungen über die Philosophie der Weltgeschichte*, ed. G. Lasson (Leipzig, 1920), 761.

Select Bibliography

I. German Texts of Hegel

Sämtliche Werke, ed. G. Lasson and J. Hoffmeister, Leipzig, 1928 et. seq.

Sämtliche Werke, ed. H. Glockner, Jubiläumausgabe, Stuttgart, 1927 et. seq.

Briefe von und an Hegel, ed. K. Hegel, Leipzig, 1887.

Dokumente zu Hegels Entwicklung, ed. J. Hoffmeister, Stuttgart, 1936.

II. English Translations of Hegel

Early Theological Writings. Translated by T. M. Knox. With an Introduction by and Fragments translated by R. Kroner. Chicago, 1948. New York, 1961.

The Phenomenology of Mind. Translated by J. B. Baillie. With an Introduction by George Lichtheim. New York, 1967.

The Science of Logic. Translated by W. H. Johnston and L. G. Struthers. New York, 1929.

The Logic of Hegel. Translated by W. Wallace from the *Encyclopedia of the Philosophical Sciences.* Oxford and Fair Lawn, N.J., 1892.

Hegel's Philosophy of Nature. Being Part Two of the *Encyclopedia of the Philosophical Sciences,* translated by A. V. Miller. With Foreword by J. N. Findlay. Oxford and New York, 1970.

Hegel's Philosophy of Mind. Translated by W. Wallace from the *Encyclopedia of the Philosophical Sciences.* Oxford and Fair Lawn, N.J., 1894.

Hegel's Philosophy of Right. Translated with notes by T. M. Knox. Oxford and Fair Lawn, N.J., 1942.

Hegel's Political Writings. Translated by T. M. Knox. With an Introductory Essay by Z. A. Pelczynski. Oxford and Fair Lawn, N.J., 1964.

Lectures on the History of Philosophy. Translated by E. S. Haldane & F. H. Simson. London and New York, 1892–95.

Lectures on the Philosophy of History. Translated by J. Sibree. London and New York, 1894.

The Philosophy of Fine Arts. Translated by F. P. R. Osmaston. London and New York, 1920.

Lectures on the Philosophy of Religion. Translated by E. B. Speirs and J. B. Sanderson. London and New York, 1895.

III. Commentaries on Hegel

A. Kojéve. *Introduction to the Reading of Hegel.* Edited by Alan Bloom. Translated by J. H. Nichols, Jr. New York, 1969.

J. Hyppolite. *Genèse et Structure de la Phénoménologie de l'Esprit.* Paris, 1946.

J. Hyppolite. *Logique et Existence: Essai sur la Logique de Hegel.* Paris, 1953.

E. Fleischmann. *La Philosophie Politique de Hegel.* Paris, 1964.

IV. Selected Works on Hegel

H. A. Reyburn. *Ethical Theory of Hegel.* Oxford and Fair Lawn, N.J., 1921.

W. T. Stace. *The Philosophy of Hegel.* London and New York, 1924.

H. Marcuse. *Reason and Revolution: Hegel and the Rise of Social Theory.* New York, 1941.

G. R. G. Mure. *The Philosophy of Hegel.* Oxford and Fair Lawn, N.J., 1965.

J. N. Findlay. *Hegel: A Re-examination.* London and New York, 1958.

W. Kaufmann. *Hegel.* New York, 1965.

F. Wiedmann. *Hegel: An Illustrated Biography.* New York, 1968.

J. Hyppolite. *Studies on Marx and Hegel.* Translated by J. O'Neill. New York, 1969.

W. H. Walsh. *Hegelian Ethics.* London and New York, 1969.